Running Guns

Whether in Africa, Sri Lanka, Colombia or the United States, it is not heavy weaponry or hi-tech devices that kill the most people, but cheap, easy to get, small arms that have flooded so many countries in the 1980s and 90s. A good deal of the cross-border arms trade that provides these weapons is illegal. So much so that several governments, including the United States, Canada and Mexico, are now pressing for rapid negotiation of a new global treaty on illegal trafficking in small arms, and the UN General Assembly called for a major conference on the issue to be held in 2001.

This highly readable book advances understanding of the illegal arms traffic. How is it conducted? Who are the players? What are the impacts? And, most importantly, what can be done to curb the deadly trade?

It is a fascinating, highly informative and policy-relevant investigation into an issue affecting too many of us and about which far too little is known.

***

This book provides an excellent introduction to one of the most important and complex issues in international politics today. With the United Nations considering new curbs on the illicit trade in firearms, *Running Guns* comes at a perfect time. No other source provides this breadth of detail on the operation of the global black arms market.

Michael Klare, Professor of Peace and World
Security Studies, Hampshire College

The illegal trade in deadly weapons has long been one of the blind spots in international law and human rights. This urgently needs to be rectified—a result unattainable without painstaking legal and factual research such as contained in this book.

C.G. Weeramantry, Former Vice President
of the International Court of Justice

Guns were used in South Africa to commit half of all murders in 1998; privately-held guns and military and police depots were principal sources of these crime weapons. This book makes a strong case for careful domestic gun regulation as an important means of curbing gun trafficking and misuse.

Adele Kirsten, Director, Gunfree South Africa

About NISAT and PRIO

Norwegian Initiative on Small Arms Transfers (NISAT)
www.nisat.org / tel. +47 22 05 41 66

NISAT was formed in December 1997 by Norwegian Church Aid, Norwegian Red Cross, the Norwegian Institute of International Affairs and the International Peace Research Institute, Oslo. The coalition combines the resources and networks of its partner organisations to help block the spread of small arms to areas where they are likely to contribute to conflict, violence and human rights abuse. It does so through support of government conferences, facilitating meetings and efforts of civil society in affected areas, and production of publications, videos and an Internet-based database of small arms production and transfers.

International Peace Research Institute, Oslo (PRIO)
www.prio.no / tel. +47 22 54 77 00

Founded in 1959, PRIO was one of the first centres of peace research in the world, and it is Norway's only peace research institute. PRIO is an independent, international centre in staff, audience and perspective. Its current research programme follows four broad themes: conditions of war and peace; ethics, norms and identities; foreign and security polices; and conflict resolution and peacebuilding. In addition to holding regular seminars, PRIO staff edit two scholarly journals—*Security Dialogue* and *Journal of Peace Research*. The institute also publishes a series of policy reports annually, and staff publish numerous books and articles.

Running Guns

The Global Black Market
in Small Arms

edited by Lora Lumpe

for the Norwegian Initiative on Small Arms Transfers
and the International Peace Research Institute, Oslo

Zed Books
London

Running Guns: The Global Black Market in Small Arms was first published by
Zed Books Ltd., 7 Cynthia Street, London N1 9JF, UK
and Room 400, 175 Fifth Avenue, New York, NY 10010, USA
in 2000

in association with

The International Peace Research Institute, Oslo (PRIO),
Fuglehaugsgt. 11, 0260 Oslo, Norway.

Distributed in the USA exclusively by St Martins Press, Inc.,
175 Fifth Avenue, New York 10010, USA

Cover designed by Andrew Corbett

A catalogue record for this book is available from the British Library.

Library of Congress Cataloging-in-Publication Data is available.

ISBN 1 85649 872 7 (Hb)
ISBN 1 85649 873 5 (Pb)

Printed and bound in Great Britain by Biddles Ltd
www.biddles.co.uk

Contents

Foreword

During my work as the United Nations High Commissioner for Refugees, as a UN peace negotiator in the former Yugoslavia and now as President of Norwegian Red Cross, I have witnessed the devastating effects of assault rifles, machine guns, grenade launchers and the like.

In many of the world's regions, vast stockpiles of these arms circulate and recirculate outside of state control. In some areas assault rifles are so prevalent that they are used as barter or local currency. The low cost and portability of these weapons mean that they are used by combatants of all sides—militaries, militias and insurgents alike—and their sheer abundance and ease of use make these weapons the instruments of far too many deaths. Low-tech, small arms are believed responsible for as much as 90% of the world's combat-related killing.

But it is not only combatants—soldiers—who fall victim to these weapons. In a July 1999 study, *Arms Availability and the Situation of Civilians in Armed Conflict*, researchers at the International Committee of the Red Cross estimated that, in general, more than 50% of war casualties in the 1990s were civilian. And in some recent conflicts the non-combatant mortality rate has been much higher.

The ICRC found that the global trade in cheap small arms is contributing to this alarming rise in civilian casualties, as these weapons increasingly are falling into the hands of fighters, including children, who are unconstrained by the rules of international humanitarian law—the 'laws of war' designed to protect civilians from attack. Tragically, warriors fighting both for and against governments frequently break these laws, and the violations appear to have worsened dramatically in the 1990s. According to the ICRC study, the proliferation of small arms is a 'major factor' in the new disregard for the rules of armed conflict.

Misuse of these weapons is of particular interest and concern to the Norwegian Red Cross. All too often, our humanitarian relief work is made necessary by war. And, increasingly in the 1990s, our aid workers were directly intimidated and imperiled by guns and grenades. For these reasons, the Norwegian Red Cross joined together in 1997 with Norwegian Church Aid, the International Peace Research Institute, Oslo and the Norwegian Institute of International Affairs to form the Norwegian Initiative on Small Arms Transfers (NISAT).

The Red Cross movement is not alone in its concern. Around the world, churches, women's organisations, human rights groups and others are mobilising on the issue. The International Action Network on Small Arms—launched by 165 nongovernmental organisations in May 1999—is now working as an umbrella group to encourage governments to lessen the flow of arms.

Many governments are now considering initiatives to limit small arms transfers, but most of these efforts focus rather narrowly on the illegal trade in such weapons without giving sufficient attention to the impact of the legal trade in surplus guns and grenades. Data collected by the Norwegian Initiative on Small Arms Transfers suggests that some of the same states expressing concern about the negative impact of the illicit trade on civilians, businesses and aid workers continue to produce and authorise the export of these weapons into conflict zones.

'Legal' weapons can exacerbate conflict, leading to humanitarian crises just as readily as can 'illegal' weapons. In fact, the international community currently does not have enough information to know whether the legal or the illegal trade is a bigger part of the problem—in terms of contributing to the outbreak and sustainment of conflict and violations of humanitarian law and human rights.

Running Guns: The Global Black Market in Small Arms advances the state of knowledge about both the legal and illegal arms traffic. By shedding light on the mechanisms and people involved, as well as highlighting relevant legal obligations, this study should help states, international organisations and citizens around the world work for effective measures to curb this deadly trade.

THORVALD STOLTENBERG

Preface *and*
Acknowledgements

More and more governments are speaking out in recent years against the illicit trade in guns and military-style light weapons, but the rhetorical interest in combating the global spread of these weapons is not always matched by a similar commitment to effective action. With this volume, we hope to advance understanding of the illicit arms trade—its meaning, methods, actors and impact—in a manner that will strengthen states' resolve and contribute to sound international policymaking in this area.

A principal thesis of this study is that the popular and governmental understanding of the term 'illicit arms trade' must be broadened to include weapons transfers that imperil people's lives through breaches of international humanitarian law and/or human rights law. This expanded definition includes guns and grenades trafficked to abusive state forces as well as to insurgents. It also includes certain aspects of arms deal making that currently reside in a grey area—for example, deals brokered in third countries in order to evade national laws and covert arms supply by governments.

This volume focuses almost exclusively on the supply side of the black market. It does not attempt to address the important issue of the causes of demand—insecurity, injustice, poverty, hunger, opportunism, warlordism, etc. The absence of such a focus is not meant to imply that fundamental attention to these areas is not key. Rather, it is an acknowledgement that in many cases eradicating these root causes is even more difficult than diminishing the supply of the tools of mass violence.

The book is structured to focus on the many governments—principally in North America and West Europe—that have stated opposition to the 'illicit arms trade.' We hope the essays included here will further their efforts, and those of journalists, activists and civil society groups working to curb the illegal weapons traffic that sustains combat, crime and terror around the world.

Authors in *Running Guns* use the adjectives 'illicit,' 'illegal' and 'black-market' synonymously. The terms 'smuggling,' 'trafficking' and 'gun-running' also refer to movements of arms that are clearly illegal, or that are in some shady area of the law, which we propose to clarify as illegal. While technically differing, the terms 'small arms' and 'light weapons' are also used inter-changeably throughout the book. Included in this category are all man-portable weapons—such as handguns, automatic assault rifles, sub-machine guns, mortars, grenades and grenade launchers, anti-personnel land-mines and shoulder-fired anti-aircraft missiles.

The book is divided into four sections. The first seeks to frame the issue by providing a lively—almost fictional, but true—account of how ammunition got from a manufacturer in the Slovak Republic to battlefields in Africa. A legal review then lays out the full body of relevant international law and identifies an emerging rule of customary law limiting states' actions in this area.

The second section addresses specific sources of supply. The book is not exhaustive in this regard, but rather identifies three broad themes: governments as the source of covert—and often illegal—arms; the impact of internationalisation of production on illicit arms transfers; and the interplay between domestic gun markets and international arms trafficking.

The third section provides operational details about how smugglers obtain and move weapons from point A to point B—how the deals are structured, and how the weapons and money are moved.

The final section seeks to identify points of leverage for limiting this deadly trade. It does so by reviewing the obstacles to effective national and international enforcement of laws, and it assesses the diplomatic initiatives in place or under negotiation to further develop cooperation and assistance in this area. Recommendations culled from all of the chapters lay out an agenda for curbing this deadly trade.

Running Guns is the result of a collaborative process involving not just the authors but also participants at a workshop in Oslo in November 1999, outside reviewers, the publishers and colleagues at the Norwegian Initiative on Small Arms Transfers (NISAT).

NISAT is a coalition of four Norwegian organisations that formed in December 1997 to coordinate and combine efforts against the lethal spread and misuse of military-style light weapons. Two of the partners—Norwegian Red Cross and Norwegian Church Aid—had seen firsthand the deadly impact of these weapons on civilians abroad, and on their own overseas missions. The other two partners—the International Peace Research Institute, Oslo (PRIO) and the Norwegian Institute of International Affairs (NUPI)—have played a key research and advocacy role.

NISAT is concerned equally with all sources of small arms trade that contribute to humanitarian suffering—the legal trade, the borderline trade and the clearly illegal. To advance the state of knowledge in the first area, NISAT is developing an Internet-accessible database of small arms production, state-authorised transfers and state policies relating to small arms production and export (www.nisat.org). On the borderline trade, that employing brokers or middlemen who exploit differing national laws to set up shady arms deals for profit, NISAT sponsored publication in 1999 of *The Arms Fixers*, by Brian Wood and Johan Peleman.

In addition, NISAT has undertaken several initiatives intended to reduce demand for small arms, principally in Africa. For more on NISAT's research, publications and advocacy, visit the coalition's homepage at www.nisat.org.

I am most grateful to all of my colleagues at NISAT and at PRIO, where I was based while working in Oslo during 1998-1999, for their welcome and comradeship. Dan Smith, the director of PRIO, was especially encouraging and always available to advise me—and to advise me well—in this project. Ingeborg Haavardsson, the information director at PRIO, was instrumental in finding a publisher for the book. Jan Egeland, the founding president of NISAT, and Ole-Petter Sunde, its executive director, were both extremely supportive. Preben Marcussen of NISAT has been diligent in managing the business end of this project, and he has done so with great humour. Stig Aga Aandstad and Martin Langvandslien at PRIO provided excellent support throughout the process, and John Carville, the language editor at PRIO, gave the manuscript a careful final copyedit.

Special thanks to Brian Wood, my colleague at PRIO/NISAT, who helped conceptualise the book and identify several of the authors. I also thank Brian, as well as the other ten authors, for sharp, insightful writing and analysis, timeliness and good cheer. I learned a great deal from each of them and enjoyed this collaboration mightily.

Ian Anthony, Kathi Austin, Joe Roeber, Alex Vines and Pieter Wezeman joined the authors at a two-day conference in Oslo in November 1999 to review and refine the chapters. Their input both at that session and later was invaluable. In addition, two readers reviewed the entire manuscript. My deep gratitude to Jonathan Winer and Daniel Garcia-Peña for extremely incisive comments—in terms of substance, style and organisation. Individual authors also received helpful feedback from many readers. For my chapter, I would like to acknowledge my appreciation to Ian Anthony, Peter Batchelor, Joost Hiltermann, Aaron Karp, Michael Klare and Alison Jamieson. These reviewers bear no responsibility, however, for the content of the book.

Although NISAT is supported by the Norwegian government, nothing in this book should be inferred to represent the views of the Norwegian government nor of the organisations that comprise NISAT. The views expressed are those of the authors. Any errors are my fault.

LORA LUMPE
Washington, DC

Introduction to Gun-Running

by Lora Lumpe, Sarah Meek and R. T. Naylor

Hardly any criminals, paramilitaries or insurgents, and even relatively few repressive governments produce their own weaponry.
Most rely on the illegal—or black—market for guns, grenades,
mortars and other weapons that sustain their warfare, repression,
terrorism or violent crime. Happily for them, and unhappily for
citizens around the world caught in the crossfire, the underground
market in arms is booming.

Several trends in the 1990s gave prominence to the issue of gun-
running. Newly opened borders, massive post-Cold War arms surpluses and the rapid expansion of free trade contributed to arms
availability and the ease of smuggling. And increased governmental and media attention to phenomena such as drug trafficking, international crime and civil wars raging around the globe caused
governments and nongovernmental activists to focus more on the
tools of violence, and on the markets that supply them.

In the black market, private dealers (who often have ties to various governments' intelligence agencies) knowingly violate the arms
sales laws or policies of source, transit and/or recipient states for
commercial gain. Also clearly within the black market are arms
sales to governments or insurgents who have been placed under
UN or applicable regional embargoes. 'Grey-market' sales are more
difficult to classify. They include legally questionable transfers,
such as arms supply authorised covertly by an exporting government against the wishes of the importing government.[1] While there
is no comprehensive and universal agreement on what is 'licit' and
what is 'illicit,' chapters 2 and 3 discuss aspects and interpretation
of current international law, and chapter 8 assesses negotiations
underway to establish new norms and conventions in this area.

Further complicating definitions, the interactions between legal
and illegal markets are manifold. Arms that are originally exported

legally but are not properly tracked or secured often fall into illegal circulation, as diversion, theft and capture of state security forces' arms are a major source of black-market supply around the world.[2]

The secretive nature of arms smuggling makes it impossible to know the global or even regional magnitude of the illegal arms traffic, but according to judicial and news accounts it flourished in the 1990s. No international police or customs agency renders a public guess about the magnitude of the illegal gun trade, as they do for the drug trade. Of commodities trafficked around the world, however, arms are believed second in value only to drugs.[3]

Given the concomitant lack of information about the overall dollar volume or quantities of weapons traded legally, it is doubly impossible to determine what percentage of the small arms trade is illicit, and what percentage is licit. Moreover, due to the high level of secrecy that attends legal, state-authorised small arms transfers, it is unknown whether, in general, the legal or the illegal small arms trade contributes more directly to ongoing warfare and repression around the world.

According to the International Committee of the Red Cross, the increased availability of small arms and light weapons through both 'legal' and 'illegal' channels contributed to an alarming rise in civilian casualties during the 1990s.[4] Similarly, there is a wide body of literature, much of it originating from the public health community, that shows a strong correlation between the availability of firearms and high firearms mortality rates within states that are not in war.[5] While lawfully acquired arms are, of course, just as deadly as illegally acquired ones, the latter contribute disproportionately to armed conflict and crime, since they constitute the principal supply for criminals, governments under embargo and insurgents.

Changing Patterns of Supply and Demand

The illicit arms trade is not new, but the apparent increase in arms trafficking is. This surge is attributable to growth during the 1990s in both supply of arms to the black market and demand for arms on the black market.

Weapons previously were not available in today's quantities. Even following World War II, which significantly increased the number of weapons globally, the surplus after the fighting was controlled, to some degree, by politics.[6] Throughout the Cold War, however, the major powers sustained their arms production at World War II levels, generating massive stockpiles surplus to their needs. As long as the rate of production of new material exceeded the rate at which arms were destroyed in war or rendered technically obsolete, the world's stock of weaponry inevitably rose.

On the macroeconomic level, the export of small arms and light weapons rarely, if ever, became a central earner of foreign exchange or a significant generator of jobs. On the micro-level of particular arms-producing enterprises, however, foreign sales became essential to maintaining production runs long enough to capture economies of scale, or indeed to provide an economic justification for their very existence. This reality increased pressures to sell. And each time an army upgraded, it would have a financial incentive to sell off, legally or surreptitiously, its second-hand material. By the end of the Cold War, states were increasingly willing to sell weapons for profit, as opposed to earlier more political considerations.

For smaller countries, investment in arms production often came to be seen as the best means available to them of remaining somewhere near the cutting edge of new technological developments. By pursuing military industrialisation, countries could not only maintain greater secrecy about their activities (on national security grounds), but also implement a de facto industrial policy while still nominally adhering to the terms of global trade conventions that called for reducing tariffs and subsidies. Additionally, indigenous small arms production assured that national military goals would not be hampered by international arms embargoes.

Therefore, over the course of the 1980s and into the 1990s, the number of states producing high-quality guns and munitions spread well beyond the confines of the Cold War alliance systems. Many developing countries now manufacture small arms, often under licence or with technology provided by the industrialised countries, and Brazil, Egypt, Israel and China have emerged as significant exporters. Small arms manufacturing companies established through licensing agreements frequently operate and export with less oversight than do the companies in North America and Europe that issue the production licences (see chapter 4 for more on the implications of the globalisation of small arms production).

On top of all of this new production resides large stocks of light weapons that the United States and Soviet Union supplied to Cold War proxy forces. The decade of the 1980s was one of the most violent in human history. Major conflicts raged in the Andes, the

Southern Cone, Central America, Southeast Asia, Southern Africa, the Horn of Africa, the Levant and the Persian Gulf—supported directly with arms from Moscow or Washington.

Many of these weapons vanished into zones of conflict which functioned for the arms trade the way bank secrecy havens do for the money laundering business: once inside, the weapons were lost to view, and any apparent control system therefore rendered irrelevant. In perhaps the most striking change in the structure and operation of the arms black market, places in which pitched conflicts were raging—such as Cambodia, Lebanon, the Horn of Africa and the Afghan-Pakistan border region—became exporters of weapons.

Added in the 1990s to the stocks accumulated in these conflict zones were massive amounts of weaponry being rendered, if not redundant, at least outside normal mechanisms of control by the dissolution of the Soviet Union, the collapse of the Red Army and the lunge by various republics, cities and even army units to grab and sell off local stockpiles.

At the same time, demand within the black market exploded. With the dissolution of the Soviet Union and the break-up of other states that owed their stable existence largely to the Cold War alliance system came a new set of wars in the 1990s. In addition, the traditional distinction between regular and irregular conflicts and formal and informal (insurgent) armies largely vanished. Guerrilla actions evolved into full-blown insurgencies, which in turn became civil wars that might then spill over to involve neighbouring states, with the demand for weapons of all sorts rising in step.

Certainly not least of the changes on the demand side was a shift in the use of weapons. During the Cold War, the armies of the two alliance systems acquired weapons less for use than to be stockpiled in a race in which the principal objective was to spend the other side into surrender. Meanwhile, many of their developing country allies acquired weapons, partly to impress or cow their public and partly so that purchasing officials could siphon off some corruption money. Under those circumstances, there was an incentive to buy the newest and most expensive equipment possible. (The actual ongoing insurgencies and coups required relatively little by way of equipment.)

Once the purpose of weapons became direct use, however, the choice of what to buy became much more flexible. Irregular armies at war do not much care about the appearance of their equipment, or its uniformity, provided parts are reasonably substitutable and ammunition is readily available. Furthermore, over the course of the 1980s and into the 1990s, a market for upgrade services spread, further obliterating many of the military advantages formerly conferred by purchasing new flows rather than second-hand stocks. That shift in demand helped open up a whole new range of sources from which to shop.

Will and Power

Governments vary greatly in their intention, willingness and ability to prevent their territories being used for illegal gun-running purposes. Loopholes in export control regimes exist everywhere, and in some cases illicit transfers result from governments not having a policy or a mechanism for control in place at all—whether due to acquiescence or lack of capacity. Even among wealthy countries with largely effective regulatory, law enforcement and customs practices, such as the United States and the United Kingdom, weapons trafficking occurs. The situation in countries without comparable resources can be much more serious.

Some governments are simply indifferent to arms trafficking and may even view it as the prerogative or perk of one or another component of the state (usually the intelligence agency). And in other cases covert government policy differs from official government policy and/or states aid other states in procuring weapons for either economic or political reasons.[7]

Thus far, the wealthier states, most of which produce and export small arms, have been most willing to focus on aspects of illicit arms trafficking such as helping states in the developing world devise national legislation or policies to manage stocks of weapons circulating outside of government control. While such assistance is important, these same states have been less willing to reform their own national laws concerning offshore brokering of arms deals, improved end-use certification and monitoring of transfers, all of which would reduce further inflows of illegal arms to the developing world. Nor have states grappled with the negative impacts of increased global trade in facilitating smuggling.

Generally, in order for a sale to take place, an end-use certificate is required. This certificate indicates that the recipient authorises the weapons delivery, and it is supposed to curb secondary trafficking once officially sanctioned weapons reach their intended destination. However, this system has been overwhelmed by a combination of commercial greed, political corruption and, not least, the sheer mass of material to be controlled. Today there is an active black market in these certificates, and many governments—or corrupt officials—are complicit in their abuse.[8] Chapter 1 demonstrates how smugglers readily falsify end-user certificates and other paperwork.

There are varying levels of other documentation required by states for the import and export of weapons. The granting of general import permits, which specify quantities rather than specific transactions, is one commonly exploited loophole.[9] States through which weapons transit often require no papers at all and can, therefore, be used to conceal the origin or destination of arms shipments. The trend toward common trade areas and international trade agreements has also had the effect of creating loopholes that can be exploited by commodity smugglers. The free transfer of goods through a common area can allow an illegal shipment to enter at one port and then pass through one or more additional countries undetected.[10]

Private brokers, sellers, transport agents and security companies that put together illegal deals are a key part of the global arms smuggling industry. Increasingly professionalised, those involved in arms trafficking use a chain of people and front companies, operate aircraft or ships registered under flags of convenience and exploit under-scrutinised ports, airstrips and borders to circumvent the few existing rules and regulations put up to prevent their activities. Chapter 6 covers these actors in some detail and lays out the policies that governments need to enact to contain them.

In addition, offshore banks and tax havens are used to hide and move the large amounts of cash that are central to illegal arms sales. The increasingly borderless world allows for rapid and generally anonymous money transfers to destinations that anti-money laundering efforts have not yet reached.[11] Although efforts to change bank secrecy policies and make large transfers of money more visible to law enforcement have been stepped up, common levels of transparency and information exchange do not yet exist.

Overcoming these many obstacles on the supply side would diminish the illicit gun trade by raising the financial and legal costs of participating in this deadly business. (Equally important, although not the primary focus of this book, are demand-side initiatives that focus attention onto the social and economic issues driving acquisition of arms for crime, insurgency or self-defence.)

Given the world-wide and interconnected nature of gun-running, legal and regulatory approaches in all of the above areas must be coordinated at the regional and global levels to be most effective. Even more fundamental, however, is a need for states to police themselves and to hold accountable other states that contribute to the illegal gun trade through acts of commission or omission.

Coordinated Government Action

Although a handful of governments in the South had sought for several years to focus the United Nations on the dangers of the illicit small arms traffic, the issue did not gain traction until 1995, with the UN Secretary-General's prominent call for 'microdisarmament' in his *Agenda for Peace*.[12] By the time of this speech, the United States, Russia, NATO and other major military powers were developing new, post-Cold War national security doctrine and priorities. They increasingly viewed arms trafficking as a major threat not only to human security—which had long been the case—but also to their new articulation of national security interests: regional and internal conflict, drug trafficking, international crime, terrorism and unfettered trade.

In addition, emphasis on small arms control was spurred by the work of several academics and by an influential a mix of humanitarian, disarmament, religious and violence-prevention groups. Many of the same organisations that came together to outlaw the trade and use of anti-personnel landmines subsequently set their sights on the broader category of light weaponry that was causing similar mass suffering around the world.[13]

As a result of these factors, since the mid 1990s governments have focused unprecedented levels of attention on the proliferation of light weapons—both in relation to crime (principally drug trafficking) and to humanitarian concerns.

As one of the earliest actions, in December 1995 the UN General Assembly instructed the Secretary-General to prepare a report on small arms, with the assistance of a Panel of Governmental Experts. This effort was motivated by concerns about the efficacy of UN operations in areas flooded with guns.[14] Reporting back in August 1997, the panel made 24 specific proposals—some reduction measures and others prevention measures. Among the latter, the panel recommended that the United Nations convene a conference on the illicit arms trade.

At its 53rd session (1999), the UN General Assembly endorsed this idea. The international conference, the first ever held by the UN on this topic, will likely occur in June or July 2001, in Geneva or New York. Throughout 2000 and the first part of 2001, states will come together to deliberate goals for the meeting. At this point, the most likely outcomes of the 2001 conference appear to be the development of non-binding norms relating to arms export practices and perhaps model regulations relating to controlling the activities of arms brokers and re-transfers of imported weapons.

The Mexican government opened a second diplomatic track in November 1996 within the Rio Group of Latin American nations. This effort culminated one year later in the signing by nearly all West Hemisphere governments of a convention negotiated through the Organisation of American States (OAS) against the illicit manufacture and trafficking of firearms, ammunition and related materials. Among other things, the treaty requires states to develop and implement laws and regulations setting out procedures for the legal manufacture, importation and exportation of firearms and components. As of February 2000, ten states had ratified the convention, which entered into force in 1998.

This regional treaty became a model, as several governments—including the United States, Canada and Mexico—pressed for the rapid negotiation by the end of 2000 of a global treaty on illicit arms trafficking. The 'Group of Eight' leading economic powers, which importantly includes Russia, endorsed this goal in 1998, and negotiation of this agreement is well under way as a protocol to a larger Transnational Crime Convention being negotiated by the United Nations in Vienna. Consensus appears to be growing around the protocol's general principles, but it is far from certain at the time of writing that this agreement will be completed by the end of 2000.

In addition, beginning in 1997 several other fora, including the European Union, Organisation for Security and Co-operation in Europe, Organisation of African Unity, Economic Community of West African States and South African Development Community all took up some aspect of small arms control, as did almost every part of the UN. Of particular note, the UN Security Council levied arms embargoes on 13 different parties during the 1990s and held ministerial meetings in 1998 and 1999 that focused specifically on gun-running, particularly to and within Africa.

Enforcement of these embargoes, however, has generally been weak.[15] An unusually direct Security Council report in March 2000 pointed to complicity by several states and private actors in undermining arms, diamond and oil embargoes levied against UNITA guerrillas in Angola.[16] Such sanctions-busting is a clear breach of international law obligations, as chapter 2 makes clear.

While the recently increased rhetorical and policy focus by governments on the illicit arms traffic represents movement in the right direction, this book is timed and intended to encourage governments to take *more* responsibility for and *more* action against the global trade in small arms through the above-named and other avenues. Several dangerous or suspect practices by governments and private actors that directly contribute to the international black-market arms trade are currently considered 'legal' and are not on the negotiating table at any of these fora. Many of these practices are illustrated in the following chapters. By taking a more expansive view of the factors that facilitate and fuel gun-running, and moving those activities into the realm of the controlled, if not prohibited, states might diminish this thriving and deadly trade.

Notes

[1] A good working definition is that grey sales 'violate national and international norms and policies, if not laws.' Michael Klare, 'The Subterranean Arms Trade: Black-Market Sales, Covert Operations and Ethnic Warfare,' in Andrew Pierre, ed., *Cascade of Arms: Managing Conventional Weapons Proliferation*, (Washington, DC: Brookings Institution Press, 1997), p. 47.

[2] Lack of adequate procedures to safeguard against diversion of legally-authorised arms transfers contributes to the crossover. For example, concerned about the quantity of firearms entering their countries, and the possibility for diversion to criminals, Latin American governments requested that the US government demand more extensive and careful documentation for export license applications by US industry to their countries (US Department of State, *Defense Trade News*, Vol. 5, No. 3 (1994), pp. 6, 13).

[3] One researcher has estimated the illegal arms trade at $2-10 billion annually (Michael Renner, 'Arms Control Orphans,' *Bulletin of the Atomic Scientists*, January/February 1999, p. 24). This guess seems plausible, but dollar valuations are highly questionable, since the value of the trade is a function of price times quantity. Price is less relevant than the quantity of weapons.

⁴ International Committee of the Red Cross, *Arms Availability and the Situation of Civilians in Armed Conflicts* (Geneva: ICRC, 1999).

⁵ See note 43 in chapter 5 for a reference list.

⁶ For example, following the war a retired military man named Sam Cummings bought up tons of surplus weapons and equipment, which he resold only with US government approval. Throughout the Cold War arms brokers like Cummings were largely drawn from three, interrelated professional classes—ex-arms company executives, veteran senior military officers or former intelligence agents, most of whom maintained relations with their former employers. Those ties permitted the major powers, within limits, to control the flow of arms to a particular region by facilitating or impeding arms deals.

⁷ In West Africa, for example, Burkina Faso has reportedly acted as a conduit to channel arms procured by Libya to fighters in Liberia and Sierra Leone. Weapons allegedly were flown from Libya to Burkina Faso, sent on to Côte d'Ivoire and transported by land to rebel forces in Liberia (Abdel F. Musah, 'Small Arms and Conflict Transformation in West Africa,' in Abdel F. Musah and Niobe Thompson, eds., *Over a Barrel: Light Weapons and Human Rights in the Commonwealth* (London/New Delhi: Commonwealth Human Rights Initiative, 1999), p. 121).

⁸ For more detail, see Tom Naylor, 'The Rise of the Modern Black Market and the Fall of Supply-Side Control,' in Virginia Gamba, ed., *Society under Siege: Crime, Violence and Illegal Weapons*, (South Africa: Institute for Security Studies, 1997).

⁹ *Ibid.*, p. 237.

¹⁰ James McShane, 'Light Weapons and International Law Enforcement,' in Jeffrey Boutwell and Michael T. Klare, eds., *Light Weapons and Civil Conflict*, (Lanham, Maryland: Rowman & Littlefield, 1999), p. 180.

¹¹ For a recent study on this issue, see Jack A. Blum, Michael Levi, R. T. Naylor, and Phil Williams, *Financial Havens, Banking Secrecy And Money-Laundering* (Vienna: United Nations Office of Drug Control and Crime Prevention, 1998).

¹² For a good summary of the history of UN involvement with small arms control, and in particular efforts to curb the illegal trade, see Graciela Uribe de Lozano, 'The United Nations and the Control of Light Weapons,' in Boutwell and Klare, eds., *Light Weapons and Civil Conflict*, pp. 161-171.

¹³ In May 1999 these groups formed the International Action Network on Small Arms. See www.iansa.org for a listing of members.

¹⁴ *Report of the Panel of Governmental Experts on Small Arms*, UN Doc. A/52/298, 27 August 1997.

¹⁵ One of the authors of this chapter (Naylor) thinks that embargoes are so badly focussed and hypocritical that it is better they not be used at all. See R.T. Naylor, *Patriots and Profiteers* (Toronto: McClelland & Stewart, 1999).

¹⁶ *Report of the Panel of Experts on Violations of Security Council Sanctions against UNITA*, UN Doc. S/2000/203, 10 March 2000.

part 1
FRAMING
THE ISSUE_____

1/Anatomy of a Shady Deal

by Brian Johnson-Thomas

Prologue, August 1999

It must once have been a pretty, tranquil little town, before the central planners decided to place heavy industry there and build giant concrete rabbit hutches to house the twenty thousand or so workers who were brought in. On my left the wooded hills rose steeply to the crest of the White Carpathian Mountains, with the odd onion-domed church dotting the skyline. Ahead lay the mass, and the mess, of Dubnica nad Váhom, centre of the Slovak Republic's thriving armaments industry.

Somewhere in that forest of chipped concrete and peeling paint, of shop windows protected by stout iron grilles, amongst the crowds of pinched, pale-faced housewives and bored, aimless youths, lay my objective—the headquarters of Hermes a.s., the largest private arms exporter in the Republic.

I was there to ask some questions about ammunition that Hermes had sent from Bratislava, the country's one true international airport, to the military regime in Sudan. Arms supplies to Khartoum are prohibited by a European Union arms embargo. I had already met some of the EU citizens who were breaking the embargo, but the weapons themselves were said to come from Dubnica, and I wanted to see the scene of the crime, as it were.

Of course I had tried the simple route—telephones and faxes. But my phone calls were never returned, and my faxes went unanswered. So here I was, about to indulge in what journalists term a 'doorstep.' Doorstepping consists simply of knocking on someone's door, talking your way inside and subsequently emerging triumphantly with the desired information. A simple concept, but not always easy to put into practice.

When I finally located the office block that was occupied by Hermes, it provided both a total contrast to its surroundings and an immediate physical challenge. Standing in immaculate lawns, the modern, low building had been designed by an architect rather than by a concrete box manufacturer. As the assortment of Mercedes and BMW cars parked outside also testified, it was redolent of serious money. It was also, alas, surrounded by a stout steel fence almost two metres high and protected by closed-circuit television. The high steel gates were electrically operated by an unseen eye, and I had to search hard for an entry phone system.

Perhaps fortunately, the operator spoke no English, and my Slovak is rudimentary at best. Thus, I was able to get an escort into the building itself, where I was met by an English-speaking secretary. She was neither helpful, nor hopeful, until I showed her an article which I had written for the London *Observer* several months previously, and which named Hermes as a supplier of arms to Sudan.[1] This piece of paper got me to second base: a seat in a light, airy boardroom containing expensive, imported Scandinavian furniture, a state-of-the-art video system and a very comprehensive collection of videos on the wide range of weapons systems for sale—everything from battle tanks to flare pistols, all made in the factories of Dubnica.

Coffee was offered. More functionaries arrived, examined the copy of the *Observer* article, conferred in low tones and left. I felt a little like a patient in a rather exclusive private clinic. Then, after half an hour or so, the door again opened and a middle-aged man, well dressed in a Harris Tweed sports jacket, entered.

'This,' said one of the young ladies flanking him, 'is our General Director.' Bingo. Forty minutes after my arrival, the serious talking could now, at last, begin. Punctiliously presenting his business card, which named him as Dusan Herda, he began by stating that my article contained several inaccuracies, of which the most serious were that the destination of the shipments was incorrect and that the value of each shipment, which was said to be around $50,000, was 'greatly exaggerated.'

I asked if it was possible for him to show me the original end-user certificate from the destination government and the matching export licence from his government, as these documents would clearly refute my story.

He replied that he had already discussed this possibility with relevant officials of the Ministry of Economics, and they had agreed that, exceptionally, I could indeed see those papers. I was then handed an end-user certificate, dated 8 August 1998, from the Defence Ministry of the Republic of Chad, stating that the goods (which it failed to specify) were for the 'exclusive use of the Armed Forces of Chad,' and an export licence from the Economics Ministry of the Slovak Republic allowing export, but naming the consignee as the Deir For Trading Company, PO Box 122, Damascus, Syria. Finally, I was shown a file of receipts for the delivery of shipments to Bratislava airport, four of which had been signed by two Britons whom I knew had been—at different times—the captain of the Boeing 707 freighter aircraft used.

There was a certain Wimbledon effect here since he was sitting at one end of a long table and I at the other, with a chorus of supporting staff along one of the other sides. As one, the heads accordingly swivelled to look accusingly at me.

I produced and passed hand to hand along the big table cargo manifests, air waybills and pro forma invoices, which showed conclusively that, although the cargoes had been described as for the Republic of Chad and accordingly consigned to the airport at N'Djamena, the cargoes were all stamped and signed for by the High Tech Group in Khartoum. I then also pointed out, as politely as circumstances allowed, that the invoices all showed individual consignment values of around $50,000.

Finally, I observed, Mr Herda was welcome to take copies of my paperwork, if he would kindly give me copies of the documents which he'd shown me. Saying that he would have to take further advice, Mr Herda and the entire 'A' team then withdrew, although one very young secretary did return briefly with a copy of the company profile that I'd earlier asked for.

The wait this time was longer—nearly 50 minutes—before he returned, but this time with only one secretary and a smartly suited gentleman who was introduced only as 'our Commercial Director,' although he was subsequently also referred to as 'the owner of the company.' This person never spoke at all, and when I pointedly asked for his name, the question was evaded repeatedly. He bears a marked resemblance, though, to photographs I've seen of one Mohammed Sayed, who manages—and maybe owns—Slovtrans, the company in Bratislava that made all the transport arrangements for the sanctions-busting flights. By a strange coincidence, it appears that Deir For Trading of Damascus is also owned by a Mohammed Sayed.

Mr Herda said that under instruction—not advice, this time— from the Ministry he could not allow me to copy any documents. I said that I understood, of course, the commercial sensitivity of contract documents but that, equally, nobody outside that room would necessarily believe me when I said that he'd been good enough to show them to me. I wondered whether he'd consider writing a note stating that I had, indeed, seen those papers and ex- plaining that commercial considerations precluded their publica- tion.

The delegation withdrew. Time passed.

Finally, Mr Herda returned with a signed statement that said I had examined 'relevant documents regarding the business matter [I] was interested in,' adding that, 'In view of the keeping of com- mercial secrets we can not provide copies' of those documents.

Mr Herda then shook my hand, saying 'Now I think it's better that you go.' I went, escorted, naturally, through several layers of secure doors.

And that, one might suppose, was that. Alas, not quite. During the 15-kilometre drive back to my hotel, I was vaguely aware of being followed. After collecting my room key, I went upstairs. The telephone was ringing. A male voice asked me, in English, to wait in my hotel as 'organs of state security' wished to interview me.

Accordingly, I rang my news desk at *The Times*, then adjourned to the hotel bar to await my visitors. Two men in leather jackets, open to show shoulder holsters, arrived. The elder gave me a quick flash of an ID card.

He had short-cropped, greying black hair, brown eyes and a mouth containing many steel teeth, with the remnants of his break- fast still attached. I noticed this particularly because he put his face very close to mine and said, enunciating slowly, 'You Have Been Asking Forbidden Questions.' Since the hotel brochure, which I'd read the night before, mentioned that the castle next door had once been the home of Stefan the Brave, I at once mentally christened my interlocutor Dogsbreath the Unwashed.

Dogsbreath then sat down on a chair opposite me, and his young acolyte, who affected an all-American gumchewin' gun- totin' wisecrackin' buttkickin' style, and whom I mentally dubbed Pepsi, took up the tale. 'What the boss means is that you're kinda an embarrassment. We're supposed to take you back to Bratislava for questioning, but we don't want no hard feelings. We'll take you to the Czech border if you'd prefer. I know what I'd do.'

Not much of a choice, really. I packed, paid my bill and sat in the back of a smart Skoda with Pepsi while Dogsbreath drove the quick half-hour up the opposite valley to the frontier post. Nobody shook hands, no one said goodbye, as I walked the short ten metres to the Czech guardroom.

I left a little bit wiser. But what had led me to Dubnica in the first place…?

Bar Talk, October 1998

Before the European Union introduced new, strict noise abatement regulations in January 1999, Belgium's Ostend Airport was a haven for beat-up Boeing 707 freighters, dodgy DC-8s and some pretty disreputable aircrews. These crews usually made their home-away-from-home in the bar of the Hotel Ter Streep, ten minutes from the airport, two minutes from the casino and just one minute to Ostend's minuscule red light district.

The bar is furnished in faded 1970s modern, with a pool table at the far end, assorted tables and chairs, plus a series of stools around the bar proper for the truly seasoned topers. For the rule is, if you sit at the bar you buy a round of drinks for all the others thereat, including standees and onlookers. Very often you're looking at buying a round of a couple of dozen beers. Obviously, one then has to stay long enough for the hospitality to be returned, so an early breakfast is not a predicted outcome.

A rather preppy 747 crew out of Chicago O'Hare was 'slumming it' over two tables, and two more tables were occupied by a band of elderly Dutch package tourists who'd come in out of the rain and who were clearly mesmerised by what one can only call 'the usual suspects'—vociferously propping up the bar and its surrounds. As Michel, a barman old enough to remember the wartime occupation of Belgium, rushed orders of beer hither and yon, Zu-Zu, just landed from Kinshasa, hammered out relaxing ragtime on the piano—still dressed in regulation flying uniform.

It was the Streep at its raucous, convivial best. As we sank our fourth—or maybe sixth—pitcher, my old friend 'Bob' suddenly grew confidential. 'Another three months and I reckon I can buy this place,' he volunteered. Naturally I asked what was prompting this change in his fortunes, especially as I'd had to spring for his cheap chicken and chips supper earlier.

'Green boxes,' he said, meaning an arms flight. 'Naughty green boxes to Khartoum. At least 20 flights and five grand each in brown envelopes after every one.'

Since arms shipments to Sudan are widely illegal by virtue of a European Union arms embargo, it wasn't surprising to learn that the five-man crew of a 707 freighter would earn $5,000 each for every flight, since they presumably ran the risk of either being imprisoned *en route* or, conceivably, back in Europe if the authorities should ever find out.

What was a little surprising, however, was the scale of the operation. Twenty flights would be around a thousand metric tonnes in weight. The cargo value, even at factory prices, was thus well over a million dollars for ammunition cargoes, or up to ten million greenbacks for decent weapons. You could say that Bob had attracted my attention. As nonchalantly as I could, I ventured 'Where are you flying out of, and who's risking his aircraft?'

Bratislava, said Bob, using Willie Haas's Seven-Oh.

'That's the one you flew the Russian heavy water to India on, isn't it?'

'Yeah. And I got five grand for that trip, too....'

I bought another round or three and, finally, before navigating with care towards the elderly elevator that eventually ascended to the bedrooms, I did the deal that I needed. In recognition of sundry chicken dinners and uncountable beers over the years, Bob would ring me 'in a few week's time,' offering a meeting place where he'd bring me originals—not copies—of invoices, air waybills, cargo manifests, crew lists and flight plans. The whole nine yards.

Explication in Valencia, 8-10 January 1999

My phone duly rang one evening just after the beginning of 1999. It was Bob, calling collect from the Hotel Tilapia in the Tanzanian town of Mwanza.

'I've got your docs for you,' he bawled. 'Can you meet me in Valencia on Friday?'

January in England: snow, ice, freezing fog. January in Spain: oranges on the trees, sunshine and *tapas* bars. No contest, really.

The hotel was the standard concrete cube, anonymous international, inhabited by business people and aircrews the world over. My room had the usual exciting view of a multi-storey car park, but you could just barely see a solitary orange tree—with real oranges—behind one corner.

I rang the airport, got through to the tower and established Bob's ETA. Time for a shower, a meal and even some relaxation before—shortly after two o'clock in the morning—the distinct sound of a non-hushkitted 707 on final approach filled the sky. On the very stroke of three, the crew bus arrived and five weary men crossed the hotel lobby to the bar that I was assiduously keeping open. I left them to it, while they had the traditional post-flight drink and left for their rooms and a good night's sleep.

I ordered two fresh San Miguel beers. They came, condensation frosting the sides of the glasses. The descending lift sighed to a stop, and Bob joined me in the far corner of the bar. From his back pocket he pulled a crumpled mass of paper. 'I must be bloody mad,' he said, 'but there you are.'

There, indeed, I was. All the damning documents I'd need to prove a deception as devious as it was incontrovertibly illegal.

I read. Bob explained. We talked. I took copious notes. I don't know how long we sat there, sipping sequential San Miguels, but I do remember that—by the time I'd returned to my room and dictated a rough first version to the night copy taker at London's *Sunday Times*, the first rays of Saturday's sun were touching my tame orange tree.

This is Bob's story....

Firstly, he said, the deal was even bigger than he'd expected. They were contracted to perform 120 flights at the rate of three flights a week. The freelance crew were each getting five thousand bucks per flight, and the aircraft was, on paper, being charged at another $30,000 per southbound flight. After the drop in Khartoum they were ferrying empty to Mwanza at the Tanzanian shore of Lake Victoria and returning to Europe with frozen tilapia. The frozen fish run was worth another $20,000 for each northbound load.

The two partners running the operation were a Briton, Christopher Barrett-Jolley, and a Belgian, Ronald Rossignol. Formerly operating a Belgian company out of Ostend Airport—Occidental Aviation—they had just bought in London a £100 off-the-shelf company to formally hold the current contract. The primary reason for this purchase was that Occidental was then in liquidation, floating belly up in a sea of debt after its one remaining aircraft un-

fortunately failed to leave the runway on take-off, and an unsym-
pathetic insurance company declined to pay out on the claim because the paperwork wasn't in order. These were minor problems,
like no maintenance records and one of the pilots not having a
valid licence. Details, always details.

So the septuagenarian Dr Waldermar Haas von Waldenbruch
had been persuaded, or prevailed upon, to grant a long lease on
his aircraft to the dynamic duo. Dr Haas, who lives in Switzerland,
owns a Cypriot airline called Avistar whose one asset at that time
was an ageing Boeing 707 freighter with the registration 5B-DAZ.
One of the most notorious 707s flying, it had carried clandestine
cargoes of arms to war zones across the alphabet from Angola to
Zaire, taking in Afghanistan and Yemen *en passant*.

So well known was 5B-DAZ that a purely cosmetic makeover
was predicated, and the aircraft underwent a renaissance, becoming 9G-ROX on the Ghanaian register. This fundamental change of
identity requires nothing more than filling in a few forms, paying a
small fee and using a tin of white paint and an even smaller tin of
black gloss for the registration letters on the aircraft's tail.

Aficionados of the power-of-good-over-evil school of thought
may take comfort from the fact that the aircraft crashed on take-off
from Bratislava exactly one month after our discussion in Valencia
and the publication of my *Sunday Times* article on 10 January.
Strangely, both the crew and the cargo vanished into the night,
leaving an empty, wrecked aircraft. The insurers have declined to
pay out on the crash, citing numerous irregularities and several
discrepancies in various accounts of the event.

But, I digress. The standard operating procedure, said Bob, was
to leave Bratislava at night with a full load of green boxes and in
possession of a flight plan, manifests and other paperwork all
pointing to a flight to N'Djamena, in Chad. Every cargo, in theory,
was destined for the Defence Ministry of the Republic of Chad—a
country not under any kind of arms embargo and thus free to buy
weapons from any source whatsoever.

The aircraft did not, of course, fly to N'Djamena on any of the
ten flights which Bob had made so far. The flight plan to Chad was
an elaborate fiction, and all the green boxes were instead delivered
to Colonel Omar of the High Tech Group in Khartoum, Sudan.

'Funny how some things don't change,' I interjected. 'Chris
Barrett-Jolley was filing false flight plans to Chad—N'Djamena in
particular—back in '94 when he was running guns to South Yemen

during the civil war. He told me so in an interview he gave when I was doing an ITV documentary.'

'Predictable, but not foolish,' was Bob's response. 'There's no radar surveillance to speak of once you're over the Med, so as long as it looks legal leaving Europe, who's to know?'

More importantly, thought Bob, the conviction had grown in him that not all the arms unloaded at Khartoum were actually going to stay in Sudan. 'On several occasions we've unloaded on the apron at KRT [Khartoum] and one of Viktor Bout's Antonov-12s has been bulk loading from our pallets straight into their hold,' he revealed.

Viktor is a former Russian KGB major who has taken the West's exhortations in favour of the free market very much to heart. He now runs a thriving business supplying both weapons and mercenaries to several—if not most—of Africa's current conflict zones. His gold chip client list included at that time such luminaries as the RUF guerrillas in the jungles of Sierra Leone and the Lord's Resistance Army in the barren wastes of northern Uganda.

Paper by paper, line by line, Bob led me through the labyrinth of documentation exposing—and it's easy once you know the tricks—the inconsistencies and downright impossibilities buried in a heap of apparently mutually self-supporting paperwork.

'After Khartoum, we always go to Mwanza,' he said, 'and take twelve hours of crew rest at the Hotel Tilapia. Northbound fish flights are never a worry because that part's all legal. Southbound flights would only be a problem if we had to abort and land elsewhere in Europe shortly after take-off and, even then, who's to say at that stage that we're not going down the route to Chad?'

That was enough for one night, or morning rather. As it was, we had to wake the slumbering bartender to pay the bill. Bed for Bob, and scribbling time for me. After filing my copy, I managed a scalding power shower and a doze before breakfast and an incessant stream of phone calls from the news desk, the lawyers and a whole string of *The Times* great and good. Then, silence. 'Stay in the hotel, we'll call you back. It's running in tomorrow's rag.'[2] Three hours of blessed sleep and I was back downstairs in the lobby, discreetly watching from behind the pages of *El Pais* as a five-man crew emerged from the lift, boarded a crew bus and left to fly empty back to Bratislava.

Green Boxes in Gisenyi, 23 February 1999

Six weeks after returning to London from Valencia, I had left for the Rwandan capital of Kigali. And now I sat in an armed convoy bound for Gisenyi, heart of the war zone in the far northwest of that benighted country. We were waiting—six food trucks and two Land Cruisers—for our Rwandan Army escort through territory liable to ambush by *Interahamwe* insurgents from their bases in the eastern part of the Democratic Republic of the Congo (formerly Zaire). We had a heavy escort for a real threat. Both the convoys before and after ours had been attacked, with a total of three military fatalities. That is not happy news at 6:30 in the morning, but our escorts did arrive. They took up positions ahead and behind us, and off we roared on the four-hour trip to Gisenyi.

Two hours up the road we made a breakfast halt at Ruhengeri, gateway to the 'Gorillas in the Mist' country. There I was suddenly grateful for the size of our escort for, by one of those coincidences that normally happen only to other people, I met an army officer whom I had first known some six years ago, when today's national army was then the rebel Rwandan Patriotic Front. Over a dark, sweet coffee and a croissant, Peter let slip the intriguing information that only the previous week the Ugandan Army had passed on to their neighbours in the Rwandan Army two truckloads of ammunition captured from Lord's Resistance Army (LRA) rebels in northern Uganda.

The Sudanese government supplies the LRA following the hallowed theory that 'my enemy's enemy is my friend,' and in the somewhat pious hope that Ugandan President Yoweri Museveni's men will thus be diverted from too openly supporting the Christian Sudanese Peoples Liberation Army in the south of Sudan. Leaving aside the politics for a moment, what intrigued me was that the ammunition was allegedly of East European origin, and that it was new stock, which Peter said was very unusual. Some of this ammo was stored in Gisenyi, my destination.

I should at this point explain that I was in Rwanda as part of the entourage of Olara Otunnu, the UN Secretary-General's Special Representative for Children and Armed Conflict. We were the advance party trucking gently up country before the high brass flew directly to Gisenyi the following day. I didn't, therefore, really expect much chance to chase up my own enquiries into arms flows.

The aforementioned Special Representative decided, however, to undertake an informal peace mission to Wamba Dia Wamba, part of the leadership of the rebel alliance fighting Congolese President Laurent Kabila. The arrangements for this supposedly secret meeting necessitated a cast, if not literally of thousands, of a few score people—principally the security escorts of the main protagonists. So it was that in a former Belgian colonial villa on the shores of Lake Kivu I saw a nondescript brown wooden box bearing the stenciled legend 'Cartridges with Bursting Charge Hermes a.s. Dubnica nad Váhom.' Now in a Rwandan Army guardroom, they were part of the captured consignment Peter had told me about back in Ruhengeri.

But the caravan rolled on, back through Rwanda, all across neighbouring Burundi and back, finally, to Nairobi. So it was some three weeks later, back in the tail end of an English winter, that I looked again at Bob's cargo manifests for 9G-ROX.

There it was: flight STV102, leaving Bratislava on 13 December 1998, signed and stamped by the High Tech Group in Khartoum one day later, 'Cartridges with Bursting Charge UN 0412. CLASS 1-4E, manufactured by Hermes a.s. of Dubnica nad Váhom in the Slovak Republic.'

Back to Belgium, 11-13 March 1999

It was clearly the right time to rush back into print. Forty-six hours after returning to England, I left for Belgium with a colleague from the London *Observer* newspaper. We had just two days to chase down some details in the Low Countries and write a story for that week's edition. Our primary destination was Ostend. Our targets were the two men who were behind the whole operation, Messrs Barrett-Jolley and Rossignol. Both of these gentlemen have enjoyed what one might term interesting careers, and I can claim both of them as acquaintances, if not exactly as friends.

Along with colleagues, I've interviewed Chris Barrett-Jolley on several occasions, the first being back in 1994 for a British TV documentary, accurately entitled 'The Gun Runners,' where he'd given us a fairly frank account of the rigours of supplying weapons to the rebel forces in South Yemen earlier that year. I've followed his subsequent career with interest, through Afghanistan and various African conflict zones, and, although he tends to avoid me of late, we certainly know each other.

I first met Ronnie Rossignol in 1996, when his company—Occidental—was flying arms from Burgas in Bulgaria to the Rwandan capital Kigali at the beginning of Laurent Kabila's campaign to oust Mobutu Seso Seko from the Presidency of then Zaire. Indeed, I'd flown part of the route on the Occidental aircraft before Ronnie & Co. realised that I wasn't who they thought I was, and I was unceremoniously dumped on the apron at Istanbul Airport during a routine refuelling stop. As it happens, I'd seen Ronnie much more recently than I'd seen his partner—just a fortnight earlier, in fact, in the Burundian capital, Bujumbura.

Much could be said about the Belgian national character, but one fact is indubitably true: they know how to host a good war. Wherever one travels throughout their former domains in Central Africa, it is an expatriate Belgian who will fix your transportation, arrange a decent bed for the night or serve you with a gourmet supper. So it was at the Yacht Club, the watering hole of the smart set on the shores of Lake Tanganyika, and close to the heart of downtown Bujumbura. True, the 8 p.m. curfew was a slight inconvenience, but the local wealth was out in force that Friday night, as we arrived on the terrace just in time to watch the sun set over the limitless ranges of Congolese mountains on the western horizon. And there, just three tables away, was Rossignol in animated conversation with a man I knew (from my own visit the previous night) was protocol chief at the Presidential Palace.

I don't know, of course, what was discussed, and if I told you my suspicions then the libel lawyers wouldn't like it. Anyway, I dare say that Ronnie wasn't entirely surprised when we doorstepped his Ostend Airport office just 14 days later. Not that he spoke to us, of course. While his office manager was going through a 'Ronnie Who?' routine, I just caught a glimpse of a familiar silhouette leaving by the far door of the hangar.

So it was back to the Belair Bar, fortunately haunted that evening by several pilots heavily into the flexible export market in light weaponry, to nail down sources for our story. I'm still not sure what the cleaning lady thought when she saw three men in earnest conversation in a far corner of the gent's toilet, and I'd rather not speculate, but we managed to get enough hard facts to file copy on the following morning. The full story ran in the *Observer* on 14 March 1999. We named C. Barrett-Jolley and Ronnie R. and itemised the Bratislava-Khartoum flights—false end-user certificates and all. Apart from one inconsequential whinge from Barrett-Jolley's lawyer much later, nobody has quarrelled with our version of the events.

From Slovakia to Serbia, Spring and Summer 1999

Alas for my continuing researches, Kosovo claimed the attention of many journalists, including me. Nothing further on this subject was published until July, when we were able to update the story just a little with news of Christopher Barrett-Jolley's new home address in England.[3] This article drew forth the aforementioned protest from his lawyers, thus prompting the doorstep in darkest Dubnica with which I started this account.

Since then, nothing, absolutely nothing. Nothing, that is, apart from confirmation from what I have, by convention, to term a 'Western intelligence official' that Mohammed Sayed—of Slovtrans in Bratislava—is the same Mohammed Sayed behind the Deir For Trading Company of Damascus.

They're all still there, all still around: The men who broker these deadly deals, the men who fly them to conflict zones, the officials in sundry economics ministries who refuse to want to know the truth, even the man in the Defence Ministry of the Republic of Chad who's been signing blank end-user certificates—for a consideration—for at least the last six years. A truly worldwide network, bound together by ties of deceit and greed.

Notes

[1] *The Observer*, 14 March 1999.
[2] *The Sunday Times* (London), 10 January 1999.
[3] *The Observer*, 4 July 1999.

HERMES a.s.
Okruzna 292, 01841 Dubnica nad Vahom
SLOVAK REP.

Pro-forma Invoice No.: ZFA012972
(Faktúra pre colné účely)

Our ref.:
Dubnica nad Vahom:

4.decembra.1998

Your ref:
Contrac No.:98/04034/HE

Purchaser:
Ministry of Defence
Republic of Tchad

Transport:
Air

Station of destination:
A´Djamena Airport
Republic of Tchad

Date and place of shipment:
december 98

Terms of delivery:
FCA Euroaiport

Terms of payment:
Irrevocable L/C opened in :
CeskoSlovenska Obchodna Banka a.s.
Jilemnickeho 2, 912 50 Trencin, Slovak Republic
account No.: 01167030/7500

Item	Description of the goods/services	Quantity pcs	Price USD/pc	Amount USD
1	100 mm HE			
		1 094	45,000	49 230,00
TOTAL				
				49 230,00

Signature and stamp:

HERMES
akciová spoločnosť
DUBNICA NAD VÁHOM
-1-

Phone:
0042-(0)827-22094
0042-(0)827-25574

Fax:
0042-(0)827-21150

Bank:
CeskoSlovenska Obchodna Banka a.s.
Jilemnickeho 2, 912 50 Trencin, Slovak Republic
account No.: 01167030/7500

2/What's Legal? What's Illegal?

by Emanuela-Chiara Gillard

'Illicit' arms transfers are commonly held to mean those that occur outside the control, or against the wishes, of exporting states. This chapter provides a more accurate assessment of what is 'legal' and what is not, through a fuller consideration of international law governing the sale or transfer of arms across two or more jurisdictions.

Although at present there are only a limited number of explicit prohibitions on arms transfers, there is a considerable body of law in diverse areas which, when put together, significantly curtails states' freedom to transfer weapons.[1] Furthermore, it is possible to discern the emergence of a rule of customary law, based on non-binding codes of conduct and their counterparts in national law, which requires exporting states to assess respect for fundamental principles of international law by recipient states and to refrain from authorising exports in cases where it is foreseeable that weapons will be used in violation of these principles.

After some preliminary remarks on international law, this chapter reviews explicit prohibitions on the transfer of weapons and then turns to other legal prohibitions and restrictions. The next section addresses limitations based on 'soft law' and on national laws. The concluding part assesses the emergence of customary law rules governing transfers of small arms.

Sources of International Law

Relevant international law can arise from a number of different sources, some of which do not have direct equivalents in domestic legal systems. While it is easy to identify the process by which new rules of law are created in domestic legal systems—usually the enactment of legislation—no such law-making mechanism exists for the creation of international law, with the possible exception of binding UN Security Council resolutions. Instead, rules of international law come into being through the consent of states, either explicitly, in the form of treaties, or implicitly, through state practice which may give rise to rules of customary law.

Treaties are probably the most important source of international law today. They may be bilateral or multilateral and may cover any aspect of international relations, including arms transfers or use. Once a treaty has satisfied all formal requirements for its existence and has entered into force, it imposes binding legal obligations on all states parties to it.[2] Failure by a party to a treaty to carry out the obligations assumed under that treaty amounts to a violation of international law.

In contrast to treaties and other negotiated agreements, the development of customary law is an ongoing phenomenon in response to the changing practices of states. Not all actions of states, however, lead to rules of customary international law. There must be general, uniform and consistent practice by states, accompanied by a belief that the practice is required by law, before states' practices crystallise into a rule of customary law. Relevant practices include actual activity by states, statements made in regard to concrete situations or disputes, statements of legal principle made in the abstract (such as those preceding the adoption of resolutions in the UN General Assembly), national legislation and the practice of international organisations. Although a review of legal restrictions in national legal systems is beyond the scope of this chapter, it is important to note that the growing body of domestic laws that regulate and restrict transfers of weapons contribute to the development of important trends in this area of law.[3]

The concept of 'soft law' has two meanings in international law. On the one hand it refers to rules of law that are indefinite and imprecise, but which nonetheless constitute obligations. For instance, steps that a state must take in order to meet treaty requirements could be described as soft law. The development of more definitive rules may result from the vague obligations that were initially adopted. Soft law may also refer to mere principles that may develop into rules of international law in the future but have not yet done so. Examples of this subordinate type of soft law may be found in the final statements of international conferences or non-binding agreements, such as codes of conduct. They typically take the form of aspirations or plans for the future.

The interaction between soft law, custom and treaty is important, particularly in areas where the law is evolving. Norms often find their first expression in a non-binding statement, which, with the passage of time and usage by states, develops into a rule of customary law and is ultimately codified in a treaty. As will become apparent, while there are currently few explicit prohibitions on transfers of small arms, there are a significant number of customary prohibitions and a growing body of soft law in the form of codes of conduct increasingly limiting transfers.

Before reviewing relevant law and norms, several preliminary points bear noting. First, it is states themselves that make international law, either by concluding treaties or by their actual behaviour. Thus, the paucity of rules expressly limiting states' rights to transfer weapons is not surprising. States, which have long been the main players in the arms trade, have been understandably reluctant to fetter their own freedom in this regard.

A second point concerns the scope of international law. Its principal purpose is to lay down rules prescribing the conduct of states. States are generally the 'subjects' of international law; violations of international law result in state 'responsibility.' Under traditional international law, non-state actors, such as individuals, are generally merely the 'objects' of international law.[4] Thus, although individuals may be the beneficiaries of international law norms—most notably human rights law—international law does not regulate their behaviour. (There are situations where international law may indirectly regulate individuals' behaviour by compelling states to regulate those under their jurisdiction—for example in implementing an arms embargo.)

This being said, the role of individuals, or private actors, in international law is progressively increasing, as illustrated by the fact that individuals are facing responsibility for war crimes in the two *ad hoc* tribunals established by the Security Council in response to the conflicts in the former Yugoslavia and Rwanda and, more importantly, under the recently adopted Statute of the International Criminal Court.[5] However, the interaction between international law and individuals is still uncertain and may give rise to loopholes in the law. Given the increasing role of private actors as suppliers, recipients and users of weapons, this problem is directly relevant to efforts to curb gun trafficking.

A final preliminary point concerns responsibility under international law. If a state commits a violation of international law, it bears primary liability for it. However, there may also be circumstances where a state has 'secondary' responsibility for a violation committed by another state. Many of the restrictions on transfers of weapons arise from this secondary, or derivative, responsibility.

In 1999 the International Law Commission (ILC), the UN body established to promote the development and codification of international law, addressed the issue of the responsibility of a state in regard to the actions of another.[6] In the same year, the drafting committee of the ILC adopted a draft article that addresses 'Aid or assistance in the commission of an internationally wrongful act.' According to this article,

> A State which aids or assists another State in the commission of an internationally wrongful act by the latter is internationally responsible for doing so if: (a) that State does so with knowledge of the circumstances of the internationally wrongful act; and (b) the act would be internationally wrongful if committed by that State.[7]

Thus, in situations where state A carries out an act, not necessarily illegal in itself, which assists state B in committing a wrongful act, if state A was aware of state B's (intended) wrongful act and this act would have been wrongful if state A had committed it, state A may bear secondary responsibility for the wrong committed by state B.

The commentary to an earlier version of the draft article gave a number of examples of this derivative responsibility. They included a state granting overflight or landing rights to another state for an unlawful military operation, or—more to the point—'a State that knowingly supplies arms to another State for the purpose of assisting the latter to act in a manner inconsistent with its international obligations.'[8] An obvious example would be if the recipient state was perpetrating a genocide. It should be noted that the current version of the draft article does not require state A to *intend* to assist state B in the commission of the wrongful act. Rather, a lower threshold of liability is adopted: It is sufficient that state A is aware of circumstances of state B's conduct.[9] The effect of this principle is that the manner in which the recipient state will use the weapons may affect the lawfulness of the transfer.

Finally, it should be noted that throughout this chapter the term 'transfer' is used to cover two scenarios: that where the state is the actual exporter, and that where the exporter is a private entity and the state is merely *authorising* the transfer. Although factually different, the two scenarios can be assimilated because they are governed by the same rules of international law. The limitations that the state must respect if it is itself exporting the weapons are identical to those it must respect when authorising the export by a private entity under its jurisdiction.

Express Prohibitions

The most basic form a specific prohibition on transfers of small arms could take is a multilateral or bilateral agreement banning transfers. As matters stand today, although the United Nations has sponsored multilateral negotiations for the non-proliferation of weapons of mass destruction, it has made little progress in banning conventional weapons. With the exception of anti-personnel landmines, the only specific agreement prohibiting transfers of small arms and light weapons currently in force is a non-binding moratorium discussed below. Nevertheless, explicit prohibitions of transfers are found in the rules of international humanitarian law and in embargoes.

International humanitarian law

International humanitarian law (IHL) is the body of rules that, in times of armed conflict, protects persons who are not or no longer taking part in the hostilities. It also restricts the methods and means of warfare employed. In so doing, IHL also imposes a number of limitations, some explicit and others implicit, on states' freedom to transfer weapons. Not only have multilateral conventions been concluded expressly prohibiting transfers of certain small weapons, but customary rules of IHL prohibit the use of certain other weapons. Furthermore, states' duties to ensure respect for and compliance with IHL further limits the circumstances in which states can transfer weapons, even those not unlawful under IHL. This section only addresses specific prohibitions; additional limitations imposed by IHL are discussed later in this chapter.

States have negotiated a number of conventions prohibiting the use of certain weapons. These include the 1868 St Petersburg Declaration Renouncing the Use, in Time of War, of Explosive Projectiles

under 400 grammes Weight; the 1899 Declaration concerning Expanding Bullets; the 1925 Protocol for the Prohibition of the Use in
War of Asphyxiating, Poisonous or Other Gases and of Bacteriological Methods of Warfare; the 1972 Biological Weapons Convention; the 1980 Convention on Prohibitions or Restrictions on the Use
of Certain Conventional Weapons which May Be Deemed to be Ex-
cessively Injurious or to Have Indiscriminate Effects (commonly
known as the Conventional Weapons Convention); the 1993
Chemical Weapons Convention; and the 1997 Convention on the
Prohibition of the Use, Stockpiling, Production and Transfer of
Anti-Personnel Mines and on their Destruction (the Landmines
Convention).

Several of these conventions prohibit outright the transfer of the
weapons in question.[10] The others merely proscribe the use of the
weapons and do not address the question of their transfer. Silence
on the issue of transfers should not, however, be equated with
freedom to transfer the weapons. Considering that the most recent
conventions expressly prohibit not just the use of the weapons but
also their transfer, it can be argued that they reflect the development that has taken place in the law since the adoption of the other
conventions and that this prohibition on transfers should be read
into the other instruments. This conclusion is supported by the fact
that it would be difficult to reconcile a state's right to transfer a
weapon, the use of which is prohibited, with that state's duty to ensure respect for IHL.

Embargoes on arms transfers

More general prohibitions on transfers of *all* weapons to specific
states or regions can be established by the imposition of embargoes
on such transfers by the United Nations or by other international
organisations. For the sake of brevity, this section focuses only on
embargoes imposed by the United Nations, but regional organisations—such as the European Union—have similar powers.[11] In addition, states can and do impose unilateral embargoes on transfers
of arms to particular states.

In the exercise of its responsibility for the maintenance of international peace and security, the UN Security Council has, in recent
years, made increasing use of its power to impose binding sanctions in situations that it determines amount to a 'threat to the
peace, breach of the peace or act of aggression' under Article 39 of

the UN Charter. These sanctions have often included the imposition of embargoes on transfers of arms to the state found to be in violation of international law and, in certain cases, to neighbouring states. An interesting development is the imposition of embargoes on non-state actors such as UNITA guerrillas in Angola and the remnants of the former *forces armées rwandaises* and the Rwandan militia.

The Security Council first imposed an arms embargo in 1965, on Southern Rhodesia.[12] This resolution called upon member states to refrain from 'providing [Southern Rhodesia] with arms, equipment and military material.'[13] Subsequently, the Security Council enacted similar arms embargoes on South Africa in 1977;[14] Iraq in 1990;[15] Yugoslavia in 1991;[16] Somalia, Libya and Liberia in 1992;[17] Haiti and UNITA forces within Angola in 1993;[18] Rwanda and the Bosnian Serbs in 1994;[19] states neighbouring Rwanda in 1995;[20] Sierra Leone in 1997;[21] and the Federal Republic of Yugoslavia in relation to Kosovo in 1998.[22] As of April 2000, UN-mandated arms embargoes remain in force against the governments of the Federal Republic of Yugoslavia, Iraq and Liberia; against all parties in Somalia; and against non-governmental forces in Angola, Rwanda and Sierra Leone.[23]

Security Council decisions to impose arms embargoes under Chapter VII of the Charter are binding on all members of the United Nations. Obligations of states ensue on two levels. First, states themselves are prohibited from transferring weapons to the embargoed state. In addition, pursuant to Article 25 of the Charter, states must also take the necessary measures to implement, apply and enforce the embargo internally to make it operative against individuals and companies within their jurisdiction.

Embargoes thus impose prohibitions on both states and private actors. Violations by states, or their failure to properly implement the embargo domestically, give rise to state responsibility on the international level, while violations by individuals give rise to their responsibility under national law. The precise nature of this responsibility—that is, whether transfer of weapons in violation of the embargo will be a civil or criminal offence—is left to the discretion of states in their implementing measures.[24] In a 1998 resolution, however, the Security Council called upon all states to adopt national legislation making the violation of arms embargoes a criminal offence.[25]

Although embargoes are binding on states as soon as they are adopted by the Security Council, precisely when and how they become operative as regards private actors depends on the legal mechanism adopted by each state for their implementation. Under the laws of some states, embargoes are binding on the national level as soon as they are adopted by the Security Council. More often, however, it will be necessary for the state to take some implementing measures, like the adoption of legislation or regulations.

The Security Council resolutions set the minimum requirements of the embargo, both in terms of the weapons covered and of whom it will apply to. With regard to the weapons covered by the embargo, the resolutions have varied from the very general, like the embargo on Somalia, which required states to implement 'a general and complete embargo on all deliveries of weapons and military equipment,'[26] to a very detailed list of prohibitions in terms both of activities and persons covered. An example of the latter is the embargo imposed on Libya, which required states to:

(a) prohibit any provision to Libya by their nationals or from their territories of arms and related material of all types, including the sale or transfer of weapons and ammunition, military vehicles and equipment, paramilitary police equipment and spare parts for the aforementioned, as well as the provision of any types of equipment, supplies and grants of licensing arrangements, for the manufacture or the maintenance of the aforementioned;

(b) prohibit any provision to Libya by their nationals or from their territory of technical advice, assistance or training related to the provision, manufacture, maintenance or use of the items in subparagraph (a) above.[27]

National implementation measures will generally spell out in more detail the scope of the prohibition and set out the mechanisms for domestic implementation.

In practice, however, enforcement of arms embargoes has proven problematic, as states and private actors have violated them with impunity. The Security Council recently has begun to develop mechanisms to follow up and oversee implementation. In 1995 the Security Council established the International Commission of Inquiry to investigate allegations of violations of the embargo on Rwanda.[28] More recently, in May 1999 the Security Council established a Panel of Experts to investigate violations of the sanctions imposed against UNITA guerrillas in Angola.[29] The Panel's report, issued in March 2000, surprised many with its specific identification of governments, individual politicians and private persons involved in embargo-busting activities.[30] With regard to the violations of the arms embargo, the Panel made the following recommendations, among others:

> the application of sanctions against leaders and governments found to have been deliberately breaking the sanctions relating to the supply of arms and military equipment to UNITA. Sanctions on identified embargo busters might include an embargo on arms sales to named countries for three years to be followed by three years of international probation;

> support for the Chairman of the Sanctions Committee's proposal of June 1999 that compliance with UN sanctions regimes should be among the criteria considered by NATO and the European Union when evaluating new candidates for membership.[31]

Although useful as a mechanism for limiting the influx of weapons into an area of conflict, arms embargoes are of limited use in preventing the build up of arms. The Security Council enacts embargoes only after it has made a determination that a threat or breach of the peace exists. Thus, UN embargoes do nothing to head off situations of violence deemed to be below this threshold. In addition, lack of political will within the Security Council or other relevant bodies frequently has stymied the imposition of sanctions.

Other Prohibitions and Limitations

Law regulating other areas imposes additional limitations on states' freedom to transfer arms. While the explicit limitations thus far mentioned make any transfer illegal, many of the limitations discussed in this section are dependent on how the recipient state *uses* the weapons. The exporting state's liability is based on its participation in the recipient state's wrongful act.

The UN Charter

The United Nations Charter neither expressly prohibits nor permits the use or transfer of any specific weapon. However, its provisions regulating recourse to the use of force are of relevance to the question of arms transfers. The cornerstone of the Charter is the prohibition against the threat or use of force enshrined in Article 2(4). All other provisions of the Charter, including those which permit resort to force in certain circumstances, must be read in light of this prohibition. Thus, although Article 51 of the Charter preserves states' inherent right to use force in self-defence—a right often interpreted as implying that states have the right to acquire weapons with which to defend themselves[32]—this right, and the corresponding right of other states to supply weapons, is subject to a number of limitations.

It is well established that excessive accumulation of weapons has destabilising effects and can, in certain circumstances, amount to a threat of the use of force in violation of the Charter. This finding imposes responsibilities both on exporting and on importing states to limit the quantity of imports.[33]

Moreover, if it is apparent that the receiving state will use the weapons in violation of the prohibition on the use of force against the territorial integrity and political independence of another state, the transfer will be prohibited even in the absence of an arms embargo. A state that transferred weapons in such circumstances would be participating in the illegal conduct of another state.

Also of importance are the Charter provisions dealing with disarmament and arms regulation and the initiatives of the General Assembly and the Security Council in this field. Arms regulation is of crucial importance to the United Nations' primary purpose of maintaining international peace and security.[34]

Customary law prohibitions on the use of force and interference in domestic affairs

Existing alongside the prohibition enshrined in the UN Charter, a customary law prohibition of the use of force imposes the same limits on transfers of weapons. Additional limitations are to be found in other customary law rules. One such limitation arises from the principle of non-intervention in the domestic affairs of another state. Thus, if state A transfers weapons into the territory of state B without complying with state B's domestic rules for imports and without state B's authorisation, not only does the failure to respect the applicable rules make the transfer illegal under national law, but the supply of weapons can amount to unlawful interference in state B's internal affairs. Allegations of interference are particularly the case if the weapons are supplied to assist opposition forces within the recipient state.[35]

In 1965 the General Assembly adopted the Declaration on the Inadmissibility of Intervention in the Domestic Affairs of States and Protection of their Independence and Sovereignty.[36] In addition to reaffirming the principle of non-intervention proclaimed in the charters of a number of regional organisations, the General Assembly declared that:

> No State has the right to intervene, directly or indirectly, for any reason whatsoever, in the internal or external affairs of any other State. Consequently, armed intervention and all other forms of interference or attempted threats against the personality of the State or against its political, economic and cultural elements, are condemned.

> Also, no State shall organise, assist, foment, finance, incite or tolerate subversive, terrorist or armed activities directed towards the violent overthrow of the regime of another State or interfere in civil strife in another State.

The question of interference in the domestic affairs of another state was also addressed by the International Court of Justice in a case between Nicaragua and the United States. The Court found that by arming, financing and training the *contra* guerrilla forces, the United States had broken the obligation under customary international law not to intervene in the affairs of another state.[37]

It is thus well established that transfers of weapons in such circumstances can be characterised as unlawful intervention in the internal affairs of another state and, as such, prohibited. On the basis of the 'derivative responsibility' principle discussed above, this prohibition also extends to seemingly lawful transfers if it is apparent the recipient state will use the weapons for unlawful interference in the internal affairs of a third state.

Terrorism

Closely related, numerous initiatives of the international community have outlawed the provision of weapons for use in acts of terrorism. The first attempt to codify this prohibition was the League of Nations' 1937 Convention for the Prevention and Pun-

ishment of Terrorism. It required parties to criminalise 'the manufacture, obtaining, possession or supplying of arms, ammunition,
explosives or harmful substances with a view to the commission in
any country whatsoever' of an act of terrorism.[38] The 1937 convention never entered into force, but the principles it enshrined re-
appeared in numerous other international instruments.

The General Assembly's 1970 Declaration on Principles of International Law reiterated the duty of states to refrain from 'organising, instigating, assisting or participating in ... terrorist acts in another state.'[39] A similar prohibition against the provision of direct
or indirect assistance to terrorists was repeated in the General Assembly's 1988 Declaration on the Enhancement of the Effectiveness
of the Principle of Refraining from the Threat or Use of Force in International Relations.[40] More directly, the 1989 version of the International Law Commission's Draft Code of Crimes Against the
Peace and Security of Mankind classified intervention in the affairs
of a state as crime against the peace and defined it as 'fomenting
[armed] subversive or terrorist activities by organising, assisting or
financing such activities *or supplying arms for the purpose of such activities*, thereby [seriously] undermining the free exercise by that
State of its sovereign rights' [emphasis added].[41]

International humanitarian law

As discussed above, conventions concluded in the field of international humanitarian law expressly prohibit transfers of certain
weapons. In addition, IHL imposes a number of other important
limitations on transfers of small arms. One limitation, like the prohibitions enshrined in treaties, is based on the nature of the weapons. Two of the cardinal principles of humanitarian law lay down
the basic customary law rules according to which the legality of
every weapon is assessed. The principle of distinction between
combatants and non-combatants prohibits the use of weapons that
are intrinsically incapable of distinguishing between combatants
and non-combatants.[42] The second principle prevents states from
using weapons 'of a nature to cause superfluous injury or unnecessary suffering.'[43] The conventions outlawing the use of specific
weapons discussed earlier in this chapter are just one example of
how these principles are put into practice. A number of other types
of small arms and ammunition whose use has not been regulated
by a convention may, nevertheless, be prohibited on the basis of

these customary rules of IHL. In such cases, as discussed above, an argument in favour of a prohibition on the transfer of the weapon could be made on the basis of the illegality of its use.

Secondly, the manner in which weapons that are not by their very nature unlawful are used may impose limitations on their transfer. Common Article 1 to the four Geneva Conventions of 1949, which codify customary rules of IHL, obliges states to 'respect and ensure respect' for the rules of IHL. While the primary responsibility for compliance with international law lies with the actual users of the weapons, states have the responsibility to ensure respect for humanitarian law. The International Committee of the Red Cross, the body entrusted with promoting and strengthening IHL, argues that states—and businesses—engaged in the production and export of small arms should bear some responsibility for the use made of the weapons and ammunition they transfer or sell.[44] A state that provides weapons in circumstances where it is likely they will be used to commit serious violations of IHL would clearly be failing its duty to ensure respect for IHL.[45]

Human rights law

Human rights law is another important source of limitations on transfers of weapons. If it is foreseeable that the recipient state will use the weapons to commit serious violations, then exporting states are prohibited from providing the weapons on the basis of their duty to ensure the respect for fundamental human rights. The most obvious ways that a recipient state could use weapons in violation of human rights norms would be to commit extra-legal or arbitrary executions, to torture people or to detain individuals in violation of human rights standards.

The prohibition of transfers could also be applicable where, rather than committing human rights violations itself through its agents, the recipient state is unable to control private actors who have control of the weapons. Such a situation would be a violation of the state's duty to protect the right to life. Thus, states should refrain from supplying weapons to states where it is likely they will fall into the hands of individuals over whom the government is incapable of exercising authority and control.

Certain provisions of human rights treaties can be suspended in times of armed conflict. However, it is well established that some core rights continue to apply. These include the right to life and the prohibition on cruel, inhuman and degrading treatment—the rights most likely to be breached by abuse of small arms.

Genocide

The 1948 Convention on the Prevention and Punishment of the Crime of Genocide prohibits and criminalises acts of genocide. Article 3 of the convention includes among the criminal activities not only genocide, but also conspiracy to commit genocide and complicity in genocide. Therefore, it is possible for not only the perpetrator but also for a state that has assisted in the perpetration of a genocide, for example by providing the weapons with which the genocide was committed, to be responsible under the convention. However, it is unlikely that states supplying weapons have the intent to 'destroy in whole or in part a national, ethnical, racial or religious group' required by Article 2 of the convention for their actions to amount to complicity in genocide. In situations falling short of this intent, states that supply weapons in circumstances in which it is foreseeable they will be used to perpetrate genocide will nevertheless be acting in violation of international law.

Non-Binding Limitations

So far this chapter has only considered legally binding limitations on transfers of weapons. However, as explained at the outset, there is an important body of norms which, although not binding at present, are proposals for development. They represent principles that could in the future become law. In the context of arms transfers these include non-binding agreements banning transfers and non-binding codes of conduct.

Agreements prohibiting transfers

To date the only agreement banning transfers of small arms is the moratorium concluded on 31 October 1998 by the members of the Economic Community of West African States (ECOWAS).[46] The non-binding moratorium quite simply prohibits the 'importation, exportation and manufacture of light weapons in ECOWAS member states' for a renewable period of three years. Accordingly, any transfer would apparently be illegal for both exporting and importing states.[47]

Codes of conduct

The idea of employing codes of conduct to regulate arms exports is not new. In 1991 the five permanent members of the UN Security Council adopted guidelines to this effect.[48] These provided that the states in question would avoid transfers likely to prolong or aggravate an existing armed conflict; increase tension or introduce destabilising military capability in a region; contravene embargoes or other internationally agreed restraints; be used otherwise than for legitimate defence and security needs; support international terrorism; be used to interfere in the internal affairs of sovereign states; or seriously undermine the recipient state's economy. The methods for implementing the guidelines were left to the individual states. Following Chinese withdrawal from the discussions in 1992, in stated reaction to a major arms sale by the United States to Taiwan, no further progress was made in implementing the guidelines.

In November 1993 the Organisation on Security and Co-operation in Europe adopted a document entitled 'Criteria on Conventional Arms Transfers,' which required states to take into account a number of factors when considering proposed transfers. These factors included the recipient state's human rights record, its record of compliance with international commitments, and the nature and cost of the arms in question in relation to the circumstances of the recipient state. The criteria provided that states would avoid transfers likely to be used, among other things, to suppress human rights, to threaten the national security of other states, to prolong or aggravate existing conflicts or to support or encourage terrorism.[49]

In addition, in 1996 the United Nations Disarmament Commission put forward Guidelines for International Arms Transfers.[50] Although these addressed a number of issues in addition to the regulation of legal transfers, they did not establish specific criteria to be considered by exporting states.

The most comprehensive initiative of this kind to date is the Code of Conduct for Arms Exports adopted by the Council of the European Union in June 1998. This instrument covers exports of military equipment—including small arms and light weaponry—and dual-use goods.[51] The European Union has left the regulation d dual-use goods.[51] The European Union has left the regulation of arms transfers to the exclusive competence of member states, and the Code of Conduct is the first step toward harmonisation of the 15 member states' policies and regulations. Its aim is to set minimum standards to be applied by all states when considering exports of weapons.

The Code of Conduct requires states to consider requests for exports of military equipment on a case-by-case basis, assessing their compatibility with eight criteria before authorising exports:

1) Respect for the international commitments of EU Member States, in particular the sanctions decreed by the UN Security Council and those decreed by the Community, agreements on non-proliferation and other subjects, as well as other international obligations;

2) The respect for human rights in the country of final destination;

3) The internal situation in the country of final destination, as a function of the tension or the existence of tension or armed conflicts;

4) The preservation of regional peace, security and stability;

5) The international security of the Member States and of territories whose external relations are the responsibility of a Member State, as well as that of friendly and allied countries;

6) The behaviour of the buyer country with regard to the international community, as regards in particular to its attitude to terrorism, the nature of its alliances and its respect of international law;

7) The existence of a risk that the equipment will be diverted within the buyer country or re-exported under undesirable conditions; and

8) The compatibility of the arms exports with the technical and economic capacity of the recipient country, taking into account the desirability that states should achieve their legitimate needs of security and defence with the least diversion for armaments of human and economic resources.

Not all criteria are accorded the same importance. If certain criteria are not met, the Code requires states to refuse to grant the export licence. These include situations in which the export would violate the exporting state's own international obligations; the existence of a clear risk that the equipment in question might be used for internal repression; or that it would be used aggressively against another country to assert by force a territorial claim. With regard to other criteria, states are merely required to 'exercise special caution and vigilance in issuing licences.' This latter approach is adopted, for example, with regard to exports to countries where 'serious violations of human rights have been established by the competent bodies of the United Nations, the Council of Europe or the EU.' Finally, with regard to the other criteria, member states are merely required to 'take into account' certain factors.[52]

The Code also contains operative provisions aimed at harmonising its application by member states and increasing transparency.[53]

The principal weakness of the EU Code of Conduct is that it is merely a non-binding statement of intent.[54] With regard to its substance, the Code has been criticised first because a number of the criteria, most notably those concerning the human rights situation in the receiving state, are not sufficiently explicit. The criteria are considered ambiguous and leave too much scope for individual interpretation to member states. Secondly, it fails to include violations of international humanitarian law in the receiving state as a ground for refusing the transfer. Under the Code, such violations are merely something the exporting state should 'take into account.' And thirdly, the Code relates exclusively to exports of weapons and does not address related issues such as brokering and licensed production of weapons.

With regard to its implementation, the principal weakness lies in the fact that the ultimate decision of whether to grant an export licence remains at the discretion of national authorities, and cannot be challenged. Moreover, critics cite the lack of transparency of the process: information exchange between states on licence denials remains confidential; the process is not open to parliamentary scrutiny; and member states are not required to report regularly and comprehensively to the public on implementation.[55]

Despite these criticisms, the establishment of such a system is an important development for the promotion of accountability and transparency in arms transfers. It is important to note that, since its adoption in 1998, the geographical scope of application of the Code of Conduct, originally limited to the 15 members of the European Union, has been considerably extended through its adoption by the states of East and Central Europe with which the European Union has concluded association agreements, Cyprus, the European Free Trade Association countries, members of the European Economic Area and Canada. Most recently, in December 1999 the United States endorsed the EU Code of Conduct principles.[56]

The idea of establishing codes of conduct for the export of weapons—be they international, regional or national—has met with support from a number of sides. In his 1995 report on the work of the Advisory Board on Disarmament Matters, the UN Secretary-General raised the possibility of establishing such a code in supplier states in Africa,[57] and in 1997 the Organisation of American States adopted a convention on illicit firearms trafficking establishing common procedures to regulate small arms exports among the majority of states in the Western Hemisphere (see chapter 8 for more on this agreement).

Efforts are also being made at the national level in a number of states to enact legislation implementing similar codes of conduct. Obviously, these internal codes are binding. For example, in 1995 South Africa adopted a new policy which imposed conditions on transfers of weapons to a number of identified states experiencing civil strife or human rights abuses, while guidelines for arms transfers adopted in 1996 require South African arms exports to be screened according to human rights and security criteria in the receiving country and to be approved by a cabinet-level minister.[58] Similarly, in June 1997 the United States House of Representatives passed legislation containing a strong code of conduct for US arms transfers based on human rights and other criteria. Although this bill failed at the House-Senate conference committee stage, a compromise bill was enacted in 1999, requiring the US government to initiate multilateral negotiations toward an international code of conduct which would prohibit arms transfers to states that fail to meet a set of strict human rights and democracy criteria.

In reality, such an effort has already been underway since 1996, in the International Code of Transfers that is being developed and promoted by a commission of 17 Nobel Peace Prize winners under the leadership of former Costa Rican President Oscar Arias. This draft code is by far the strictest and most comprehensive proposed to date, both in terms of criteria to be considered and in terms of the activities to which the code applies.[59] This proposal covers transfers of weapons, transfers of technology and brokering activities, and it includes a requirement that participating states enact the code into national law and introduce measures for effective implementation and enforcement.[60]

Codes of conduct—expressly listing circumstances in which states should refrain from transferring weapons based on the situation in the recipient state—are an innovation in international standard setting. However, they do not themselves actually impose substantive new limitations on states' freedom to transfer weapons. Rather, they bring together and codify existing limitations under international law and are a mechanism for the development of international public opinion about which kinds of arms transfers should be considered unethical and worthy of censure or sanction, and which should be considered legitimate.

Conclusions

This review of the rules and mechanisms regulating transfers of weapons shows that, although there are few explicit legal restrictions on states' freedom to transfer weapons, there are a number of situations in which transfers of weapons are prohibited because it is foreseeable that the weapons will be used by the recipient state in violation of international law. Moreover, many states—including most of the principal exporters of weapons—have adopted national codes of conduct requiring them to assess the compliance of the receiving state with fundamental principles of international law before authorising transfers. Additionally, a number of non-binding guidelines—once again, accepted by most of the principal weapons-exporting states—impose similar requirements.

As explained at the outset, customary international law is a body of rules that is constantly developing and evolving. It is therefore appropriate to ask whether any emerging rule of international law can be discerned from states' practice in this field. Apart from the ECOWAS moratorium, there have not been any instances of outright bans of transfers of small arms and light weapons. Instead, much more widespread are measures limiting the circumstances in which arms transfers can be carried out and requiring states to consider the situation in the receiving state before authorising transfers. Such guidelines exist both in international law and in domestic legal systems. Although the international instruments are not legally binding, often they mirror the binding requirements of export criteria under national law.

As also discussed in the introduction to this chapter, national laws are an important source of state practice. And when, as in the present case, there is a coincidence of approach in the national laws of the states most closely associated with a particular activity—in this case weapons-exporting states such as certain members of the European Union, the United States and South Africa—accompanied by instances of state practice on the international level where the same approach has been adopted internationally, it can be argued that a customary rule of international law is evolving.

Is it possible to identify the content of this emerging rule? National laws and international law share the requirement that exporting states establish licensing requirements for arms exports under which requests for exports are reviewed individually and assessed on the basis of a number of criteria.

The first criterion prohibits transfers that would put the authorising state in violation of its own obligations under international law if it authorised the transfers. It includes the questions of whether any treaties prohibiting the transfer of the weapons in question exist or whether there is an embargo in force against the proposed recipient.

The subsequent criteria address the situation in the recipient state and its possible violation of international law, for which the exporting state could have secondary responsibility if it were to provide weapons. Precisely what aspects of the recipient state's compliance with international law they cover is still uncertain, in view of the different approaches adopted by the various instruments. However a list of 'core' violations can be drawn up, and if it is foreseeable that the weapons will be used by the recipient state for the commission of those violations of international law, the export should not be authorised. A possible list of core violations would include:

- the violation of the prohibition against the use of force;
- intervention in the internal affairs of another state;
- the perpetration of serious violations of human rights;
- the perpetration of serious violations of international humanitarian law (although some of the codes of conduct seem to consider compliance with IHL as a secondary issue, inasmuch as

grave breaches of IHL can be assimilated to serious violations of human rights they should be included);
- the commission of genocide;
- the commission of terrorist activities.

At present the Nobel Laureates' draft code is the only instrument whose scope goes beyond transfers of weapons. It cannot presently be argued, therefore (as desirable as it may be to do so), that emerging customary law will dictate that states must apply these same criteria when granting licences to brokers or authorisations for licensed production agreements or transfers of technology.

Notes

[1] See C.G. Weeramantry, 'Traffic in Armamantry: A Blind Spot in Human Rights and International Law,' *Justice without Frontiers: Furthering Human Rights*, Vol. 1 (1997), p. 228.

[2] Different frameworks exist for giving effect to treaties at the national level. In some states, treaties automatically come into force once entered into by the government. In others, legislative ratification is necessary. Thus, treaties may serve in some countries (such as the United States) as the norm to which the national legislation must then conform, but they have no direct effect at the national level until the legislature actually drafts and passes implementation legislation.

[3] Since national legal restrictions on arms transfers can give rise to a rule of customary international law of similar content, it is necessary to sketch out the main features of national arms export regimes. The most common requirement is the need for government approval of exports by means of a licence. The circumstances in which a licence is required vary, but usually these cover transfers of weapons or related equipment appearing in an export control list drawn up by the government. In deciding whether to grant a licence, governments sometimes must consider a number of issues relating to the specified destination and end user of the weapons. A typical example is the United Kingdom's 'Export Assessment Criteria,' under which a licence is not to be granted if the arguments in favour of the export 'are outweighed by the need to comply with Britain's international obligations and commitments or by concern that the good might be used for internal repression or international aggression, or by the risks to regional stability.' In addition, many states also require an end-user certificate confirming the final destination of the weapons and their non-export, signed by a political or diplomatic authority in the recipient state.

[4] In one major noteworthy exception, Common Article 3 to the Geneva Conventions of 1949 and Additional Protocol II of 1977 to the Conventions

requires non-state actors to abide by certain norms of international humanitarian law.

[5] The International Criminal Tribunal for Yugoslavia, established by Security Council resolution 827 of 25 May 1993; the International Criminal Tribunal for Rwanda, established by Security Council resolution 955 of 8 November 1994; and the Rome Statute of the International Criminal Court adopted on 17 July 1998.

[6] The International Law Commission's usual method of work is to prepare drafts on topics of international law. When draft articles on a particular topic have been completed, the General Assembly convenes an international conference of plenipotentiaries to incorporate the draft articles into a convention to which it is then open to states to become parties. Conventions based on ILC draft articles include the 1961 Vienna Convention on Diplomatic Relations; the 1969 Vienna Convention of the Law of Treaties; and the 1978 Vienna Convention on Succession of States in Respect of Treaties.

[7] International Law Commission, 51st session, 3 May–23 July 1999, State Responsibility, Titles and texts of draft articles adopted by the Drafting Committee, UN Doc. A/CN.4/L.574 as corrected, article 27.

[8] *Yearbook of the International Law Commission* 1978, Vol. II, Part 2, p.103.

[9] For a detailed discussion of the question of intention or knowledge of wrongfulness, see the report by the Special Rapporteur, International Law Commission, 51st session, 3 May–23 July 1999, Second report on State Responsibility, UN Doc. A/CN.4/498/Add.1, paras. 178-179.

[10] Article 1 of the 1972 Convention on the Prohibition of the Development, Production and Stockpiling of Bacteriological (Biological) and Toxin Weapons and on Their Destruction; Article 1 of the 1993 Convention on the Prohibition of the Development, Production, Stockpiling and Use of Chemical Weapons and on their Destruction; Article 1 of Protocol IV to the 1980 Conventional Weapons Convention; Article 8 of Protocol II to the 1980 Conventional Weapons Convention on Prohibitions or Restrictions on the Use of Mines, Booby-Traps and Other Devices as amended on 3 May 1996; and Article 1(b) of the 1997 Landmines Convention.

[11] For example, at the beginning of 2000 the European Union maintained eleven arms embargoes against: Afghanistan, Bosnia and Herzegovina, Burma, China, the Democratic Republic of Congo, Croatia, Indonesia, Nigeria, Sierra Leone, Sudan, and the Federal Republic of Yugoslavia. The European Community's common list of material covered in a 'full scope embargo' includes: 'weapons designed to kill and their ammunition' (the first item in this category being 'small arms and machine guns, and specially designed components thereof'); 'weapon platforms'; 'non-weapon platforms' and 'ancillary equipment.'

[12] Security Council resolution 217, 20 November 1965.

[13] Security Council resolution 217, 20 November 1965, para. 8.

[14] Security Council resolution 418, 4 November 1977.

[15] Security Council resolution 661, 6 August 1990.

[16] Security Council resolution 713, 25 September 1991.

[17] Security Council resolution 733, 23 January 1992; resolution 748, 31 March 1992 and resolution 788, 31 March 1992 respectively.

[18] Security Council resolution 841, 16 June 1993 and resolution 864, 15 September 1993 respectively.

[19] Security Council resolution 918, 17 May 1994 and resolution 942, 23 September 1994 respectively.

[20] Security Council resolution 1011, 16 August 1995.

[21] Security Council resolution 1132, 8 October 1997.

[22] Security Council resolution 1160, 31 March 1998.

[23] www.un.org/News/ossg/sanction.htm

[24] For example, in the United Kingdom all violations of an embargo are considered criminal offences carrying prison sentences, while in Italy embargo violations are considered 'administrative' offences, punishable with a fine based upon the value of the prohibited transaction but falling far below this value.

[25] Security Council resolution 1196, 16 September 1998, para. 2.

[26] Security Council resolution 733.

[27] Security Council resolution 748 , para. 5.

[28] The International Commission of Inquiry was established pursuant to Security Council resolution 1013, 7 September 1995 and was reactivated by Security Council resolution 1161, 9 April 1998.

[29] The Panel of Experts was established pursuant to Security Council resolution 1237, 7 May 1999.

[30] Report of the Panel of Experts on Violations of Security Council Sanctions against UNITA, Enclosure to Annex I to UN Doc. S/2000/203, 10 March 2000.

[31] Report of the Panel of Experts on Violations of Security Council Sanctions against UNITA, paras. 52-56.

[32] See, for example, General Assembly resolution 50/70B, 12 December 1995 and the Report of the Panel of Governmental Experts on Small Arms, 27 August 1997, UN Doc. A/52/298, para. 45, which recognises that 'States have the right to export and import small arms and light weapons.'

[33] See Report of the Disarmament Commission, *Guidelines for international arms transfers in the context of General Assembly resolution 46/36 of 6 December 1991*, UN Doc. A/51/42, 22 May 1996, paras. 20 and 21.

[34] *Guidelines for international arms transfers*, Annex I, para. 6.

[35] See chapter 3 in this volume for more on legal and policy issues relating to arms supply by states to insurgents in other states.

[36] General Assembly resolution 2131 (XX), 21 December 1965. These principles were reiterated in the Declaration on Principles of International Law concerning Friendly Relations among States in Accordance with the Charter of the United Nations adopted by the General Assembly in resolution 2625 (XXV), 1970.

[37] *Military and Paramilitary Activities in and against Nicaragua (Nicaragua* v. *United States of America), ICJ Reports* 1986, para. 292(3).
[38] Convention for the Prevention and Punishment of Terrorism, 16 November 1937, série de publications de la Société des Nations, *Questions Juridiques*, 1937, Vol. 10, Article 2.5.
[39] *Ibid.*
[40] General Assembly resolution 42/22, 17 March 1988, para. I.6.
[41] *Yearbook of the International Law Commission*, 1989, Vol. II, part 2, p. 67. Similar statements prohibiting states from providing direct or indirect assistance to terrorist activities have been made at a regional level in the Conference on Co-operation and Security in Europe and by the representatives of the G7/G8 nations.
[42] Article 51(4) Protocol Additional to the Geneva Conventions of 12 August 1949, and relating to the Protection of Victims of International Armed Conflicts ("Protocol I").
[43] Article 35(2) Protocol I. See also *Legality of the Threat or Use of Nuclear Weapons*, Advisory Opinion, *ICJ Reports* 1996, p. 226, para. 78.
[44]International Committee of the Red Cross, *Arms Availability and the Situation of Civilians in Armed Conflicts* (Geneva: ICRC, 1999).
[45] Such violations of humanitarian law include the 'grave breaches' identified in all four Geneva Conventions, applicable in international armed conflict. These include 'wilful killing, torture or inhuman treatment, including biological experiments, wilfully causing great suffering or serious injury to body or health, unlawful deportation or transfer of a protected person and extensive destruction and appropriation of property not justified by military necessity and carried out unlawfully and wantonly.' Articles 50, 51, 130 and 147 respectively of the four Geneva Conventions of 1949.

In addition are those violations identified in Common Article 3 to the Conventions, applicable in internal conflicts, including: 'violence to life and person, in particular murder of all kinds, mutilation, cruel treatment and torture; the taking of hostages; outrages of personal dignity, in particular humiliating and degrading treatment; and the passing of sentences and carrying out of executions without previous judgement pronounced by a regularly constituted court affording all the judicial guarantees which are recognised as indispensable by civilised peoples.'
[46]Economic Community of West African States, *Declaration of a Moratorium on Importation, Exportation and Manufacture of Light Weapons in West Africa*, 21st ordinary session of the Authority of Heads of State and Government, Abuja, 30-31 October 1998.
[47] ECOWAS heads of state agreed to a code of conduct for this moratorium in December 1999, which authorises ECOWAS governments to import weapons for peacekeeping operations or hunting, training or sporting purposes. See chapter 8 for more on this initiative.
[48] Guidelines for Conventional Arms Transfers agreed by the five permanent members of the Security Council in London, 18 October 1991, as re-

ported in *SIPRI Yearbook 1992* (Oxford: Oxford University Press, 1992), p. 304.

⁴⁹ Decision of the OSCE Forum for Security Co-operation, November 1993, *FSC Journal,* No. 49 (24 November 1993).

⁵⁰ *Guidelines for international arms transfers in the context of General Assembly resolution 46/36 of 6 December 1991,* UN Doc. A/51/42, 22 May 1996.

⁵¹ The European Union Code of Conduct for Arms Exports, *SIPRI Yearbook 1999* (Oxford: Oxford University Press, 1999), p. 503.

⁵² Thus, for example, with regard to criterion 6, the Code provides that: 'Member States will take into account, *inter alia,* the record of the buyer country with regard to:

   a. its support or encouragement of terrorism and international or-
       ganised crime;

   b. its compliance with its international commitments, in particular on
       the non-use of force, including under international humanitarian
       law applicable to international and non-international armed con-
       flicts; and

   c. its commitment to non-proliferation and other areas of arms con-
       trol and disarmament.'

⁵³ Among other things, it imposes an annual reporting obligation on states. Although originally intended to be confidential, in 1999 the Council de-cided to make the report public. See 'Annual Report in conformity with Operative Provision 8 of the EU Code of Conduct on Arms Exports,' 3 No-vember 1999, (1999/C315/01).

⁵⁴ The Code was adopted by the Council as part of the Common Foreign and Security Policy under Title J of the Treaty of European Union and, as such, is only politically and not legally binding. The fact that Code was re-ferred to in a Joint Action of the Council under Article J.3 of the treaty did not alter its status. (Joint Action of 1 December 1998, adopted by the Coun-cil on the basis of Article J.3 of the Treaty on European Union on the Euro-pean Union's contribution to combating the destabilising accumulation and spread of small arms and light weapons, 1999/34/CFSP.)

⁵⁵ See, for example, B. Wood and J. Peleman, *The Arms Fixers: Controlling the Brokers and Shipping Agents* (Oslo: PRIO/NISAT/BASIC, 1999), p. 127 and B. Adam, 'Efforts to Control the International Trade in Light Weapons,' *SIPRI Yearbook 1999,* p. 512.

⁵⁶ *US–EU Joint Statement of Common Principles of Small Arms and Light Weap-ons,* 17 December 1999, www.useu.be/summit/arms1299.html.

⁵⁷ Advisory Board on Disarmament Affairs, *Review of the Implementation of the Recommendations and Decisions adopted by the General Assembly at its Tenth Special Session,* UN Doc. A/50/391, 30 August 1995, para. 13.

⁵⁸ *Defence in a Democracy: White Paper on National Defence for the Republic of South Africa,* May 1996.

⁵⁹ The draft code prohibits transfers of weapons which would foreseeably contribute to gross violations of human rights; grave breaches of the laws

and customs of war; acts of armed aggressions and forcible deprivation of the right to self-determination; or violent suppression of fundamental democratic rights; or would seriously undermine respect of international arms embargoes, non proliferation treaties and transparency arrangements, the promotion of human development and disarmament, or the prevention of systematic violent crime by non-state actors. International Code of Conduct on Arms Transfers, November 1999 draft, article 1. Each of these criteria is described in detail on articles 2 to 9 (available at www.arias.or.cr/fundarias/cpr/code2.shtml).

[60] *Ibid.,* articles 11 and 12.

part 2
SOURCES OF
SUPPLY_____

3/Government Gun-Running
to Guerrillas

by Lucy Mathiak and Lora Lumpe

The legacy of military aid by governments to guerrilla or insurgent forces during the Cold War era can be seen in a significant portion of today's violent conflicts. That legacy goes well beyond the billions of dollars worth of light weapons still in circulation and in use as a result of such operations. It also encompasses the complex logistical, political and economic networks established to move weapons to combatants while masking the true identity of the supplier government. For the most part, these structures remain in use today, although they have been reshaped by post-Cold War political and economic trends.[1]

Governments generally provide arms to sub-state groups in an effort to undermine or overthrow the government in the recipient state. States also may supply arms for purely commercial reasons. Regardless of motivation, such transfers may be illegal under domestic or international law, and they usually are cloaked in secrecy in order to evade laws or policies prohibiting or restricting state-organised arms transfers to insurgents.

States can generally tap into and mobilise vastly greater resources for gun-running than can private traffickers. Moreover, the line between government operation and transnational crime is blurred when governments rely on smugglers to carry out procurement and delivery of weapons. However, it is reasonable to speculate, although impossible to prove, that such 'grey market' operations eclipse the private black market in terms of magnitude.

Official gun-running was not unique to the Cold War. Armed destabilisation campaigns have been a frequent component of the foreign policy of big states and small, driven as often by internal domestic political pressures as grand geopolitical goals. There is ample evidence that governments continued the practice throughout the 1990s. Nonetheless, Cold War competition in the developing world produced an increase in the number and types of conflicts where states armed sub-state groups, and the absence of East-West hostilities today presents the international community with an important opportunity to consider the development of international norms and laws to limit this practice.

This chapter uses a detailed study of the Afghanistan case to explore the practical operation and legacy of one US government gun-running operation during the Cold War. It then examines the phenomenon in the post-Cold War period and includes an overview of current international law related to the practice. The chapter concludes with a positive critique of a recent proposal by the Canadian government for an international treaty explicitly barring governments from arming non-state actors in other states. Although imbued with some moral and practical complexities, such a policy would have a profound positive impact on reducing armed violence and terror around the world.

Cold War Cases

The superpowers, China, and their allies delivered large quantities of light weapons ranging from landmines to surface-to-air missiles to non-state combatants in civil and regional conflicts throughout the Cold War. In recent years, scholars and journalists have begun to examine the lethal legacy of these practices. However, much of the work to date focuses on the consequences, rather than on the policies through which covert arms supply to insurgents was operationalised. China, South Africa, Israel and other states that armed guerrillas are generally the subject of footnotes or referential paragraphs within larger monographs.

Most studies of the Soviet Union's arms trade focus on transfers of major conventional weapons, and those that focus on light arms transfers emphasise shipments to states, rather than to non-state actors. One of the most authoritative English-language accounts available to date confirms that the Soviet Union provided arms to a range of independence/liberation movements, including the opposition to Haile Selasse in Ethiopia; the MPLA in Angola from 1964 onwards; SWAPO in Namibia from 1961 onwards; FRELIMO in

Mozambique prior to and following independence from Portugal; the ANC in South Africa; the Palestinian Liberation Organisation and the Polisario in Western Sahara.[2] Nevertheless, even this analysis fails to address key questions of policy formation, volume and types of weapons supplied and implications of such aid.

Given the paucity of specific public information on small arms transfers from governments other than the United States to insurgent forces, we present here an in-depth analysis of one US Cold War case, as well as some analysis based on other US cases. Extensive open source information exists on the United States' practice in this area, due largely to the efforts of private groups, like the National Security Archive, to cause the government to declassify relevant Cold War-era documents. Such information has been augmented by the large amounts of previously classified information that became available due to the investigations of the 'Iran-*contra*' gun-running scandal of the late 1980s.

Throughout much of the Cold War, the US government engaged in covert political and military operations, including secret arms supply to state and guerrilla forces, authorised under the National Security Act of 1947. The use of small arms and light weapons supply increased during the late 1970s, when backlash against the Vietnam War made direct US military engagement an unacceptable policy option for reversing several revolutionary governments that emerged at the close of the decade. Although the policy of military aid to anti-Soviet insurgents is known as the 'Reagan Doctrine,' in fact Ronald Reagan was building on initiatives of his predecessor, Jimmy Carter, in arming guerrilla movements against the governments of Afghanistan, Angola, Cambodia and Nicaragua.

The Reagan administration's Afghan policy emphasised arming multiple resistance groups known collectively as '*mujahideen*' in order to draw the Soviet Union into a costly and damaging war for control of Afghanistan. This case is unique among the Reagan Doctrine cases in that the administration and the Central Intelligence Agency (CIA) had an unambiguous green light from Congress to arm the insurgents. As a result, the full extent of the programme did not require concealment, as was the case with arms supply to groups in Angola, Cambodia and Nicaragua. Unlike the latter cases, which used covert delivery systems to hide war making from Congress and the public, the arms pipeline to Afghan rebels relied on channels with little accountability because of preconditions set by the intelligence and military services within Pakistan, which served as a primary staging ground for the rebel groups and which did not want to be seen as engaging in direct confrontation with the Soviet Union.

Arms in the Afghan Pipeline

Soviet tactics required Afghanistan's *mujahideen* to wage a ground war while defending against helicopter, airborne and bombing attacks. The guerrillas received aid to wage these wars in two stages: 1979-1984 and 1985-1989. During the first phase, the *mujahideen* operated with weapons that were on hand before the invasion—arms pilfered from Democratic Republic of Afghanistan (DRA) and Soviet stocks and small amounts supplied through China or the Pakistan pipeline. Significant external supply began in 1985-1986 and permitted the guerrillas to upgrade and expand their arsenals.

Few guerrillas had sophisticated weapons of any kind at the time of the Soviet invasion in 1979. One analysis suggests that many fighters had little more than bolt-action Lee Enfield .303 rifles, while a much smaller number had looted AK-47s or Pakistani-supplied FN-FAL assault rifles. The insurgents came into large supplies of light weapons as a result of upheaval in the DRA military during 1980 and began receiving arms through the Pakistan pipeline the same year. By 1988 the *mujahideen* arsenal reportedly included AK-47s, AK-74s, SKS 7.62mm rifles, Iranian 7.62mm G3 rifles, 9mm Sten guns, shotguns, Chinese-made Type-56-1 assault rifles, and light machine guns (7.62mm RPD and RPK, the 7.262mm PKM, and older Czech weapons).[3]

Afghanistan's *mujahideen* are best known for their use of shoulder-launched missiles, becoming practically synonymous with 'Stinger' missile systems. But the Aghan rebels had been using a range of surface-to-air missiles long before the first 150 Stingers arrived in summer 1986, and Stingers represented only a small portion of the missiles they employed to counter Soviet aircraft.[4]

Advocates for the *mujahideen* had listed 'shoulder-fired air defence missiles,' specifically Stinger missiles, as the highest priority for combat effectiveness from the early 1980s onward. Due to opposition from the CIA, however, US supplies were restricted to replicas of Soviet SA-7 and SA-9 surface-to-air missiles until 1985. The Carter administration had included such replicas in its first shipments of covert aid in 1980, and these shipments were arranged through Egypt in order to further mask US involvement.[5] The *mujahideen* also secured variants of the SA-7 through the Afghan army during the early years of the war. The Soviet Union curtailed this practice, however, when it removed the missiles from the Afghan Army's arsenal.[6] China, acting on its own interest in countering Soviet influence, eventually emerged as the *mujahideen's* primary supplier of SA-7s, accounting for an estimated 70 percent of missile deliveries to the guerrillas over the course of the war.[7]

By mid-1985 the Central Intelligence Agency had turned to British Blowpipe and American Redeye missiles for its Afghan operations because of technical and supply problems with SA-7 and SA-9 missiles. Also in 1985 the Congress approved the transfer of a limited number of Stinger missiles to the *mujahideen* and to UNITA rebels in Angola. The transfers happened over the objections of the CIA, which expressed serious reservations about the security of the weapons, the ability of the recipients to use the weapons successfully and the precedent of providing state-of-the-art weapons to such groups. As a result, the quantity of missiles supplied and the chain of transfer were relatively restricted. After the Soviets withdrew, the Stingers were alleged to be used in other conflicts and ultimately became the focus of a highly publicised and fruitless effort to collect the missiles and return them to the United States.

The Effect on the Primary Conduit State

The United States' Cold War covert operations were heavily reliant on co-dependent alliances with developing states, which masked the nature and depth of US aid to sub-state groups in exchange for economic and military aid, control over weapons distribution and other *quid pro quo* arrangements. Such relationships were particularly important when, as often was the case, there were compelling policy reasons for public or Congressional objection to decisions to arm one or more specific groups.[8]

Arms supply lines worked in several ways. The United States typically channelled weapons through one primary ally in a given region of conflict, working with other countries on an ad hoc basis. Weapons and other military equipment intended for resistance groups were included in military modernisation packages for primary conduit states—Pakistan, Zaire, Thailand, Honduras—which were expected to send their obsolete and overstocked equipment to the respective sub-state group. While a portion of such weapons did make it to the intended recipients, enterprising members of the conduit-state militaries often took advantage of such surpluses by entering the lucrative black-market trade.[9]

Pakistan emerged as the fourth largest recipient of US aid in exchange for its role as arms conduit to the *mujahideen*.[10] During 1980, Congress appropriated $30 million in covert programmes directly intended to aid the *mujahideen* and $1.5 billion in overt military and other aid for the government of Pakistan in exchange for playing this role.[11] This arrangement constituted a de facto reversal of American policy toward Pakistan. Before the Soviet Union invaded Afghanistan, the United States had drastically curtailed diplomatic, foreign aid and military cooperation with Pakistan due in large part to that government's refusal to join the 1968 Non-Proliferation Treaty and its initiation of a nuclear programme in 1971. In addition, Pakistan exhibited many signs of instability—a weak government, tensions between military and civil governance structures and frequent reports of human rights violations.[12]

The Soviet invasion of Afghanistan in 1979, however, caused US policymakers to override their reservations and abruptly restructure the relationship. Pakistan was the only country bordering Afghanistan through which the United States could arrange covert arms shipments to the Afghan resistance (Iran, China and the Sov-

Table 3.1 US Allies in Supplying Arms to Sub-State Groups in Selected Conflicts

Conflict state	Primary conduit states	Regional allies	Relatively autonomous suppliers*
Afghanistan	Pakistan	Iran	China, Egypt
Angola	Zaire	South Africa	China, South Africa
Cambodia	Thailand		China, Singapore
Nicaragua	Honduras	Argentina, Costa Rica, Guatemala, Panama	Israel

* Saudi Arabia did not directly purchase or deliver arms to insurgent groups, but it emerged as a major financier of such arms transfers.

iet Union being the other bordering countries). At the same time, Pakistan could point to legitimate new security concerns of its own as a result of the invasion. In late September 1980, Pakistan's President Zia-ul-Huq reported more than 200 Soviet violations of Pakistan's airspace since the occupation.[13]

With the first deliveries of economic and military assistance in 1981, Pakistan experienced a windfall. Security assistance included funds for military training and a lengthy list of major weapons, including tanks, armoured personnel carriers, howitzers, multiple rocket launchers and surface-to-air missiles. Light arms included 30mm grenade launchers, mortars, RPG-7 and SPG-9 rocket launchers and recoilless rifles and anti-aircraft guns.[14]

In addition to bilateral American aid, the Pakistani government received significant financial input from international agencies, the government of Saudi Arabia and other sources during this period. Pakistan also profited from humanitarian aid to Afghan refugees as $600 million of $716 million in funds allocated for this purpose went to groups living within Pakistan's borders. In short, the Soviet invasion created a multi-billion-dollar international aid industry for Pakistan during the 1980s.

The arrangement gave Pakistan substantial operational rewards as well. Pakistan's intelligence service, Inter-Services Intelligence (ISI), demanded and received control over the arms pipeline and the choice of recipients as a precondition for that country's help in channelling weapons to the *mujahideen*.[15] Control over the supply lines gave the ISI enviable access to vast stores of weapons. Between 1979 and 1989, the CIA channelled $2 billion in weapons aid, or an estimated 80 percent of the agency's covert aid budget, to the *mujahideen*.[16] Viewed in terms of market prices for small arms and light weapons, it becomes clear that a stunning volume of weapons and ammunition were poured into the hands of the ISI and its clients within a decade.

Echoing the behaviour of the military and intelligence establishments in Honduras, Thailand and Zaire, the ISI used its role in the pipeline to appropriate for its own purposes between 50-70 percent of the military resources intended for the *mujahideen*.[17] Pakistan's intelligence services and their military partners used the diverted weapons for self-aggrandisement through black-market sales. They also retained a portion of the weapons to consolidate their own power within Pakistan's military and civil society. The diversions were known at the time within the region and within the

United States but were accepted as an unpleasant but necessary element of the aid programme. Congressional proponents of the Afghanistan programme quashed attempts to investigate or audit the use of US-supplied resources, arguing that such an accounting was counterproductive to US national security interests.[18]

The ISI exercised significant power over the types of weapons supplied and opposed delivery of Stinger missiles and other advanced weapons as potentially threatening to Pakistan itself. Such opposition became increasingly problematic for the United States, as advocates for the *mujahideen* pressed for more powerful weapons, arguing that 'the guerrillas are not being supplied with weapons that are effective against the Soviet helicopter threat.' The Reagan administration already had rejected demands for greater firepower, such as the Redeye shoulder-fired ground-to-air missile, 'on grounds that some deniability be preserved and that in the main the resistance should be given Soviet bloc weapons.' More importantly, Pakistan 'strongly objects to providing these and other sophisticated arms, both because they could be turned against Pakistani forces under other circumstances and because they would invite Soviet retaliation.'[19] As a result, parts of the Pakistani government were 'perceived by many as an obstacle to providing more effective arms to the resistance, especially anti-aircraft weapons.'[20]

Secondary Suppliers

Iran's newly installed Islamic leaders allowed refugee camps and training bases inside their country, helped to arm the *mujahideen* and sent troops to fight alongside resistance movements inside Afghanistan. A significant US-Iranian partnership was unlikely, however, due to the virulent anti-Americanism of the Khomeini regime and the equally anti-Iranian views of the post-hostage crisis American public and policymakers. The president and members of the administration knew of but did not officially acknowledge or challenge Iran's supporting role during either the Carter or Reagan administrations despite the latter's placement of Iran on the list of nations exporting terrorism in 1984 and the implementation of 'Operation Staunch' to deny Iran weapons and spare parts for its war against Iraq.[21] The Reagan administration subsequently entered into informal partnership with Iran during the 1980s when Oliver North and Richard Secord arranged for Iranian groups to receive one thousand TOW anti-tank missiles with the understanding that Iran would turn one hundred of the TOWs over to the *mujahideen*.[22]

Saudi Arabia also supported the *mujahideen* but did so as a major behind-the-scenes financial backer, echoing its contributions to other Reagan-era covert operations. Despite their financial role, the Saudis had little direct involvement with the *mujahideen* aside from low-level attempts to influence the behaviour and direction of the groups that they supported.[23]

Finally, China ran an independent supply operation to the guerrillas that was defined by its own objectives and shaped by its rivalry with the Soviet Union. The extent of the aid is not known, although China is known to have provided 'a range of military hardware, including small arms, mortars, anti-tank mines, recoilless rifles, RPG rocket-propelled grenade launchers, anti-aircraft machine guns and ammunition.' Beginning in 1981 China preferred to supply its weapons directly to *mujahideen* groups, due to concerns over corruption in the Pakistani-operated pipeline.[24]

The 'Freedom Fighters'

The term *mujahideen* masks the number of resistance groups and their diverse sources of support. At least twelve factions received aid from multiple sources, of which the US government was the largest contributor.

Pakistani leaders were loath to supply weapons to groups that might spawn armed ethnic separatist movements within its own borders. As such, the ISI channelled weapons to groups that were perceived as controllable, or allied with the Pakistani vision, rather than to groups that were particularly dedicated to or successful at military operations against Soviet forces in Afghanistan.[25] Under ISI management, most of the aid went to the six main *mujahideen* groups based in Peshawar, Pakistan, rather than to groups actively engaged in combat inside Afghanistan.

The major share went to Gulbuddin Hekmatyar, who was anything but the democracy-loving freedom fighter depicted in Reagan administration rhetoric. A 1985 Congressional study described him as 'a relatively young leader often compared to the Ayatollah Khomeini in his intense ideological fundamentalism. He is antagonistic both to the West and to the Soviets, and was in opposition to the Daoud regime with Pakistani support, before 1978. Gulbuddin's

Hezb-e-Islami often clashed with other groups in the field, especially the *Jami'at (-e-Islami).*' In addition, Hekmatyar and *Hezb-e-Islami* were accused of trafficking narcotics and American weapons, carrying out political assassinations and violently enforcing strict Islamic norms for women.[26]

The second largest recipient of American aid, *Jami'-at-e-Islami*, was led by Burnhanuddin Rabanni. While this group was described as the 'largest and militarily most effective group' among the Peshawar organisations, it also was built on 'intellectual underpinnings that call for the replacement of both secular traditionalism and communism by an Islamic society.'[27] Thus, the ISI's practice of channelling a disproportionate share of American aid to Hekmatyar and Rabbani's groups produced two major fundamentalist groups that emerged from the war as 'the most well-equipped and disciplined' elements of the resistance alliance.[28]

These choices of most favoured clients had consequences at all levels of the conflict. Just as Pakistan's ISI skimmed a large percentage of the aid off the top, its clients diverted additional arms from Afghan resistance fighters in the field. The Peshawar groups stockpiled a portion of the weapons for use in enforcing their ideal Islamic state following the Soviet withdrawal. They also diverted weapons for sale on the black market and forced commanders inside Afghanistan to buy American-supplied weapons at inflated prices. These problems were noted and documented in the US press and in Congressional studies and testimony throughout the decade. As was the case with reports of corruption within Pakistani aid channels, however, proponents of the aid programme dismissed corruption within the resistance groups as a necessary evil.[29]

Thus, there were three disparate sets of interests at work in the US-Pakistan-Afghanistan triangle. Just as Pakistan's security interests differed in perspective and practice from those of the United States, the ideological objectives of the Peshawar groups varied dramatically from those of either Pakistan or the United States. As a January 1982 report noted, 'The political parties in Peshawar have the additional specific goal of trying to build constituencies inside Afghanistan that will acknowledge their pre-eminence. This brings Peshawar client bands into conflict with local leadership and with bands affiliated with rival exile leaders. In the ensuing, usually costly, turf fights, the *mujahideen* often lose sight of the more important overall goals of the resistance movement.'[30]

The Legacy

The infusion of large amounts of new weapons into local wars raised the level of lethality by increasing the quantity and the sophistication of weapons in the field. Groups that mobilised against Nicaragua's Sandinista regime in 1979 and the early 1980s, for example, typically had little more than hunting rifles, shotguns and .22 pistols, if they were armed at all. Prior to the US covert arms supply operation, only a small portion of combatants that collectively became known as *contras* had sophisticated weapons.[31]

The short-term focus by the US government on defeating, or at least impeding, revolutionary regimes meant that little if any thought was given to the disposition of the arms or the groups to which they were given once US objectives were met (in the unlikely event that they were met). As a result, the sub-state recipients were able to accumulate stocks of weapons and ammunition sufficient to sustain combat for extended periods after external support ended. Moreover, many groups used their protected status as US clients to enter lines of licit and illicit trade through which they are now able to finance wars without external aid. Of the four main Reagan Doctrine cases, Nicaragua is the only case where a peace process has held to date.

Most lasting is the impact these significant weapons inflows have on entire surrounding regions and the people living there. The weaponisation of Pakistan's Northwest Frontier Province is legendary, as is the gun violence rate in Lahore. Similarly, despite the absence of any industrial-scale arms production in these locales, Central America, Cambodia and Angola have been transformed into some of the most heavily militarised and deadly societies on earth, in large part due to the legacy of the Reagan era gun-running operations.[32]

These military aid programmes have also had serious political impacts within recipient countries. All of the states that served as primary conduits for US supply operations could be described as fragile if not marginal democracies. The accumulation of large stocks of sophisticated weapons and financial inputs increased tremendously the power of military and intelligence establishments within those states and helped them repress dissent. The difficulty of establishing stable civilian rule is clear in Pakistan, where the 1999 coup by Army General Pervez Musharraf provides a recent demonstration of the ways in which covert arms supply operations have often undermined civil society and democratic development in partner countries.

In addition, imbalances among recipient groups in Cambodia, Nicaragua and Afghanistan created further tension. Military and intelligence services charged with funnelling aid to the resistance used that position to support and promote particular groups. Such groups—the FDN in Nicaragua, the *Hezb-e-Islami* in Afghanistan and the *Khmer Rouge* in Cambodia—used their privileged positions to promote their own agendas. They also used their control over material for profit through arms deals on the black market, to build their own power bases against other resistance groups and to extort money from other groups by refusing to turn over supplies unless paid. Such disproportion in power among resistance groups has played a significant role in the more recent eruption of violence in Afghanistan and in Cambodia, as erstwhile anti-Soviet allies used their stores of Cold War weapons to launch attacks on each other before the peace agreement was less than a year old.

Finally, in the case of Afghanistan, the secret arms supply operation contributed not only to an ongoing humanitarian crisis and to state and regional instability, but it also strengthened a global network of fundamentalist, virulently anti-Western—and in particular anti-American—terrorists.

It appears clear that states cannot readily 'undo' the flows of weapons within and between states resulting from covert supply operations to non-state actors during the last decades of the Cold War, nor the societal changes they have wreaked.

Contemporary Cases

Despite a conventional wisdom that state supply of arms to non-state actors ceased following the end of the Cold War, the practice appears to be alive and well, albeit at a diminished pace than during its heyday in the 1980s. During the 1990s, sub-state arms supply has been used to pressure governments, as in alleged Russian support to insurgents in Georgia and Moldova in order to persuade the newly independent governments not to stray too far.[33] In other cases, arms to insurgents appear to have been commercially motivated. If, as is sometimes reported, elements of the Russian government have been aiding insurgent groups such as the PKK in

Turkey or the forces of Shah Massoud in Afghanistan, the motivation is more likely to be commercial than ideological.

Numerous other states reportedly have or are engaged in covert destabilisation programmes in recent years, including small arms supply. The list of recent allegations includes: Uganda and the United States in southern Sudan; Sudan in northern Uganda[34]; Uganda in Angola; Turkish support for rebels in Chechnya; support by Greece, Syria, Armenia and Russia for Kurdish guerrillas in Turkey; official Pakistani aid to Kashmiri militants; official or popular Indian support for Tamil fighters in Sri Lanka; French government support for the ex-armed forces of Rwanda and for the *Interhamwe* militia; and multiple regional states sponsoring multiple warring militias in central Africa. Chinese arms supply to rebel forces in Africa is also often alleged, with the motivation apparently commercial rather than ideological.

In the 1990s some liberal government officials, human rights organisations and media called, paradoxically, for the provision of arms to sub-state combatants on humanitarian grounds. In the face of gross international inaction during the carnage in Rwanda and Bosnia, and during the escalating repression in Kosovo, arming a group of combatants for self-defence might offer a seductive solution. The debate over international response to such crises, however, is increasingly posed as a false dichotomy between sending weapons for self-defence or enabling genocide. Such an analytical structure inherently stunts the necessary process of developing viable, non-violent/non-military strategies for pre-empting or ending localised wars of attrition that have marked the past decade.

The highest profile case in this regard involved the tacit or explicit provision of arms and training by some NATO member states to the Kosovo Liberation Army (KLA) prior to NATO's 1999 bombing of Serbia. As the level of Serbian police repression increased in Kosovo in 1997-1999, often in response to provocation by the KLA, commentators in many Western countries voiced support for arming the guerrillas for the defence of the wider Kosovar population. Responding to such talk, the UN Security Council passed a binding resolution in March 1998 stipulating that all states 'shall prevent arming and training for terrorist activities in Kosovo.'[35] Whether or not NATO states provided arms to the KLA, the record of postwar armed violence carried out by men in Kosovo, many of them identified as KLA, has included several grenade attacks on Serb-frequented market places and a rocket attack on a UN vehicle. Disarmament initiatives among the KLA required under the terms of the NATO-Serbian ceasefire agreement obviously have been inadequate.

The other major case invoking the humanitarian arms justification is that of 'non-lethal' military aid and training to Kurdish rebels and other opposition forces in Iraq.

Northern Iraq

Surely the most overt covert operation currently under debate, or underway, is US governmental arms supply to some of the 90 Iraqi opposition groups seeking to participate in the overthrow of Saddam Hussein.[36] This case illustrates well how internal domestic politics drive covert arms supply programmes.

According to a remarkable on-the-record interview with the former director of the CIA's Iraq operation, the CIA ran guns and arranged military training for Northern Iraqi opposition forces beginning in late October 1994. The operation absorbed at least $100 million of US funds.[37] When John Deutsch became the Director of US Central Intelligence in May 1995, the operation shifted from a gradual strengthening of the Iraqi opposition to a plan for a quick coup. That effort blew up in June 1996, resulting in the capture and likely deaths of hundreds of CIA 'assets' in Northern Iraq, the evacuation of 5000 Iraqi Kurds to the US territory of Guam and renewed internecine fighting between the two main Kurdish militias in Northern Iraq.

Calls to arm the Iraqi opposition began anew in America following the withdrawal of UN arms inspectors from Iraq in 1998 and the US/UK bombing run which began in December of that year. Throughout 1998 a mix of prominent Republicans and Democrats in the US Congress pressed the Clinton administration to provide military training and arms to the fractious Iraqi opposition, both within and outside Iraq. This push culminated in the quick passage by the Congress of the Iraq Liberation Act of 1998, which President Clinton was persuaded to sign into law, despite his administration's oft-stated opposition to the legislation.[38]

The law encourages the executive branch to provide up to $97 million of arms and training to Iraqi opposition groups. It also requires the administration to publicly identify those Iraqi groups that met certain democracy criteria and which would, therefore, be eligible to receive military and financial aid. In early 1999, the State Department appointed a special representative for 'the transition in Iraq,' who coordinates the effort to organise the opposition and disperse the $97 million.[39] This special representative designated seven opposition groups as eligible for military assistance, although the three main militias in Iraq have said they want nothing to do with the plan.

The main proponent of the aid seems to be the London-based Iraqi National Congress. After at least three major betrayals by the US intelligence and military community in the past 20 years, Iraqi-based militants are understandably cool to US 'aid.' In addition, Turkey and Saudi Arabia, America's closest allies in the region, have voiced loud opposition to arms supply to the insurgents. Finally, the head of US military operations in the Persian Gulf, General Anthony C. Zinni, and US Under Secretary of Defense for Policy, Walter B. Slocombe, have also opposed arming the guerrillas.

An unnamed senior State Department official was quoted as saying: 'We are not interested in supporting an insurgency against the Iraqi military.'[40] At the same time, four Iraqi rebel leaders, including two former officers in Iraq's armed forces, attended a ten-day training course at the Air Force's special-operations headquarters in Florida. American officials reportedly schooled them on how to organise a military in an emerging state and other subjects.[41] And General Zinni has hinted at the possibility that the US intelligence establishment has some truly clandestine plans underway.[42]

In October 1999 the Clinton administration reiterated its commitment to provide non-lethal aid and training to the exile groups. This show of support coincides with growing pressure in the US Congress, by Republican lawmakers in particular, for a more aggressive programme of military assistance. Former Director of Central Intelligence James Woolsey, a prominent Republican, testified before the Congress in early 1999 in favour of recognising an Iraqi government-in-exile and arming it 'with light weapons, including anti-armour.'[43] This hardening of Republican positions took place in the context of a presidential campaign, which resulted in the Democratic administration taking a similarly hardline position, lest the Democratic candidate be painted as 'soft on Saddam.' Thus, domestic politics might well result in the repetition of a just-recently, and spectacularly, failed policy.

Assuming that all states are equally driven by internal political rhythms, armed support for insurgencies around the world can be expected to continue both frequently and indefinitely—barring the establishment of laws or norms to govern such behaviour.

The State of Law

Some states interpret existing international law as prohibiting them from supplying arms to non-state actors in other states, without the permission of the recipient state government.[44] Given the fact that many states frequently arm insurgent groups, difference in interpretation obviously exists on this point.[45] In fact, there is an inherent tension in international law relating to arming sub-state groups that leaves the matter subject to widely varying interpretation.

The UN Charter enshrines two fundamental principles that have special significance for the issue. One is the principle of respect for human rights and the self-determination of peoples. The other is non-intervention and the suppression of aggression against nations. As one legal scholar noted in 1988:

> Whether support of insurgency is either permissible or desirable in any particular situation ultimately will depend upon the relative weights one accords these principles. In light of the Charter's stated purposes, these two principles were designed to be mutually reinforcing. In the context of insurgencies and national liberation movements, striking the balance between these has become a continuing source of controversy within the international legal community.[46]

UN General Assembly resolution 2625, the 'Declaration of Principles of International Law Concerning Friendly Relations and Cooperation Among States,' is one of the most authoritative statements on the Charter principles of self-determination and human rights. It defines self-determination as the right of all peoples 'freely to determine, without external interference, their political status and to pursue their economic, social and cultural development.' It imposes on states the duty to refrain from any forcible deprivation of that right. In opposing or resisting the deprivation of these fundamental rights by a state, peoples 'are entitled to seek and receive support in accordance with the purposes and principles of the Charter under the Resolution.' At the same time, the resolution requires that states respect the territorial integrity and political independence of states that are in compliance with the resolution. This statement, along with a subsequent decision by the International Court of Justice, implies that respect for territorial and political integrity is grounded in the presumption that fundamental human rights and other protections are being provided by the state to its populace in compliance with its duty under the UN Charter.

Non-aggression is primarily a principle protecting the sovereign authority of the state government within its territory, including over its people, from all external influences adverse to its interests. Article 2(4) of the Charter imposes an obligation on all states to refrain from 'the threat or use of force against the territorial integrity or political independence of any state' in the conduct of foreign affairs. The term 'aggression' has never been fully defined in an international legal sense.[47] In general, however, three categories of aggression define the means by which states may affect the interests of other states: armed aggression (direct military force); indirect aggression (covert acts against the civil government, such as by aiding resistance movements); and economic or ideological attacks. State support of insurgency might, therefore, be viewed as indirect aggression and a violation of principles of international law.

In 1986 the International Court of Justice addressed relevant issues in considering the legality of the United States' supply of arms and training to the *contra* rebels in Nicaragua.[48] Ruling against the United States, the court held that no general right to intervene in support of an opposition group exists in international law. The court further ruled that in this particular case the United States' extensive arming and training of rebel groups in Nicaragua amounted to an armed attack (the 'threat or use of force') under customary international law. Despite the World Court's condemnation of US actions, nothing happened, as the court lacks enforcement mechanisms.

During the Cold War, many developing nations and Soviet bloc countries asserted that armed intervention and support for armed insurgency were justified in order to oust colonial powers and racist regimes.[49] 'Self-determination,' however, like many legal concepts, is open to subjective interpretation and can be manipulated by states seeking to justify intervention. It is not always clearcut whether opposition groups are true representatives of a people, as defined under international human rights law. Similar difficulty exists in some cases in defining racism and even genocide.

On the flip side of the ideological spectrum, the Reagan Doctrine was the anti-revolutionary, 'pro-democracy' counterpart to the developing world/Soviet bloc anti-colonialism/self-determi-nation argument, and it was equally open to subjective determina-tion. Most notably, the extent of the opposition groups' commit-ment to democracy and human rights was highly questionable, as noted above. The new swing toward humanitarian justification for arming people facing state repression would likely be as open to subjective and politicised interpretation as either of these earlier justifications for arming sub-state actors.[50]

In its 1997 report, the UN Panel of Experts on Small Arms noted that, 'During the Cold War and in the current period, states have secretly carried out transfers of small arms and light weapons. Such transfers are not necessarily illicit. Any transfer not approved by the competent authorities in the recipient state could, however, be classified by that state as interference in its internal affairs and therefore illegal.'[51] None of the report's recommendations dealt ex-plicitly with curbing covert or overt arms supply to non-state ac-tors. One recommendation did, however, call for the UN to con-vene an inter-Afghan forum to help account for, retrieve and de-stroy the small arms and light weapons left unaccounted for in Af-ghanistan by the United States, China, the Soviet Union and other states that sponsored sides in the civil war.

Although it would appear that some clarification of the law and/or new legal approaches are warranted, or at least worthy of discussion, the 1999 Report of the Group of Governmental Experts on Small Arms included no recommendations in this area.[52] Some legal scholars have called for a new conference on the law of war to set some limits on state intervention—including the provision of arms—into civil wars.[53] In addition, one government has called for the development of new international treaty law in this area.

The Canadian Proposal

The Canadian government recognised in 1998 that, in concert with efforts to limit the illicit trade in small arms, an equally important effort must be made to make the licit trade more open, accountable and responsible. According to Foreign Minister Lloyd Axworthy, one of the principle problems surrounding the legal trade is 'delib-erate sales by governments to non-state actors.'[54] Seeking to ad-dress this problem, the government of Canada floated a proposal at a July 1998 meeting of 21 states concerned about small arms proliferation.[55] The basic idea was that international law should be developed to enshrine the principle that states should not:

> engage in acts that inappropriately arm non-state actors, either directly or indirectly. This principle would hold that small arms and light weapons designed and manufactured to military specifications for use as lethal instruments of war are reserved for the possession and use of the armed forces. Non-state actors should not be armed and equipped as though they were armies themselves.[56]

Included among the possible elements of the convention was a recognition that:

- States would need to adjust national laws and regulations to incorporate and enforce the principle that military small arms and light weapons are not to be transferred to insurgents or other non-state actors.

- Definitions would need to be included for 'international trade,' 'transfer,' 'state actor' and 'military small arms and light weapons.' The Canadian draft proposes that a definition of the latter could be adapted from the formulation of the 1997 report of the UN Panel of Governmental Experts on Small Arms, excepting pistols, rifles and carbines. According to the Canadian draft, 'the definition of "international transfer" might be needed to ensure that transfer arrangements other than sales, such as gifts or loans, to non-state actors are similarly prohibited.'

- Perhaps most challenging would be defining 'non-state actors.' Instead of trying to do so, the draft proposal suggests a positive listing of what is meant by 'state actors,' with any organisation *not* captured by that list logically a non-state actor. Any listing of state actors would need to ensure that only government-controlled military and police organisations and law enforcement agencies are included, and that paramilitary organisations are excluded. Law enforcement agencies would include prison guards, border patrol and the coast guard.

- A 'Settlement of Disputes' article would allow for the investigation of breaches of the prohibition on international transfers to non-state actors. Additional articles could require consultations among states parties to solve problems and call meetings of parties to exchange information and review the operation of the convention.[57]

The proposal has been criticised on a number of grounds. First, some have found its focus on military small arms and light weapons unduly restrictive, omitting categories of non-military weapons, such as handguns, hunting rifles and shotguns. Others perceive the proposal as discriminatory against non-state actors, insufficiently rooted in international humanitarian and human rights law and/or unduly inflexible. Critics have said that a convention of this type would unjustly deny arms to non-state actors who might be opposing repressive regimes, while those repressive regimes could legally arm themselves against their citizens.

In response to the latter view, Foreign Minister Axworthy said that barring state arms supply to foreign insurgents does not give *carte blanche* to governments regarding treatment of their nationals or residents. He noted that many states already control sales of arms to other governments on the basis of their human rights and non-aggression record, and he suggested that states further strengthen the application of such criteria.[58] 'Prohibiting transfers of military small arms and light weapons to non-state actors must *not*, in our view, be interpreted as providing any right for states to acquire and use these weapons in any way they wish.'[59]

The British, Norwegian and German governments all expressed some degree of public support for the Canadian treaty proposal, but the idea seemed hobbled by a lack of enthusiasm by non-governmental organisations and by the strong opposition of the US government, which views it as inflexible and unenforceable.[60] In December 1998, however, the principle embodied in the proposal was picked up the 15 states of the European Union through their adoption of the Joint Action on Small Arms. This agreement commits member states to ban small arms exports to non-state actors and to work to universalise this principle.[61] Several other states, including Switzerland and Canada, already have as part of their national arms export legislation a prohibition on arms supply to other than state entities. And the Russian government has reportedly expressed some support for the notion as well.[62]

Given the spread of this norm through regional and national laws, as well as the merit of the idea based on historical analysis of such policies in practice, the treaty proposal deserves support. Writing in the early 1990s, Aaron Karp noted a need for codified restrictions of arms supply to sub-state groups based on international consensus in order to avoid some future resumption of the destabilising practice at Cold War-era levels. Directly addressing one of the stated points of opposition to the treaty idea, Karp believed it should be possible to finesse

> the circumstances when the international community wants to encourage arms transfers, especially to ethnic nationalists whose situation is dire and whose demands are legitimate. ...[A] credible policy to stifle the flow of small and light arms may have to be balanced with consultative mechanisms to permit such transfers in desperate cases. At a minimum, the international community can establish standards determining when such arms transfers are permissible and when they must be stopped at all costs.[63]

Conclusions

Covert gun-running by governments to foreign insurgent groups became a major source of small arms proliferation during the Cold War. Arms pipelines established to supply combatants in South Asia, Southern Africa and Central America during the 1980s continue to spill over today, as the weapons have been recycled to other conflicts, to bandits or to terrorists. Moreover, the networks established to run those pipelines continue to operate, following their own agendas and dynamics.

These transfers, of course, fuel armed conflict and instability, as they are generally intended to destabilise and topple governments. Because of the unaccountable nature of covert arms supply, such operations also feed directly into the global black arms market. Compounding the dangers, guerrilla forces often lack an adequate chain of command and an authority structure sufficient to ensure physical control of weaponry. In addition, sub-state actor recipients are often less susceptible to pressure to observe the laws of war when employing the weapons.

In many cases, arms trafficked to insurgents arms now pose a direct threat to the state that previously supplied them. And, while the shipments are intended to further the political and/or economic interests of the supplier state, the supplier rarely if ever takes responsibility for the impact of its policies.

While apparently greatly diminished since the 1980s, governments continue to arm sub-state groups in foreign states for political or economic reasons. Developing clear international law barring small arms supply (usually covert) to sub-state actors would be one of the most meaningful policies that concerned governments and non-governmental organisations could pursue to curb further dangerous small arms proliferation. Past and continuing practitioners of covert arms supply cannot be expected to embrace the proposal immediately. But for the group of like-minded states and non-governmental organisations that came together first in support of the landmines ban treaty, and then in support of the establishment of an International Criminal Court, this proposal would seem to be a most worthy effort to explore and further develop.

At the same time, cutting off the state supply of arms to guerrilla forces must be balanced with responsible state-to-state arms transfer policies. Such policies would bar arms and military support to repressive governments. In addition, international mechanisms and responses must be developed or strengthened to protect people from repressive governments.

Notes

[1] See chapter 7 for more on brokering and shipping networks, many of which were spawned by covert arms supply operations run by various states and their intelligence agencies.

[2] Academician General Yuriy Kirshin, 'Conventional Arms Transfers During the Soviet Period,' in Ian Anthony, ed., *Russia and the Arms Trade* (Oxford: Oxford University Press, 1998), pp. 66-70.

[3] Anthony Cordesman, *The Lessons of Modern War, Vol. III: The Afghan and Falklands Conflicts* (Boulder, CO: Westview Press, 1999), p. 146.

[4] Cordesman, *Lessons of Modern War, Vol. III*, pp. 172-173.

[5] Egypt also included other weapons, such as shoulder-fired anti-tank and anti-aircraft rockets, guns and ammunition. Department of State cable, 'Aid to Afghanistan Insurgents,' 2 June 1980; Department of State cable, 'Anti-Aircraft Missiles Reported Provided to Afghan National Islamic Insurgents,' 24 July 1980; Department of State cable, 'Sadat Interview on Arms to Afghan Freedom Fighters,' 23 September 1981; 'US Flies Weapons to Rebels In Afghanistan, Sadat Says,' *Washington Post*, 23 September 1981.

[6] Cordesman, *Lessons of Modern War, Vol. III*, p. 172.

[7] US Defense Intelligence Agency, 'Chinese Opposition to Soviet Afghan Invasion is Reflected in Aid to Resistance,' 6 March 1981; Cordesman, *Lessons of Modern War, Vol. III*, p. 147.

[8] Zbigniew Brzezisnski could have been describing relations in several other conflicts when he boasted of the roles of China and Thailand in sup-

plying weapons to the Khmer Rouge: 'I encouraged the Chinese to support Pol Pot. Pol Pot was an abomination. We could never support him but China could.' As quoted in Elizabeth Becker, *When the War Was Over* (New York: Public Affairs, 1998), p. 435.

9 A portion of the arms taken out of service by the Honduran military may have been sold to FMLN forces in El Salvador rather than turned over to the *contras*. Yet until late 1983, interdiction of alleged arms flows from Nicaragua to the FMLN was the basis of the Carter and Reagan administrations' arguments for their *contra* operations. Department of State cable, 'Alleged Involvement of Honduran Officers in Arms Trade to Salvadoran Guerrillas,' 11 September 1981.

10 Richard P. Cronin, *Pakistan: US Foreign Assistance Facts,* Congressional Research Service Issue Brief 85112, 20 July 1987, p. 1.

11 Diego Cordovez and Selig S. Harrison, *Out of Afghanistan: The Inside Story of the Soviet Withdrawal* (NY: Oxford University Press, 1995), pp. 54-58.

12 Cronin, *Pakistan: US Foreign Assistance Facts*, pp. 4-6, 10; Leonard Spector, *The Undeclared Bomb* (Cambridge, MA: Ballinger Publishing Company, 1988), pp. 120-125; Tim Weiner, *Blank Check: The Pentagon's Black Budget* (NY: Warner Books, 1990), p. 147.

13 *Washington Post*, 27 September 1980.

14 Cordesman, *The Lessons of Modern War, Vol. III*, pp. 20-21.

15 According to military analyst David Isby, the ISI established this precondition because it did not trust the CIA to mount a successful operation. Interview by L. Mathiak with David Isby, Washington, DC, 10 June 1986.

16 Prepared for the US government by the Orkan Corporation June 1986, reproduced by permission of the Near East/Southeast Asia Division, CIA for use in a course at the National Defense University, *The Soviets in Afghanistan: Adapting, Reappraising, and Settling in*, June 1986, p. 33; United Nations Report, *Afghanistan: Questioning the Future*, 26 July 1989, p. 3.

17 Cordesman and Wagner estimate that as little as 30 percent of supplies reached the *mujahideen*. Cordesman, *The Lessons of Modern War, Vol. III*, p. 20; *The Soviets in Afghanistan*, p. 33.

18 In February 1987, Representative William Gray III requested that the GAO investigate 'repeated reports that much of this assistance is not reaching the intended recipients.' Gray was later persuaded to withdraw this request in deference to the Afghanistan aid initiative. Letter, Representative William Gray III to Charles A. Bowser, Comptroller General of the United States, 27 February 1987.

19 *The United States, Pakistan, and the Soviet Threat to Southern Asia*, Congressional Research Service Report no. 85-152F, September 1985, pp. 23-24.

20 *Ibid.*, pp. 14-19.

21 Geoffrey Kemp, *Forever Enemies? American Policy & the Islamic Republic of Iran* (Washington, DC: Carnegie Endowment for International Peace, 1994), pp. 22-23.

22 Oliver North, 'Release of American Hostages in Beirut,' background memo, 4 April 1986; 'US-Iran Dialogue,' National Security Council Memorandum of Conversation, 26 May 1986; 'Rundown of Visitor's Comments on 19/20 September 86,' Internal National Security Council Report (North and Secord), 20 September 1986.

23 The amount of Saudi funds involved has not been documented, although one source implies that the figure is in the $500 million range. Bob Woodward, *Veil: The Secret Wars of the CIA 1981-1987* (New York: Simon & Schuster, 1990), p. 582; see also Selig Harrison, 'Afghanistan: Soviet Intervention, Afghan Resistance, and the American Role,' in Klare and Kornbluh, eds., *Low Intensity Warfare* (NY: Pantheon Books, 1988), pp. 200-201.

24 'Chinese Opposition to Soviet Afghan Invasion is Reflected in Aid to Resistance,' US Defense Intelligence Agency Weekly Intelligence Summary, DIAWIS 10-81, 6 March 1981; 'China and Afghanistan: PRC Concerns and Ability to Influence Events,' Defense Intelligence Estimates Memorandum, DDE-2200-197-83, March 1983; *The Soviets in Afghanistan: Adapting, Reappraising, and Settling in*, p. 25.

25 *The United States, Pakistan, and the Soviet Threat to South Asia*, pp. 16-17; Richard Cronin, *Afghanistan After Five Years: Status of the Conflict, the Afghan Resistance and the US Role*, Congressional Research Service Report No. 85-20 F, January 1985, pp. 5-8; *Afghanistan: Questioning the Future*, pp. 3-4.

26 United Nations, *Afghanistan: Questioning the Future*, pp. 2-3

27 Cronin, *Afghanistan After Five Years*, p. 11.

28 United Nations, *Afghanistan: Questioning the Future*, p. 3-4; Cronin, *Afghanistan After Five Years*, pp. 6, 11.

29 *The Soviets in Afghanistan: Adapting, Reappraising, and Settling in*, p. 33; Cronin, *Afghanistan After Five Years*, pp. 6, 11; United Nations, *Afghanistan: Questioning the Future*, p. 3.

30 *Afghan Resistance Movements in 1981*, p. 2.

31 Christopher Dickey, *With the Contras: A Reporter in the Wilds of Nicaragua* (New York: Simon and Schuster, 1985), pp. 118-119.

32 A 1999 field study by the International Committee of the Red Cross in a region of Afghanistan showed light weapons injuries decreased by only 30 percent when the war ended. The continuing high rate of rifle and fragmentation wounds were attributed to the widespread availability of weapons in the region. See ICRC, *Arms Availability and the Situation of Civilians in Armed Conflict* (Geneva: ICRC, 1999), pp. 39-41.

33 Ian Anthony, 'Illicit Arms Transfers,' in Ian Anthony, ed., *Russia and the Arms Trade* (Oxford: Oxford University Press, 1998), pp. 217-232.

34 On 8 December 1999 the Presidents of Uganda and Sudan agreed to restore diplomatic ties and stop supporting rebel movements trying to topple each other's governments. The eleven-point agreement requires each side to disarm and disband guerrilla groups operating on their territory—the Lord's Resistance Army in Southern Sudan and the Allied Democratic

Forces operating on Uganda's western frontier, and camps of the Sudanese People's Liberation Army in northern Uganda. See Karl Vick, 'Uganda Signs Peace Deal with Sudan,' *Washington Post*, 9 December 1999.

35 Security Council resolution 1160, 31 March 1998.

36 The two principal exile groups seeking the mantle of leadership for the opposition are the Iraqi National Accord (www.iraq-free.demon.co.uk) and the Iraqi National Congress (www.inc. org.uk).

37 Jim Hoagland, 'How CIA's Secret War on Saddam Collapsed,' *Washington Post*, 26 June 1997; see also, John Lancaster and Jonathan C. Randall, 'CIA and Northern Iraq Dissidents: Little to Show for $100 Million,' *Washington Post*, 15 September 1996; Hugh Davis, 'Secret operation that became a public disaster,' *The Daily Telegraph*, 11 September 1996.

38 See *Congressional Record*, 5 October 1998, pp. H9486-ff.

39 Thomas W. Lippman, 'US Builds Support For Ouster Of Saddam,' *Washington Post*, 29 January 1999.

40 John Lancaster and Colum Lynch, 'Iraqi Exiles Meet to Mount An Opposition,' *Washington Post*, 2 November 1999.

41 Steven Lee Meyers, 'US to Aid Iraqi Opposition to Develop a Military Cadre,' *New York Times*, 28 October 1999.

42 Vernon Loeb, 'General Wary of Plan To Arm Groups in Iraq—Commander in Gulf Fearful of "Rogue State",' *Washington Post*, 29 January 1999.

43 Hearing before House Armed Services Committee, 10 March 1999, statement of James Woolsey.

44 The Swiss Federal Department of Foreign Affairs conducted a review of a proposal by the Canadian government calling for the negotiation of a convention barring state-backed transfers of arms to guerrilla groups (see below) and determined that the measure was unnecessary, as the Swiss government considers the practice illegal under existing international law. Private communication between L. Lumpe and official of Swiss Federal Department of Foreign Affairs, 23 November 1999.

45 Moreover, the fact that the UN Security Council has specifically included non-state actors in arms embargoes on several recent occasions (concerning Angola, Rwanda, Sierra Leone, and with reference to 'terrorist activities in Kosovo') would seem to indicate that the international community does not consider the practice of arming insurgents already sufficiently illegal.

46 Captain Benjamin P. Dean, 'Self-Determination and US Support of Insurgents: A Policy-Analysis Model,' *Military Law Review*, Fall 1988.

47 *Ibid.*

48 *Military and Paramilitary Activities in and against Nicaragua* (Nicar. Vs. US), 1986 ICJ 14 (Judgement of the Merits of June 27).

49 See UN General Assembly resolutions 2383 and 3103.

50 For example, during debates about the possible provision of military support by NATO member governments to the Kosovo Liberation Army (KLA) as a means of protecting the broader Albanian-Kosovar population,

many people noted the sharp distinction in policy toward the quite analogous Kurdish Workers Party (PKK) in Turkey and the economic, political and cultural repression suffered by Turkey's Kurdish nationalist population. Many of the same governments lending material or moral support to the KLA have labelled PKK fighters as 'terrorists' despite the similar fundraising and operational methods employed by the two insurgencies.

51 *Report of the Panel of Governmental Experts on Small Arms*, UN Doc. A/52/298, 27 August 1997, para. 51.

52 See *Report of the Group of Governmental Experts on Small Arms*, UN Doc. A/54/258, 19 August 1999.

53 Robert W. Gomulkiewicz, 'International Law Governing Aid To Opposition Groups In Civil War: Resurrecting The Standards Of Belligerency,' *Washington Law Review*, January 1988, footnote 29.

54 Notes for an Address by the Honourable Lloyd Axworthy, Minister of Foreign Affairs, to the International NGO Consultation on Small Arms Action, speech 98/50 as prepared for delivery, Orilla, Ontario, 19 August 1998.

55 'An International Agenda on Small Arms and Light Weapons: Elements of a Common Understanding,' final communiqué from the Oslo Meeting on Small Arms, 13-14 July 1998 (available at www.nisat.org).

56 Canadian Ministry of Foreign Affairs, Discussion Paper, 'A Proposed Global Convention Prohibiting the International Transfer of Military Small Arms and Light Weapons to Non-State Actors,' undated, obtained from the Canadian Mission to the UN, New York.

57 *Ibid.*

58 Notes for an Address by the Honourable Lloyd Axworthy.

59 Canadian Ministry of Foreign Affairs, Discussion Paper.

60 Private communication by L. Lumpe with US and Canadian government officials, November-December 1999.

61 European Union Joint Action on Small Arms (1999/34/CFSP), 17 December 1998 (available at www.sipri.se/projects/expcon/euframe/eusmja.htm). The operative language in the agreement is that the states of the EU 'shall aim at building consensus in the relevant international forums, and in a regional context as appropriate, for a commitment by exporting countries to supply small arms only to governments (either directly or through duly licensed entities authorised to procure weapons in their behalf) in accordance with appropriate international and regional restrictive arms export criteria.' A Joint Action is legally binding, though it is up to the Member States to implement it through national laws and policies.

62 Private communication by L. Lumpe, with Ian Anthony, Stockholm International Peace Research Institute, November 1999.

63 Aaron Karp, 'Arming Ethnic Conflict,' *Arms Control Today*, September 1993, p. 13.

4/Manufacturing Trends – Globalising the Source

by Pete Abel

Most arms that are trafficked outside of state control—or on the margins of it—were initially produced and traded legally. As more countries, and more companies within those countries, produce small arms, sources and possibilities for diversion onto the illegal market increase. A greater number of producers also renders enforcement of embargoes more difficult. In order to reduce the risk that weapons are diverted from the licit into the illicit realm, one area where states need to exert the utmost care and responsibility is in regulating production of small arms, light weapons, associated materials and ammunition.

This chapter provides an overview of trends in the global production of small arms and ammunition since the 1960s. It does not provide a comprehensive listing of small arms and light weapons producers around the world. Such a listing would be (and is) the subject of entire reference books. Rather, this chapter lays out some of the factors influencing the scope and structure of small arms production today. In particular, through several case studies this chapter emphasises the role that licensed production agreements have played in the proliferation of small arms. It details the impact such production has had in undermining human rights policies of several states and concludes with the need to bring licensed production agreements within existing arms export control systems.

Proliferation of Small Arms Producers

A United Nations report noted in July 1999 that there is 'little information publicly available on either official or private international transfers and sales of small arms.'[1] Indeed, the majority of governments provide no data on manufacture within their jurisdiction, authorised transfers or national inventories of small arms and ammunition. Where data is given, it is usually aggregated to such an extent that detailed analysis is difficult, if not impossible.

A number of nongovernmental initiatives have recently begun to gather, organise and analyse the available information. Most notable are an Internet database being developed by the Norwegian Initiative on Small Arms Transfers[2] and the Swiss government-backed *Small Arms Survey*, an annual yearbook to begin publication in 2001. These and other efforts aimed at promoting control over the trade are reliant on national governments and international agencies to provide accurate and comprehensive data. Given the scope and scale of small arms manufacture and trade, and the small size of the commodities, nongovernmental researchers can never hope to quantify these trends precisely or independently from official sources.

Analysis of trends in small arms production is further complicated by differing definitions of 'small arms' and 'light weapons.' For example, NATO has defined small arms as 'all crew-portable direct fire weapons of a calibre less than 50mm and will include a secondary capability to defeat light armour and helicopters.'[3] Other definitions include any weapons that use gunpowder or another propellant to fire a projectile through a barrel, and that can be carried by one or two persons, a pack animal or light vehicle. Distinctions between 'civilian,' 'law enforcement' or 'military' small arms further confuse analytical comparisons.[4] For this chapter, 'small arms' are limited to pistols and revolvers; shotguns, rifles and carbines; sub-machine guns; machine guns; ammunition (12.7mm and below); and hand portable grenade launchers and mortars.

The differing definitions have led to varying estimates for the number of manufacturers and of countries producing such weapons. A report by the UN Institute for Disarmament Research identified nearly 300 companies in 52 countries as manufacturing small arms and related equipment in 1994.[5] Another survey reported a lower figure for the same year, 252 manufacturers in 69 manufacturing countries.[6] And in a 1999 report, a UN Group of Governmental Experts on Small Arms said that light weapons 'continue to be produced in large numbers, mostly in developed countries, although they are now manufactured in over 70 countries on an industrial scale and in numerous countries as a craft industry.'[7] At great variance with these reports, an unpublished estimate by an international law enforcement agency, provided to the author in January 2000, placed the number of worldwide small arms-producing companies at 1900.[8]

Table 4.1 seeks to document and quantify trends in production by updating these previous studies and integrating open source material from a range of publications. According to this research, 385 companies in 64 countries were manufacturing small arms and/or ammunition in the 1990s. Given the secrecy that attends the business of gun manufacturing in many parts of the world, this table undoubtedly errs on the side of caution, under-reporting manufacturing. It does, nevertheless, clearly identify two trends in small arms manufacturing from 1960 to 1999—an increasing number of countries producing small arms and an increasing number of manufacturing enterprises within those countries.

It is important to note that more manufacturers do not necessarily denote an increase in total manufacturing capacity for small arms and ammunition. In the 1960s there were ten small arms manufacturers in six countries in Eastern Europe. By the end of the century, this figure had grown to 66 manufacturing firms in 15 countries. Much of this 'growth,' however, was caused by the creation of new states following the dissolution of the Soviet Union. In addition, information sources and reporting on Eastern European

Table 4.1 Proliferation of Small Arms Production, 1960-1999

		Africa	Asia / Pacific	West Europe	East Europe	Middle East	South / Central Amer.	North Amer.	Total
1990s	Firms	22	31	137	66	13	17	99	385
	States	7	14	15	15	6	5	2	64
1980s	Firms	10	23	88	12	6	15	42	196
	States	5	14	15	7	4	5	2	52
1970s	Firms	2	17	63	12	4	8	36	142
	States	2	10	16	7	2	4	2	43
1960s	Firms	1	7	29	10	2	3	17	69
	States	1	5	14	6	2	2	2	30

Sources: *Jane's Infantry Weapons, Jane's Security & Counter Insurgency Equipment, British Defence Equipment Catalogue, International Defence Equipment Catalogue*, technical and advertising brochures from law enforcement equipment manufacturing companies and the Omega Foundation's database of military, security and police companies.[9]

arms industry during the Cold War often only included state arsenals—complexes that each comprised several production facilities. These state arsenals were each broken up into several new private companies. With the exception of improvements generated from greater private investment in new production technologies, such changes of ownership do not necessarily imply any increase in manufacturing capacity. However, the 1990s did see a major increase in the number of manufacturing companies in Eastern Europe, each pursuing a profit through export sales.[10]

There has been little change in Western Europe in the number of countries manufacturing small arms between the 1970s and 1990s, but there was a doubling of companies involved in production during this same time. At least two conflicting dynamics are reflected within this trend: The consolidation of the arms industry and the privatisation of previously state-owned industries.

Other regions of the world experienced more modest increases in the number of manufacturing companies and countries. For example, during the 1980s and 1990s there was no increase in the number of manufacturing countries in either the Asia/Pacific or South/Central America regions, and both areas saw only modest increases in the number of companies—from 23 to 31 and 15 to 17 respectively. However, these figures likely under-report the situation, since most sources refer to China North Industries (NORINCO) and Chinese State Arsenals as the two manufacturers in China, while other sources cite 16 arms producing factories there.[11]

Overall, between 1960 and 1999 there has been a doubling of the number of countries that produce small arms and a nearly sixfold increase in the number of manufacturing companies. While some of this increase can be explained by factors previously outlined—privatisation of state industries, creation of more nation states and the availability of more accurate reporting—the data indicates steady increases in the production of small arms and ammunition throughout the past decades. Much of this growth in the number of producers is a result of licensed manufacturing agreements (more below). However, very little information is available on the actual manufacturing capacities of these small arms factories, or of particular countries.

The United States is one of the most transparent of all small arms supplying states, and it might have the largest small arms industrial capacity in the world today. Since 1996, US export law has caused the US government to publish an annual report listing out the amount of arms—including small arms, light weaponry, ammunition and components—that the State Department cleared for export during the preceding year.[12] Reports for 1996-1998 indicate that the State Department authorised manufacturers to export more than $1.5 billion of such items, including more than 1.6 million guns of various types, nearly 200,000 grenades, and more than two billion rounds of ammunition.[13] It is important to note that this information only denotes licences granted by the State Department, rather than actual delivery of items, but these figures point to a massive industrial capacity. While it is impossible to compare the level of US arms exports to those of other major suppliers, due to secrecy on the part of the other suppliers, given the magnitude of licence authorisations and the size of the US domestic market, it is reasonable to speculate that the United States currently produces more small arms than any other country.[14]

Unauthorised, or Illegal, Small Arms Production

Most of the companies counted in table 4.1 will be known to relevant government agencies within their country of operation, since most states authorise the production of weapons by requiring producers to register. Similarly, states generally control exports from these manufacturers through some sort of export licensing procedure. This does not mean that all trade by such enterprises is licit, but any unlawful transfers will probably be due to loopholes in export control regimes, governmental incompetence (perhaps due to lack of capacity) or local corruption.

Coexisting with these legal manufacturers in some states are unauthorised and completely unregulated private arms producers. While generally crude in nature and small in terms of global production, the illegal or unauthorised manufacture of small arms can have a major impact on conflict and human rights violations in some countries and regions. Many private workshops are devoted solely to production of 'single-shot' weapons used only for ceremonial, hunting or sporting purposes, but some undertake production of militarily significant weapons.

There is currently very little systematic information available on 'craft' production of small arms and ammunition. The arms bazaars of Pakistan's Northwest Frontier are perhaps the best known example of small-scale production of small arms. Hundreds of one-room operations manufacture copies of AK-47s and other rifles and pistols. Individual craftsmen manufacture small numbers of weap-

ons, with a pistol taking three days and an AK-47 between seven
and ten days. Because there are many hundreds of such arms sellers, the overall production figures run into the thousands of weapons. Recent reports have suggested, however, that business is suffering due to a glutted market.[15]

Home-made or unauthorised weapon production has been reported in a wide range of other countries as well, including: Brazil,[16] Cambodia, Colombia, East Timor, India, Northern Ireland and
Palestine.[17] Guerrilla forces combating state forces most often undertake this production. For example, *Khmer Rouge* militia were reported to have established factories that could produce 500-600
landmines and rocket-propelled grenades each day,[18] and both the
LTTE (Tamil Tigers) in Sri Lanka and the Revolutionary Armed
Forces of Colombia (FARC) have produced improvised tanks, built
from farm tractors or bulldozers with cabs protected by armour
plate and machine guns mounted on top.[19] FARC guerrillas have
also manufactured simple mortars and cylinder bombs.[20] Similarly,
Irish Republican Army militants became very skilled at producing
explosives from fertilisers for use in home-made weapons such as
nail bombs and 'drogue bombs' (an anti-vehicle grenade consisting
of 230g of explosive packed into a baking tin).[21] The Tamil Tigers
are also reported to have produced small-sized suicide body-suits,
denim jackets with concealed explosives, to allow child soldiers to
undertake suicide missions.[22]

Many of these home-made weapons are quite simple. For example, 'Kraal shotguns' in KwaZulu Natal often consist of nothing
more than a hollow pipe with a spring inserted inside, operated by
a nail.[23] But some home production can achieve surprisingly good
standards. Indian police officers describe some handguns produced
by illegal gun makers in the Bihar State as being as good as their
service revolvers.[24]

Governments sometimes overstate reports of home-made
weapon production, in an effort to deflect scrutiny of their own activities or to raise support for their procurement of more arms. For
example, autumn 1999 killings in East Timor carried out by militia
forces opposed to Timorese independence were widely acknowledged to have been armed by the Indonesian army. An Indonesian
general denied that his forces had armed the militias, showing
journalists two home-made guns with crude metal barrels. These
weapons supported his claim that the militias made their own
weapons, but the General made no mention of the SKS, M16 and G3
rifles that had also been confiscated from the militias.[25]

The 1997 Inter-American Convention against the Illicit Manufacturing of and Trafficking in Firearms, Ammunition, Explosives and Other Related Materials (the OAS Convention) obliges parties to the treaty to establish legal and regulatory structures for authorising and controlling manufacture of small arms and light weapons. It also requires record keeping and the exchange of information with other parties on authorised producers of firearms, ammunition and explosives.[26] The global Firearms Protocol being negotiated in 1999-2000 under the auspices of the UN Economic and Social Council will likely contain similar provisions.

Most home-made production of small arms is unauthorised, if not illegal, from the point of view of the state in which it occurs. In some cases, however, the state itself engages in unauthorised small arms production by reverse engineering another country's or a company's products, or by exceeding its permissible licensed production quotas. Such production is 'illicit' in that the owner of the original product has not given permission for production, but the manufacture of such weapons is often undertaken by state-owned companies or by private companies that are authorised by state agencies. For example, China North Industries has allegedly made an unlicensed (and therefore illegal) version of the Israel Military Industries 9mm sub-machine gun.

Licensed Production Agreements

One of the principal factors behind the steady increase in the number of manufacturing countries and companies noted in table 4.1 is the widespread transfer of arms production technology through licensed production agreements.[27] In such deals, a corporation in one country contracts with a foreign corporation to permit the manufacture of its military equipment. The licensing company will provide technical data or copies of the item to be produced, and sometimes it provides machine tools or sets up the production line.

Throughout the Cold War, small arms manufacturing companies in the leading arms-supplying states provided licensed manufacture agreements to client countries in order to gain access to the local market. The licensee companies or enterprises inevitably became independent of their patron by creating minor variations on the weapons they produce. Having thus developed an 'indigenous' weapon design and an independent industry, these firms are free to seek their own export markets. In the process they spawn additional small arms industry through further manufacturing technology transfer.

Licensed production is not unique to the manufacture of weapons. A wide range of other industrial sectors utilises such agreements to extend the production and marketing of products and services to specific countries or world regions. What is perhaps unique about small arms licensed production, however, compared to other industry sectors is the level of secrecy (or commercial confidentiality) surrounding these agreements. Also unusual is that, with the exception of the United States, the licensed products are not generally destined for the domestic market of the licensing company. For example, there is little if any domestic market in the UK for the Heckler & Koch (owned by British Aerospace) HK33 assault rifle production commencing in Turkey. The fact that most developed countries do not face the consequences of the weapons industry they are licensing may explain in part the lack of effective controls on such production agreements.

Licensed production is not a new concept. *Fabrique Nationale d'Armes de Guerre* (FN) was founded in Belgium in 1889 to produce German Mauser rifles under licence for the Belgian Army. A number of licence agreements were established immediately after World War II in European countries, as well as in other regions.[28] Nevertheless, there has been little research into small arms licensed production agreements, either in terms of the number and range of weapons manufactured, the impact on employment in the country that is exporting the production or on any 'third party' (unauthorised) exports.[29]

From 1960 to 1999, 14 countries established small arms and ammunition licensed production agreements with some 46 countries.[30] One 1995 report estimated that licensed production was taking place in at least 21 developing countries, 16 of which were also exporting the small arms they manufactured. These countries included Brazil, Chile, Egypt, India, Indonesia, Iran, North and South Korea, Pakistan, Singapore, South Africa and Turkey.[31]

It is not clear whether new licensed production agreements are increasing in recent years, or whether there is simply better reporting on the trend. Many ongoing production agreements for the most popular small arms—such as the Heckler & Koch G3 rifle and MP5 sub-machine gun, and the FN-FAL rifle—have been operational since the 1950s. The FAL provides a good example of the wide range of countries producing specific weapons under licence. It has been manufactured in Argentina, Australia, Austria, Brazil,

Canada, India, Israel, Mexico, South Africa and Venezuela. Similarly, China, East Germany, Egypt, Finland, Hungary, Iraq, North Korea, Poland, Romania and Yugoslavia have all produced the Russian/Soviet AK-47 rifle (and variants).[32]

Irrespective of whether the phenomenon is occurring more or less frequently in recent years, the identification of a licensed production agreement does not provide meaningful information on the quantity of weapons or ammunition being produced. However, it does provide a framework for beginning to analyse whether licensed production agreements are contributing significantly to the proliferation of small arms, and to the illegal supply of such weapons in particular. The available information indicates a marked increase in exports of small arms by licensee companies, as these companies face the same — or greater — pressures to export as do companies in developed economies. In many cases, these exports appear to contradict the terms of the licence agreement.

Heckler & Koch's Global Reach

Edmond Heckler, Alex Seidel and Theodore Koch, former employees of the *Mauser Werke* gun company, founded Heckler & Koch GmbH in Germany in 1948. The design for H&K's most famous rifle, the G3, was originally developed by CETME in Spain but was later transferred to Heckler & Koch.[33] This 7.62mm rifle has been the German Army's standard assault rifle since 1959, and the armed forces of more than 45 armies have adopted it as well, with licensed production taking place in twelve countries.[34] Heckler & Koch also designed, developed and manufactured the MP5 sub-machine gun, which has become the weapon of choice of many law enforcement and special forces units around the world. Table 4.2 shows where the G3 rifle, MP5 submachine gun and other H&K small arms have been, or are being, manufactured under licensed production agreements.

Most licensed production agreements for the Heckler & Koch G3 rifles and MP5 sub-machine guns were signed long before the British Aerospace subsidiary Royal Ordnance purchased Heckler & Koch in the Spring of 1991. However, Royal Ordnance had previously established close connections and licensed production agreements with H&K through the Royal Small Arms Factory (RSAF) in Enfield. The first licence agreement was signed in April 1970. Under its terms, RSAF Enfield manufactured various Heckler & Koch weapons and sold these to Heckler & Koch (UK) Ltd, which was incorporated in March 1973 and existed as a sales company. The Royal Ordnance factory in Nottingham later began manufacturing H&K arms as well. Most of this production was exported, as there was little domestic requirement for G3 rifles. Exports peaked in 1994 at £22 million.[35]

This close manufacturing arrangement between Heckler & Koch (Germany) and Royal Ordnance (UK) raised serious concerns that the two companies were exploiting inconsistencies between German and UK export controls in order to evade arms export embargoes. After reports emerged that H&K MP5 weapons had been identified in Bosnia and Serbia, apparently breaching the UN arms embargo levied in 1991, Heckler & Koch stated that the weapons in question 'were made under licence by Royal Ordnance at its small-arms factory in London, before 1987,' and that H&K did 'not know how many MP5 barrels have been delivered to Enfield.'

Prior to the UN embargo, it was not illegal for UK firms to export to Yugoslavia, although it was for German firms. A company spokesman for Royal Ordnance reportedly stated that, 'Heckler and Koch [UK] has never delivered weapons to Yugoslavia,' and

Table 4.2 Heckler & Koch Small Arms Licensed Production

Pistols	Rifles	Sub-machine guns	Machine guns	Other
P7M13 9mm Pakistan	*7.62mm G3* Burma* France Greece Iran* Mexico Norway Pakistan Portugal Saudi Arabia Sweden Turkey UK *5.56mm HK33* Greece Thailand Turkey	*MP5* Greece Iran* Mexico Pakistan Saudi Arabia Turkey UK	*7.62mm HK21A1* Greece Thailand UK *5.56mm HK53* Greece	*40mm Riot gas launcher* Italy

*The Heckler & Koch company has stated that these licensed production agreements have lapsed.

that it abides 'scrupulously by the requirements of Her Majesty's Government and only export[s] to places for which we have approval. We cannot be responsible for what may end up in the hands of third parties.'[36] A spokesman for British Aerospace emphasised that the alleged events took place before 'Royal Ordnance bought Heckler & Koch in 1991.'[37]

This disingenuous statement, implying that the company had no links with H&K prior to 1991, effectively deflected attention. In a pattern that would be repeated with licensed production in other countries, neither company technically had broken its national laws, but H&K weapons had ended up in a conflict zone.

Turkish Licensed Production and Exports

Makina ve Kimya Endustrisi Kurumu (MKEK), part of Turkey's state-owned Machine and Chemicals Industries Board, manufactures a wide range of small arms, ammunition and other weapons systems under licensed production agreements. Individual agreements often contain more than one component or weapon system. For example, in 1992 Giat Industries of France won a contract to supply guns and turrets for armoured personnel carriers that Turkey was producing in collaboration with the American company FMC.

Under the $116 million contract, in-country production would account for $53 million of the contract value. Turkey's Under-Secretariat for Defence Industry mandated that additional direct offsets of $29 million would be used to import components for the guns and turrets, while, under a $29 million indirect offset programme, Giat would give MKEK 25mm ammunition production technology and would also export existing MKEK military products. In addition, Giat would supply 60 Oerlikon (Swiss) guns, 60 Giat-produced guns and 67 turrets off the shelf. On the co-production side, 455 guns and 448 turrets will be manufactured locally in conjunction with MKEK. According to one report, GIAT was giving away its 25mm ammunition technology 'free of charge' to successfully win the larger contract.[38] This form of offset—or deal sweetener—may explain why some companies are willing to provide small arms licensed production agreements at commercially unsustainable prices.

MKEK also manufactures a range of Heckler & Koch small arms under licence. It has made the G3A3 and G3A4 assault rifles since the 1970s and the MP5A2, MP5A3 and MP5K sub-machine guns since the 1980s. In January 1998 it was reported that Heckler & Koch had won an $18 million contract for the licensed production by Turkey of 200,000 HK33 5.56mm assault rifles, to be produced over the next ten years.[39]

The Turkish military and police have been involved in repressive fighting against Kurdish guerrillas and Turkey's broader Kurdish population since the mid-1980s. Several West European states have cut off arms supply to Turkey at various times over the past 15 years due to serious human rights concerns about the conduct of this counter-insurgency. Local production of small arms frees the Turkish military from such external pressures, as MKEK's licensed production is displacing weapons imports. MKEK doubled its revolver sales within Turkey in 1998 to 20,583 at a total value of 3.3 trillion Turkish lira. At the same time, imports of foreign-made arms decreased.[40]

MKEK has also increased its exports in recent years, including many weapons made under licence. In 1995 the company reported that it had sold its products to some 38 countries, including Botswana, Brazil, Chile, Ecuador, Hong Kong, Kuwait, Libya, Macau, Pakistan, Peru, Singapore and Tunisia. Its most popular products were MP5 machine guns, 66mm anti-tank rockets, eight-inch shells and 81mm and 120mm mortars with a six- to eight-kilometre range.[41] In 1996 MKEK reported that it had exported nearly $50 million of products, with the principal recipients being Jordan, Norway, Pakistan, Switzerland, Tunisia, the Turkish Republic of Northern Cyprus and the United Kingdom.[42] For the first eleven months of 1998, MKEK's exports were reported significantly lower, at $5.8 million, to 22 different countries. According to the MKEK Directorate-General, the leading importer was Bosnia, and other recipients were Burundi, Tunisia and the United Arab Emirates.[43]

Turkish gun exports can be expected to increase in the coming years. In 1998, while signing a contract for production of the new HK33 assault rifle, it was reported that MKEK would continue to produce the older G3 assault rifle for export.[44] And in July 1998 the Turkish News Agency reported that MKEK would export 500 MP5 sub-machine guns valued at $400,000 to the Indonesian Police.[45] This announcement of a small shipment of MP5 sub-machine guns provides an important illustration of the problems that licensed production agreements raise for export controls.

In 1997 two British documentaries showed film footage of Indonesian Special Forces (Kopassus) training with Heckler & Koch MP5 sub-machine guns.[46] British Aerospace admitted that these weapons had been supplied from its Nottingham facility in 1996. At first the UK government denied that it had issued any export licences for Indonesia for the licence category covering the MP5 submachine gun.[47] Despite questions from Members of Parliament asking specifically about the export of MP5 sub-machine guns to Indonesia, the government's response was that 'readily available records (since 1991) show no licences granted for export of these weapons to Indonesia have been issued.'[48] Even when the Department of Trade recognised that 'Heckler and Koch MP5 sub-machine guns are manufactured in the UK by Royal Ordnance,' there was still no record of export licences having been granted for MP5 sub machine guns.[49]

The then new Labour government reported in July 1997 that it had received four licence applications for the export of sub-machine guns and other automatic weapons to Indonesia.[50] A letter from the Department of Trade and Industry to a Member of Parliament in July 1998 declined to name which company had requested the export licences, but it specified that the four applications covered a total of 366 weapons for the Indonesian Armed Forces. In early 1998 the government stated that three of these export licence applications had been refused, and in February 1999 it divulged that the unnamed company had withdrawn the fourth export application.[51]

It seems a remarkable coincidence that a few months after a British company is refused new export licences for Indonesia, MKEK would announce that it was supplying the same weapon to the Indonesian Police. Another British documentary provided evidence that MKEK had shipped 500 of the sub-machine guns to Indonesia in September 1999, at the height of the massacres in East Timor around the independence referendum.[52] The European Union had embargoed arms to Indonesia in 1999, due to human rights concerns. This policy meant that neither Heckler & Koch in Germany nor in the United Kingdom would have been allowed to export MP5 guns to Indonesia. But Turkey, which is not a member of the European Union, could do so.

British Aerospace has argued that the licensed production agreements with MKEK for the G3 rifles and MP5 sub-machine guns were negotiated and signed long before British Aerospace purchased Heckler & Koch in 1991. However, there is evidence that Heckler & Koch has continued to provide engineering blueprints, technical assistance, training and other services for MKEK in subsequent years.[53] In addition, the licensed production agreement for the newer H&K rifle, the HK33, was signed in 1998.

Moreover, the exports of H&K weapons made under authorised licensed production agreements with MKEK in Turkey and with Pakistan Ordnance Factories (see below) appear to contradict statements by Heckler & Koch officials that the right to re-export was excluded in agreements signed with Turkey, Iran, Saudi Arabia, Pakistan and Thailand. This same official said that, in 1982, the German government placed further regulations on the export of completed weapons. As a result, to obtain the approval of the German government, weapons manufactured under licensed conditions must be for the sole use of the country concerned, and they may not be re-exported. Exemptions from this re-export exclusion can only take place after previous consultation with the German government.[54]

It is not clear whether either the German or UK governments or British Aerospace has given permission for MKEK to export MP5 sub-machine guns to Indonesia. Nor is it clear whether any re-export controls will be enforced by the German government or British Aerospace for the production agreement signed in 1998 for Turkish manufacture of the HK33 assault rifle.[55] A spokesman for British Aerospace recently noted that it was 'difficult, if not impossible' to control the production quantities.[56]

In early 2000 negotiations are underway by Colt Manufacturing (USA) to purchase H&K.[57] According to a 1997 State Department report on US arms exports to Turkey, it is 'US policy to restrict the sale of arms that clearly could be used to repress a civilian population, such as small arms and violent crowd-control devices.'[58] If the purchase goes through, it will be interesting to see whether the US government ends H&K's arms production contracts with MKEK.

Pakistan Ordnance Factory

Pakistan Ordnance Factory (POF) is a state-owned weapons manufacturer, established after partition from India. It now has a complex of 14 independent factories that manufacture a wide range of weapons, including small arms and ammunition, as well as medium and heavy artillery and anti-tank weapons. In 1986 the company was reported to employ some 40,000 people and to have military exports of $30-35 million annually, with a stated goal of $150 million per year in the near future.[59]

Small arms manufactured under licensed production agreements include Heckler & Koch's G3A3 and G3A4 assault rifles, MP5A2 and A3 sub-machine guns and P7M13 pistol. In addition, POF reportedly manufactures Rheinmetall MG3 machine guns and Royal Ordnance Factories' 105mm anti-tank ammunition.[60]

In a 1992 interview, a Pakistani arms manufacturer was surprisingly frank in revealing one reason for establishing licensed production agreements with POF. According to him, POF, which had long maintained close ties with German arms manufacturers, had recently begun providing a new service — end-use certificates to cover German arms shipments to Kuwait.[61] Arms exports to the Middle East are illegal under German law, and they have frequently aroused controversy. By going through Pakistan, a legal destination, many German companies had found a convenient route to enter the Middle East market. Some of Germany's largest weapons manufacturers had granted production licences to the Pakistan Ordnance Factories, so sales to Pakistan did not raise problems in Bonn. The article also described another variation of the end-user scheme in which German companies would negotiate a contract with a Middle Eastern client, then hand it to POF for the actual deliveries, in essence 'selling' their contract to the Pakistanis.

POF has exported arms to a number of countries, including, allegedly, 150 machine guns, 50,000 rounds of ammunition and 5000 120mm mortar bombs to the repressive junta in Burma in March 1989.[62] Other small arms recipients have included France, Morocco, Sri Lanka, the Gulf states,[63] the Philippines National Police and South Africa.[64] Spokesmen for POF also revealed that the enterprise had shipped G3 rifles to Kenya in 1997 as part of a deal brokered by Lightweight Body Armour, a company based in Daventry, UK. Officials at the British company were unable, or unwilling, to identify when exactly in 1997 this deal was brokered, but shortly after the election in May 1997 that brought in the Blair government, a number of UK export licences for body armour, ammunition and small arms to Kenya were refused.

During a 1999 investigation for a British documentary, a POF sales manager offered to sell anti-personnel landmines to undercover reporters seeking to buy small arms and ammunition for a 'resource company' operating in Sudan.[65] Despite providing the reporters with detailed specification sheets for the mines, POF spokesmen denied the state enterprise is currently manufacturing such mines. However, *Jane's Infantry Weapons 1999/00* edition notes that the ARGES grenade, originally from Austria and produced by

POF under a licensed production agreement, is 'also employed as the warhead for the POF bounding anti-personnel mine.'[66] It is unknown at the time of writing whether the licensed production agreement between POF and ARGES has been rescinded.

Impact on Export Controls and Human Rights

The ease with which Pakistan Ordnance Factories and Turkey's MKEK can continue to supply weapons to the security forces in countries that are engaged in external aggression or internal repression illustrates the impact of licensed production agreements in undermining export controls. The same weapons, if manufactured in the home countries of the licensing companies, would be denied export licences. If not clearly illegal, such practices skirt the spirit of national laws and regional policies, such as EU embargoes.

As noted in the cases above, if production and export limits are embedded in the licensed production agreements, as some arms company officials have stated, they are being violated with apparent impunity. There is no recent evidence of enforcement of these provisions by either European governments or companies. This lack of enforcement action stands in sharp contrast to patterns in other industrial sectors, such as pharmaceuticals and the music industry, where strenuous efforts are made to prevent foreign companies from making unauthorised use of intellectual property.

Moreover, arms companies have, in the past, taken action to prevent unauthorised use of their products. For example, Krupp — Germany's largest munitions firm in the early 1900s — successfully sued a British company for producing its hand grenade fuses in Britain during World War I.[67] More recently, Russia cancelled the supply of T-80 tank parts to a Ukrainian company that was manufacturing the tanks under a licensed production agreement and supplying tanks to Pakistan. The object of this action was not to stop exports of the weapons. Rather, Russia wanted to export the same tank to India.[68]

The international community has made very little effort to control the proliferation of small arms production. While some states, including the United States, Sweden and Germany, have limited controls on licensed production agreements, there is a lack of consistency and enforcement. There is an urgent need for coherent and effective controls, especially across the European Union, to shut down this shady source of arms supply.

European Union

During preliminary discussions on the EU Code of Conduct on Arms Transfers (see chapter 2), a Europe-wide coalition of arms control, human rights and development organisations called for 'harmonised, extensive control lists which cover exports (or licensed production) of major conventional weaponry, all types of small arms and light weapons, police and paramilitary equipment, military and paramilitary training equipment and services, and dual-use technologies.'[69] Subsequently, the European Parliament passed a resolution on arms clearly stating that the proposed code should apply to exports and licensed production.[70] Unfortunately, when EU governments introduced the EU Code of Conduct on Arms Transfers in June 1998, it included no export control measures relating to licensed production.

United States

Export control law in the United States treats licensed production agreements as a physical export and requires prior approval from the State Department. In addition, the State Department must notify the Congress before licensed production agreements valued at more than $50 million may go forward.[71] US licensed production contracts usually limit production levels and prohibit sales or transfers to third countries without prior US government consent. Recent reports have suggested that the United States' European and NATO allies have lobbied to have such restrictions removed, but the State Department reportedly does not favour doing so.[72]

Despite these control procedures, overproduction and illegal transfer of licensed production occur. In a rare example that was caught and prosecuted, in 1992 Japan Aviation Electronics Industry (JAE) was fined $10 million for illegally selling weapons components to Iran. JAE had been authorised under a US licence to manufacture gyroscopes and accelerometers for the Japanese military's F-4 fighter jets. Between 1984 and 1987, the company transferred navigational components in defiance of the US policy prohibiting arms sales to Iran.[73] In another case in the late 1980s, a South Korean firm producing US-designed M16A1 assault rifles violated the terms of its licence by manufacturing greater quantities than permitted and exporting them without US government approval.[74] No penalties were levied, as South Korea was able to claim that the exported guns were an indigenous 'Koreanised' version of the weapon.

United Kingdom

Several Members of Parliament sought clarification in 1999 about UK government controls on companies establishing licensed production abroad. The Trade Minister told them that 'Companies wishing to license overseas production of their products do not require [Department of Trade and Industry] approval, nor are they required to notify DTI of agreements entered into.'[75] When asked recently whether he could do something about licensed production of weapons by UK firms abroad, specifically the Heckler & Koch deals conveyed above, Prime Minister Blair reportedly said, 'I can't actually.'[76] Moreover, at least one arms industry executive does not believe that the UK government is concerned about circumvention of UK export controls via licensed production arrangements.[77]

While the government may not choose to control the establishment of licensed production agreements, the United Kingdom has laws that could be used as a legal basis for doing so. Within the Export of Goods (Control) Order, there are several categories of products that are identified as requiring export licences. These include category ML18, which would cover the type of design, test and manufacturing equipment needed to produce components, to test and assemble weapons. Other export categories that could cover equipment required to establish small arms production are ML22, which covers 'technology,' and PL5017, which includes equipment and test models for the development of military goods.

In addition, the UK government does not currently include controls on 'third country' exports by licensees.[78] In early 1999 the government stated that it might consider the issue, possibly in the context of the Wassenaar Agreement, a forum of 33 arms-exporting states, based in Vienna.[79]

Gaining Control

Consumer groups and public interest organisations can and have exerted enormous retail and political pressure on corporations, such as Nike, that license manufacture of their products, particularly with regard to child labour, wage levels and unionisation practices of their affiliates abroad. Consumer pressure may not be applicable to arms companies that have established licensed production agreements in developing countries, but the analogy may encourage Western arms companies and governments to implement and enforce re-export controls on companies producing small arms under licence. At a minimum, to protect against diversion and undermining of their own national laws and policies, as well as the undermining of supranational arms embargoes, national governments should:

- ensure that all licensed production agreements for small arms and light weapons manufacture, ammunition and components are subject to authorisation within national export control legislation. Authorisation criteria should be at least as stringent as those for direct arms exports. In addition, the European Union should bring licensed production within the scope of the EU Code of Conduct on Arms Transfers. In all cases, licensed production agreements should be subject to the following:

i.   they should not be permitted for recipient states where an export licence application for a direct weapons transfer would be refused;

ii.   they should not be permitted where the recipient state cannot demonstrate sufficient accountability in terms of end-use control; and

iii.   they should not be permitted to states that have a record of violating UN and other international arms embargoes;

- ensure that licensed production agreements include provisions stating authorised production quantities and enforce adherence to these provisions;

- enforce re-export controls for existing licensed production agreements and make such controls mandatory for any future agreements;

- require end-use certification and end-use monitoring for licensed production agreements; and

- take collective action to prevent small arms proliferation through unauthorised licensed production by companies and governments.

In addition, increased transparency around licensed production agreements would reduce the propensity of these deals to undermine, or circumvent, national and regional export controls. Transparency could most easily be achieved through unilateral decisions by states that authorise licensed production agreements to make public the specifications of such agreements, for instance in parliamentary or government digests such as is currently done in the United States.[80] In a more complicated arrangement, states could exchange information on licensed production arrangements they have entered into through regional arms registers or other notification systems.

Notes

[1] United Nations, *Report of a consultative meeting of experts on the feasibility of undertaking a study of restricting the manufacture and trade of small arms...*, UN Doc. A/54/160, 6 July 1999.

[2] See www.nisat.org, 'database of small arms production and transfers.' This project is acquiring publicly available government export data, culling out small arms data, converting the values into current-year US dollars for comparability and entering the figures into a searchable, online database.

[3] 'Proliferation of Small Arms and Minor Weapons,' *Strategic Analysis*, Vol. 17, No. 2, May 1994, p. 189.

[4] With the availability of 'military spec' weapons to civilian markets, the growing militarisation of police and the use of the military in law enforcement roles, distinctions between 'civilian', 'police' or 'military' small arms are being blurred. This trend is apparent from the advertising of a number of small arms manufacturers.

[5] 'Arms Control Orphans,' *Bulletin of the Atomic Scientists*, Vol. 55, No. 1, January 1999.

[6] An analysis of *Jane's Infantry Weapons 1993/4*, presented in C. Louse, 'The Social Impact of Light Weapons Availability and Proliferation,' *Journal of Humanitarian Assistance*, 1995.

[7] The experts on small arms made the link between the increase in the number of legitimate and illegitimate producers and the excessive and destabilising availability of small arms. United Nations, *Report of the Group of Governmental Experts on Small Arms*, UN Doc. A/54/258, p. 8.

[8] Unpublished data on 'worldwide small arms producers,' provided to the author from an international law enforcement agency, January 2000.

[9] The Omega Foundation (UK) database contains records on some 8000 companies that manufacture or provide military, security and/or police equipment or services. The database uses open source information to compile a company record that provides corporate, product and transfer data. E-mail contact: Omega@mcr1.poptel.org.uk.

[10] The increased availability of East European guns is not only due to changes in ownership of factories. The off-loading of Warsaw Pact standard weapons in the 1990s was a major source of supply, as the armed

forces of many countries re-equipped to NATO standard arms. See 'Eastern Europe's Arsenal on the Loose: Managing Light Weapons Flows to Conflict Zones', *BASIC Papers*, No. 26, May 1998.

11 S. Rana, 'Small Arms and Intra-State Conflicts,' conference paper, 7-11 November 1994, (Geneva: UNIDIR, 1994).

12 L. Lumpe, 'US Policy and the Export of Weapons,' in Jeffrey Boutwell and Michael T. Klare, eds., *Light Weapons and Civil Conflict* (Lanham, MD: Rowman & Littlefield, 1999).

13 US Department of State and Department of Defense, 'Foreign Military Assistance Act Report to Congress, Fiscal Year 1996, 1997 and 1998' as posted on www.nisat.org.

14 According to one knowledgeable source, the United States accounts for 66 percent of all new firearms production in recent years, and yet it is still a net importer of firearms for the civilian and police markets. M. Barnes, outside legal counsel to the US National Rifle Association, March 2000. On US imports of Austrian, Brazilian, Chinese, German, Italian and other weapons, see T. Diaz, *Making a Killing: The Business of Guns in America* (New York: The New Press, 1999).

15 'Gun dealers fight for trade,' BBC News, 27 January 2000.

16 See for example 'Rio's weapons of Crime,' www.geocities.com/Pentagon/Quarters/2928/07dig.html.

17 'A new weapon, made in Ramallah,' *Israel Wire*, 14 June 1998.

18 'Notorious killer's changed role,' *Bangkok Post*, 1 February 1998.

19 'Colombia rebels wheel out secret weapon in war: Home made tanks,' Reuters, 1 April 1998.

20 Information provided by D. Garcia-Peña, March 2000.

21 'Uncovering the Irish Republican Army,' *Jane's Intelligence Review*, August 1996.

22 'Tiger cubs and childhood fall as casualties in Sri Lanka,' *Jane's Intelligence Review*, July 1998.

23 J. Honwana and G. Lamb, 'Small Arms and Drug Trafficking in Southern Africa: A conceptual paper,' Centre for Conflict Resolution, University of Cape Town, South Africa, 1998.

24 'Gunsmiths' cottage industry poses growing threat,' Gemini News Service, February 1998 (available at www.oneworld.org/gemini/feb98/india.html).

25 'Timor visit by Andrews shatters democracy illusion,' *Irish Times*, 19 April 1999.

26 See chapter 8 for more on these initiatives.

27 Licensed production agreements are often also referred to as licensed manufacturing agreements, co-production agreements, technology transfer agreements and sometimes classified within the general term of 'offsets.' While there are technical differences between these terms, for the sake of brevity this chapter will use the term licensed production.

[28] For example *A/S Kongsberg Vapenfabrik* in Norway produced the Heckler & Koch G3A3 rifle under license after World War II (*Jane's Infantry Weapons 1987/8*, p. 181), and *Fabrica Militar de Arma Portatiles* in Argentina manufactured nearly 75,000 Colt *Modelo* 1927 (M1911A1) pistols under license from Colt Firearms between 1947 and 1966 (E. Ezell, *Small Arms Today* [Boston: Stackpole Books, 1988], p. 38).

[29] Three early 1990s sources reported generally on the trend of licensed arms production, including especially small arms, in developing countries: R. Sanders, *Arms Industries: New Suppliers and Regional Security* (Washington, DC: National Defense University Press, 1990); US Office of Technology Assessment, *Global Arms Trade: Commence in Advanced Military Technology and Weapons* (Washington, DC: US General Publications Office, 1991); and M. Klare and D. Andersen, *A Scourge of Guns: The Diffusion of Small Arms and Light Weapons in Latin America.* (Washington, DC: Federation of American Scientists, 1996)

[30] The 14 licensing states are: Austria, Belgium, Czech Republic, France, Germany, Israel, Italy, Portugal, South Africa, Singapore, Sweden, Switzerland, United Kingdom and United States. The 46 licensees are: Argentina, Australia, Belgium, Brazil, Bulgaria, Burma, Canada, Chile, China, Colombia, Czech Republic, Egypt, France, Germany, Greece, India, Indonesia, Iran, Iraq, Italy, Japan, Kenya, Malaysia, Mexico, Morocco, Nigeria, Norway, Pakistan, Philippines, Poland, Portugal, Romania, Saudi Arabia, Singapore, South Korea, Spain, Sweden, Switzerland, Taiwan, Thailand, Turkey, Switzerland, United Kingdom, United States of America, former Yugoslavia and Venezuela.

[31] M. Klare, 'Light Weapons Diffusion,' in Jasjit Singh, ed., *Light Weapons and International Security* (Delhi: Pugwash Conferences on Science and World Affairs, 1995).

[32] M. Klare, 'The New Arms Race: Light Weapons and International Security,' *Current History*, April 1997.

[33] *Jane's Infantry Weapons 1977/8*, p. 141.

[34] *Infantry Equipment Update*, Vol. 26, No. 10, p. 71. *Jane's Defence Weekly*, 4 September 1996.

[35] Heckler & Koch (UK) Ltd annual records from Companies House (the UK agency with statutory responsibility for regulating companies and their activities), record dated January 1998.

[36] 'Germany: Sniper rifles supplied to Serbs despite sanctions,' *Independent*, 30 December 1993.

[37] 'Germany: Royal Ordnance "helped send arms to banned countries",' *Guardian*, 29 December 1993.

[38] 'Turkey reveals offset details on Giat contract,' *International-Trade-Finance*, 6 November 1992.

[39] *Jane's Defence Weekly*, 14 January 1998, p. 10.

[40] *Turkish Daily News*, 25 January 1999.

41 *IDEF Magazine*, 20 September 1995.

42 *Turkish Press Review*, 7 October 1996.

43 *Aksam*, 28 December 1998.

44 *Jane's Defence Weekly*, 14 January 1998, p. 10.

45 Anadolu (Turkish News Agency), 25 July 1998.

46 'Making a Killing' and 'Profit before Principle,' ITV, UK broadcast on 2 and 9 June 1997.

47 *Hansard*, 23 July 1997.

48 *Hansard*, 21 July 1997, col. 450.

49 *Ibid.*

50 *Hansard*, 23 July 1997.

51 *Hansard*, 20 January 1998.

52 'Licensed to Kill,' Channel 4 Dispatches programme, UK broadcast on 9 December 1999.

53 'Licensed to Kill,' Channel 4 Dispatches programme.

54 Presentation by Georg Stevens, Bonn Bureau of Heckler & Koch, to workshop on Small Arms organised by the Swiss Government, Geneva, 22-23 November 1999.

55 MKEK officials told undercover reporters that instead of the 200,000 production figure that was reported in the press, the company was in fact going to produce some 600,000 rifles and that exports could begin as early as June 2000. ('Licensed to Kill,' Channel 4 Dispatches programme.)

56 *Defence Industry*, December 1999, p. 9.

57 'Royal Ordnance to sell Heckler & Koch,' *Guardian*, 7 January 2000.

58 US State Department report to the Senate Foreign Relations Committee and House International Relations Committee, 'US Military Equipment and Human Rights Violations in Turkey,' July 1997, paragraph 8.

59 'POF: the hidden giant,' *Military-Technology*, Vol. 10, No. 9 (September 1986), pp. s62-s67.

60 'Episcope: 100 mm APFSDS ammunition from POF,' *Heracles*, No. 53 (August 1986), p. 6.

61 'Pakistan serves as German arms export front,' *Middle East Defense News-Technology Watch*, 20 January 1992.

62 *Index on Censorship*, October 1991.

63 *Far Eastern Economic Review*, 15 November 1990.

64 Pakistan Ordnance Factories, fax communication, October 1999.

65 'Licensed to Kill,' Channel 4 Dispatches Programme.

66 The Pakistan Ordnance Factories plastic hand grenade is a licence-produced ARGES (Austrian) model, known as the 84-P2A1. The ovoid plastic body contains approximately 5000 steel balls packed around 95g of plastic PETN explosive. As the grenade explodes, it scatters the steel balls over a lethal radius of 20 metres (*Jane's Infantry Weapons 1999/00*).

67 For example, during World War I the English company Vickers appropriated Krupp's special fuse for hand grenades. When the war was over,

Krupp sued Vickers for violation of patent rights, demanding payment of one shilling per fuse. The total claimed by Krupp was 123,000,000 shillings. The case was settled out of court and Krupp received payment in stock of one of Vicker's subsidiaries in Spain. H. C. Engelbrecht and Hanighen, *Merchants of Death* (New York: Dodd, Mead & Co., 1934).

[68] 'Delivery of Tanks to Pakistan sets off sales war with Russia. Moscow stops licensing parts exports to Ukraine,' *Los Angeles Times,* 2 May 1997.

[69] 'The EU Code on Arms Transfers: Essential Standards,' December 1997.

[70] EP Resolution on Arms, Minutes of 15/01/98 - Provisional Edition, Code of Conduct on Armaments.

[80] Arms Export Control Act, section 36(d).

[72] 'Requests for Third-Party Transfers raise "Serious concerns" at State,' *Arms Trade News* , February 1999, p. 2.

[73] L. Lumpe, 'Sweet Deals, Stolen Jobs,' *The Bulletin of the Atomic Scientists*, September/October 1994.

[74] US Congress, Subcommittee on Investigations of the Committee on Armed Services, House of Representatives, Review of Arms Co-production Agreements, hearing held 22 March 1989 (Washington, DC: US Government Printing Office, 1989).

[75] *Hansard*, 22 March 1999, col. 118.

[76] 'Cook's War Machine,' *Daily Mail* (London), 2 September 1999, p. 16.

[77] Paul Greenwood (a director of Pains Wessex, a UK manufacturer of tear gas), 'Mark Thomas Comedy Product,' UK broadcast on 20 January 1999.

[78] A Member of Parliament asked the President of the Board of Trade (Mrs. Roche) what control she had over the transfer of armoured vehicles and personnel carriers to Indonesia and other countries from the GKN Defence licensed production facility in the Philippines. Mrs Roche replied that: 'The control of exports from the Philippines is a matter for the Philippine Government. Any export of licensable goods from the UK to the Philippines would be subject to UK export controls.' (*Hansard*, 15 July 1997).

[79] *Hansard*, 12 January 1999, col. 150.

[80] Arms export notices, including for licensed production agreements, are printed in the *Federal Register*.

5/Domestic Gun Markets: The Licit-Illicit Links

by Wendy Cukier and Steve Shropshire

Domestic controls on firearms are crucial to curbing international gun trafficking. This is so because domestic and international markets are inextricably linked, as are licit and illicit supplies. For instance, the same distribution networks that serve warring factions also supply organised criminals. And whether one's focus is on armed conflict or on armed crime, the firearms used stem from three principal sources: misuse of firearms by their legal owners (whether the owners are in the military or private citizens); diversion of firearms from their legal owners to illegal purposes (through loss or theft); and firearms manufactured and/or traded on illicit markets.

Both domestic and international efforts to stem illicit flows of firearms seek to reduce the misuse of these weapons. In both contexts, stemming the illegal supply and misuse requires an ability to track legal possession and trade. Efforts to license firearm owners, register firearms and license dealers are all examples of controls on legal firearms aimed at reducing their misuse and diversion into the illegal trade. While many factors shape domestic demand for firearms, mechanisms addressing the supply side have proven effective.[1]

These principles, which have long been applied in the context of domestic firearm regulation, have recently been extended into the international arena. For example, the protocol that states began negotiating in 1999 against the illicit manufacturing of and trafficking in firearms, to supplement a UN Convention against Transnational Organised Crime, proposes controls on the legal commercial arms trade in order to curtail illicit international trafficking.[2]

This chapter explores the relevance of domestic gun markets and gun regulation for efforts to curb the illicit trade. It begins by reviewing the sources of guns used in crime and violence, the interactions between legal and illegal markets and the mechanisms for diversion. It then reviews principles of domestic firearm regulation and international norms regarding firearm regulation.

Sources of Firearms, Legal and Illegal

On a global basis, information about the legal firearm trade is limited. No intergovernmental body currently compiles annual statistics on the regional or global gun trade, and very few states provide public data on the firearms exports or imports that they authorise.[3]

Information on illicit trafficking is even more incomplete. Surveys conducted by INTERPOL and by the United Nations Commission on Crime Prevention and Criminal Justice have yielded some anecdotal information, but they do not provide a comprehensive picture.[4] Several governments recently have sponsored specific research projects to analyse the sources of firearms that they recovered in the commission of crimes. These studies contribute to our basic understanding of the phenomenon of firearms trafficking, domestically and internationally. Highlights follow:

- The US Treasury Department's Bureau of Alcohol, Tobacco and Firearms (BATF) is the agency responsible for investigating illegal arms dealing within the United States, and it also works with other countries to trace weapons of US origin used in crimes abroad. BATF funds research to assist its enforcement efforts. Many of these studies suggest that, within the United States, illicit firearms often originate in particular regions and from particular dealers.[5] A study based on BATF data revealed that during 1996-1998 nearly 35,000 weapons recovered from crime scenes originated in 140 stores (less than 1% of all licensed US gun dealers). Of those guns, 87% were not in the hands of the original purchaser at the time they were used in crime, suggesting that resale and theft are major issues for gun trafficking within the United States and, by extension, internationally.[6]

- In Canada, studies undertaken in 1995 and 1997 in a number of jurisdictions revealed that the firearms most often recovered in crime were rifles and shotguns, most of which originated in domestic markets.[7] This finding contradicted previous claims based on anecdotal studies, that handguns were most frequently used.[8] Canada historically has had very strict controls on such weapons, and only about 20% of the firearms recovered were handguns. Of those that could be traced, 40% previously had been registered in Canada, while the remainder had not.[9] Based on this finding, on seizures of illegally imported handguns at the border and on the results of police investigations, the Canadian government's Smuggling Work Group concluded that a large percentage of the handguns used in crime in Canada were illegally imported, primarily from the United States.

- Japanese officials recover a relatively small number of firearms each year, but of these 30% are said to originate in the United States and 30% in China.[10]

- According to a recent analysis of guns recovered in Rio de Janeiro during 1994-1999, the vast majority (over 44,000, or 83%) were manufactured in Brazil. Just over one thousand guns (2.5%) were made in Argentina, and three thousand (6.7%) were manufactured in the United States.[11] Paraguay is believed to be a major conduit for guns entering Brazil illegally.[12]

- In South Africa, efforts by the South African Police Service to track the supply of firearms recovered in crime are relatively recent; however, detailed analysis has revealed that the bulk of the weapons used are actually handguns, many of them at one time legally owned. Military-style weapons, such as assault rifles, have represented a small proportion of guns used in crime, contrary to widely repeated claims.[13]

As these studies indicate, weapons frequently cross over from the realm of the legal to the illegal, and they frequently cross international borders. Some of the ways in which this transformation occurs are listed below. In general terms, though, the sources of weapons used for illegal purposes—the commission of a crime—fall into three broad categories: 1) legally held firearms that are misused by their lawful owner; 2) the 'grey' market—originally legal firearms that are resold illegally or stolen, etc.; and 3) illegally manufactured and traded firearms.

Theft

Governments participating in the United Nations' *International Study on Firearm Regulation* reported more than 100,000 firearms lost or stolen in 1996, but this figure is considered quite conservative. For example, while the US government reported more than 12,000 stolen guns to the study, some estimates of gun theft in the United States run as high as 500,000 per year.[14] South Africa reported nearly 17,500 stolen in 1995 but, again, this figure is believed to be quite low. And Canadian citizens annually report around 3000 firearm thefts, but the actual number is likely much higher. Until recently in Canada it was mandatory to report only the loss or theft of handguns and assault weapons, not rifles and shotguns. Given that Canadians own an estimated six million rifles and shotguns compared to 1.2 million handguns and assault weapons, and given that regulations regarding transfer, storage and illegal possession of handguns are much stricter than those for rifles and shotguns, it is reasonable to assume that the reports of stolen guns represent only a fraction of the total number stolen each year.

Small-scale theft of firearms sent via mail order has been identified as a problem in several countries, including Canada, the United States and Australia.[15] A private delivery company in the United States, United Parcel Service (UPS), currently delivers approximately three quarters of all firearms shipments in the United States from manufacturers to distributors, as well as nearly 99% of all firearms sent from distributors to dealers. In 1998 alone, 941 firearms were reported stolen in UPS interstate shipments.[16] A single dealer reported that 60 of his guns had been stolen en route over the past 18 months.[17] Mail order distribution of prohibited components is a related problem. Cheap and anonymous gun advertising on the Internet has been identified as a contributing factor to the latter phenomenon.

Police and army stocks

Recent news from around the world illustrates the ways in which state-owned firearms leak into illicit markets through theft, corruption or other forms of diversion. In Australia military personnel falsified records to conceal the theft of an undisclosed number of firearms from national stockpiles.[18] And from 1990-1999, police in South Africa reportedly lost or had stolen more than 14,636 firearms.[19]

In the United States, several police departments upgrading their firearms recently came under widespread criticism for inadvertently supplying illicit markets when they sold their old guns, rather than destroying them.[20] In addition, investigators from the US General Accounting Office discovered that gun parts were routinely stolen from US military bases and resold at gun shows or to gun dealers. Investigators were able to purchase such parts at 13 of the 15 gun shows they targeted.[21] In 1997 undercover FBI agents arrested six US marines and seven civilians for weapons trafficking after recovering over 50 machine guns, explosives, rockets and other military devices. These arrests were part of a larger investigation in the southeastern United States that focused on gun shows, military bases and dealers.[22]

In Mexico, weapons destined for the Army, including 16,000 handguns and 6000 rifles, were seized by Mexican police from drug gangs.[23] And over 3000 firearms recovered in crime or surrendered in amnesties to the Metropolitan Toronto Police Service in Canada were discovered missing in 1998. Officers and civilians working in the unit were found to have sold them illegally.[24]

Straw purchases and other resales

Firearms that are purchased legally and then resold or given to a second owner are a problem in many countries, particularly in those with less restrictive domestic controls. Within countries that have divergent domestic regulatory standards there is ample evidence that illegal guns flow from areas with weaker regulation. For example, within the United States 'straw purchases' and other mechanisms are used to move guns from states with lax controls to states with stricter ones. A recent study of guns recovered in crime revealed that one quarter of all weapons that came from outside the state in which they were recovered came from Georgia, South Carolina and Texas.[25]

Similarly, weapons flow from countries with weaker regulation to those with tighter gun ownership laws and practices. A high percentage of the handguns recovered in crime in Canada, for example, originate in the United States, and investigations have revealed that straw purchases are frequently used.[26] Similar mechanisms have been documented for cross-border gun-running from the United States to Mexico.[27] Other examples of guns from the United States being diverted into illegal markets abroad follow:

- Two hundred firearms were seized in Colombia from drug lord Ivan Urdinola. All of the weapons had been legally purchased and imported from the United States and registered in Colombia before being used by paramilitary hit-men to commit a series of murders.[28]
- In Jamaica authorities confiscated 338 assorted firearms, mostly originating from the United States, including US Army standard issue M16 assault rifles. The weapons were intended for market distribution in Jamaica, reportedly for robberies and drug-related crimes.[29]
- US Customs agents thwarted an attempt by Colombian nationals to export 53 AR15 rifles (a police version of the M16) to Colombia without proper authorisation and an effort by a former Venezuelan security officer to ship 120 firearms from the United States to Venezuela illegally.[30]

In a number of countries, including the United States and South Africa, initial sales of firearms are regulated, but secondary sales are not. In addition, gun shows, which are largely unregulated, have proven to be a major source of illicit guns within the United States and also for international illegal markets. For example, an individual was arrested having purchased a consignment of 30 Lorcin pistols at gun shows in Miami and Dallas. The weapons were destined for Romania.[31]

Falsification of export documents

Smugglers have used 'short-orders,' false documentation, misreporting and concealment with other commodities to ship weapons commercially from the United States to Canada.[32] Similarly, a major consignment of parts for M2 automatic rifles originating in Vietnam and destined for Mexico was found in a sealed container in San Diego falsely labelled as hand tools and strap hangers.[33] An effort was made to import a large quantity of Chinese-made AK-47 assault rifles into Canada, where they are prohibited. The weapons were mislabelled as hunting rifles.[34]

Illegal sales by dealers

There is considerable evidence that some federally licensed fire-arm dealers in the United States are willing to violate national and local laws to provide guns to juveniles and adults who are ineligible to purchase guns.[35] More than half of the weapons submitted by local and state police to the BATF for tracing originated with less than one half of one percent of the United States' 180,000 licensed dealers.[36] In some cases, dishonest firearms dealers have engaged in legal firearms trade while also diverting some of their firearms to illicit markets. Several cases of this type have been identified in Canada (Operation Pinball), in the United States and in United Kingdom (Operation ABONAR).[37]

Illegal manufacture and reactivation

While relatively few countries report serious problems with illegal manufacture of weapons, there are some striking exceptions. For example, of the firearms seized in South Africa by the South African Police Service in 1998, approximately 15% (3066) were home made.[38] In addition, a number of illegal weapon production workshops were discovered in Kazanluk, Bulgaria, in 1998.[39] (For more on illegal production of weapons, see chapter 4.)

In some cases, the illegal or unauthorised manufacture of weapons is facilitated by the use of components that have been imported or stolen. The domestic manufacture and assembly of firearms from imported parts, for example, is cited as a major source of illicit weapons in Australia. A related problem is posed by the reactivation of firearms that were legally owned at one time but that have been deactivated because of a change in local law. Loopholes in the law have sometimes allowed such weapons to be reactivated and resold.[40] For example, up to 100 deactivated machine pistols were legally exported as collectors' items from the United States before being reactivated and sold to criminals in Britain.[41]

Principles of Domestic Firearms Regulation

Firearms regulation is usually considered in the context of opportunity reduction—that is, by reducing access to firearms, opportunities for violence and the severity or lethality of violence can be reduced.[42] There is, by now, ample evidence to conclude that rates of firearm death and injury are linked to firearm availability.[43] Similar effects have also been suggested in the post-conflict context.[44]

In addition, as indicated above, some significant portion of supply for the illicit firearms trade originates with weapons that were at one time legally owned but that have been diverted to illicit markets and uses. Consequently, improved regulation of legal markets for firearms will raise the bar against diversion of firearms to black markets and also aid in enforcement of initiatives targeting trafficking.

Firearm regulations operate at several levels. Licensing measures are intended to reduce the accessibility of firearms and the risk that owners will misuse them or handle them irresponsibly. These measures also raise the costs, discouraging casual ownership and reducing proliferation. General principles of firearm regulation are outlined here.

Licensing owners

Licensing regimes typically collect information about prospective gun owners in order to assess risks. In some cases people with criminal records are not eligible to own guns. In others, much broader criteria are applied. For example, prospective owners are sometimes required to provide references and personal information, medical or psychological certification and/or spousal approval. Screening can occur on a regular basis when the permits or licences are renewed. In Canada, validity checks are continual, meaning that if a firearm owner is the subject of a complaint or a charge, flags are raised requiring an investigation into the appropriateness of continued gun ownership by that individual.

Regulating sales and dealers

Regulation of firearms manufacturing and sales is intended to increase the responsibility of manufacturers and dealers and deter illegal sales. The rationale for licensing gun dealers is to set more rigorous standards by increasing the effective cost of a licence. Regulatory restrictions and litigation have also been used to encourage suppliers of firearms to control sales responsibly.[45]

Registration

Firearm regulation also facilitates law enforcement efforts to re-duce trafficking of weapons. In this regard, the registration of fire-arms has been critical in police investigations and in enabling the police to lay charges for illegal possession of firearms. In order to identify firearms that are illegally possessed, it is necessary to be able to separate out those that are legally held. This is accomplished through registration. The same principle applies to the international movement of firearms. International law enforcement and customs officers must have a system for identifying legally exported weap-onry before they can identify firearms that are being imported or exported illegally.

Tracing and enforcement

The ability to determine where a gun was manufactured, where it was retailed and who bought it is invaluable in criminal investi-gations—whether the object is to uncover a particular low volume straw purchaser or to identify a large trafficking operation.[46] Im-proving such ability, and increasing transparency, is considered to have a deterrent effect in the context of both domestic regulation and international arms control. Dealers are likely to be more careful about whom they distribute guns to if they know police can more easily trace guns to their source. Moreover, investigations and legal cases can be built on such information, further raising the stakes for traffickers. The US Bureau of Alcohol, Tobacco and Firearms has found that tracing studies have proven a useful tool in identifying firearms trafficking patterns, illegal purchasers, problem firearms dealers and source areas supplying firearms both on a domestic and international basis.

Prohibitions of firearms where risk outweighs utility

As stated above, most domestic firearms control regimes are based on the assumption that controlling access will reduce death, injury and crime. Measures aimed at controlling access include out-right prohibitions of some firearms, where the risk of proliferation is considered to outweigh the utility. Most countries prohibit pos-session of some firearms, and some countries prohibit possession of most firearms. Nearly all prohibit civilian ownership of military-style weapons.

Canada prohibited civilian ownership of fully automatic weapons in 1979, semi-automatic weapons that could be converted to fully automatic fire in 1991 and semi-automatic versions of military weapons in 1995. In most cases, current owners were 'grand-fathered,' or allowed to keep their weapons under certain conditions. Great Britain banned the civilian possession of handguns in 1997. Owners were entitled to compensation, but possession of the prohibited guns became illegal. Similarly, Australia banned semi-automatic firearms and shotguns, except for individuals who could demonstrate compelling need. The state bought back more than 500,000 guns from its citizens.

Safe storage

There are a variety of ways in which barriers can been increased between individuals and firearms in order to prevent impulsive use or unauthorised access. In the United States attention is being focused increasingly on technological changes to reduce unauthorised access, such as the development of personalised guns.[47] Measures to encourage safe storage include the use of locked containers, trigger locks, disabling firearms and separating ammunition from the gun—all practices that are standard in most industrialised countries. Educational programs have focused on increasing awareness of safe practices and compliance with them.[48]

Limiting the number of guns

Some countries have implemented regulations that limit the number of firearms an individual may own. In the United States, some states have passed laws limiting gun purchases to one a month. Such restrictions appear to have had a positive impact in diminishing trafficking to other states.[49]

Collection and destruction programmes

Many countries have undertaken projects intended to remove unwanted, unneeded and illegal weapons from circulation. Sometimes, as in the cases of Great Britain and Australia, these efforts accompanied changes in the law, which made certain weapons illegal after a given point in time. Compensation was offered to those who surrendered their weapons, and severe penalties were imposed on those who did not. In other cases, voluntary amnesties have led gun owners to reassess their need for guns. The Canadian amnesty of 1991, for example, collected about 50,000 firearms, many of them old hunting rifles. Research on amnesties and buybacks has suggested that the results are uneven. While the impact of these programs has been questioned, they may have educational effects that cannot easily be measured.[50] Where amnesties are not accompanied by destruction of the weapons, there are risks that the surplus stocks will leak back into the illicit market.

International Norms Regarding Regulation

Stricter controls on firearms both reflect and help shape values. Countries with stricter controls send a signal about the acceptability of violence in the same way that legislation in one state on slavery, smoking, drunk driving and drug use may influence that of another state.[51] Moreover, as public opinion changes, many gun owners may begin to question whether they, in fact, need or want to maintain their weapons. Half the firearm owners in Canada have not used their guns in the past year.[52] Thus, without taking direct steps to prohibit or confiscate firearms, regulatory measures such as those listed above reduce the availability of firearms, cause citizens to take more care with their firearms and may cause citizens to decide that they no longer need guns.

It is also worth noting that despite rhetoric from some gun associations about 'the right to bear arms,' a review of international laws on firearms reveals a general lack of recognition in constitutional documents of a right to own or possess firearms. Judges and officials of several countries, in upholding or advocating measures designed to protect human rights through firearms regulations, have pointed to the lack of constitutional protection for firearms ownership and possession.[53] Instead, the international community is acknowledging increasingly that careful regulation of the legal arms trade has as important a part to play in achieving worldwide protection of human rights and promotion of governance as do efforts to curb the purely illegal arms traffic.[54]

A review of international legislation and jurisprudence reveals many common elements and principles among various states' regulatory regimes.[55] Some countries , particularly industrialised ones, have long prohibited some types of firearms and regulated the use of those that are permitted to be in the hands of the citizenry. Most industrialised states require licensing of firearm owners and registration of firearms.

The recommendations of the 1997 UN Commission on Crime Prevention and Criminal Justice provide a minimum standard for domestic firearm legislation. The Commission concluded that states that had not already done so should introduce:

- regulations relating to firearm safety and storage;
- appropriate penalties for firearms misuse or unlawful possession;
- amnesty or similar programs to encourage the surrender of illegal, unsafe or unwanted firearms;
- a licensing system, including for firearms businesses, to prevent those with serious criminal records or who are prohibited from firearms ownership in other member countries from owning or possessing firearms; and
- a record-keeping system for firearms to cover commercial distribution, marking at the point of manufacture and at import.[56]

Most industrialised countries already exceed these standards. One notable exception is the United States, which is one of few industrialised countries in the world that allows civilian possession of military weapons or widespread access to handguns for civilian 'self-protection.'[57] Firearms are controlled in the United States through a patchwork of state and municipal regulations. While a background check established by federal law has recently been implemented for primary sales, secondary markets in the United States (like gun shows and private sales) for the most part remain completely unregulated.

Given the frequent diversion of weapons of US origin noted above, many countries in the Western Hemisphere (and as far away as Japan) would benefit if the United States were able to introduce stronger controls, particularly on handguns. Most promising would be national standards to help control the secondary markets, measures such as safe storage to reduce gun theft, increasing accountability of owners through a licensing and registration system and measures to reduce firearm proliferation, such as a national one-gun-a-month law and restrictions on types of guns that may be owned.

The United States is by no means the only case where domestic gun markets feed into the illegal gun trade. There is scarcely a country that can be considered without fault in terms of supplying arms traffickers. The extent of the problem seems to grow, however, in proportion to the weakness of the firearm legislation in place, the supply of guns available and the policing and governance infrastructure in place. Therefore all of these aspects of domestic regulation must be considered.

In 1996 the United Nations Commission on Crime Prevention and Criminal Justice undertook a study of the extent of firearm regulation in member countries.[58] Seventy-eight states took part in the most recent (1999) version of this study, representing a wide cross-section of the world community. The vast majority of the study's original respondents (39 of 46) required licensing of all firearm purchases. Another six required licensing for at least some firearms. Import and export controls on guns were virtually universal, a strong majority required registration of firearm owners, and safe-storage regulations were in place in approximately three quarters of responding countries.

Since the initial survey, more than half of the participating national governments reported that they had recently amended their legislation and administration of civilian firearms ownership. Major legislative reform is underway in Brazil, Canada, China, Denmark, Finland, France, India, Jamaica, New Zealand, Poland and South Africa. These reforms are, for the most part, focused inward, and aimed at improving safety within the country's borders. Since efforts to control legal markets will reduce the availability of firearms to illicit markets, they will also have implications for curbing international gun trafficking.

Proposals

The misuse and trafficking of firearms pose complex challenges. Firearms are diverted from legal domestic markets to illegal ones in many ways. In addition, the same mechanisms that supply illegal domestic markets fuel international gun-running. Consequently, a wide range of measures at the national and international level are required to stem the flow of guns.

Raising standards of firearm regulation

Given that virtually all illegal firearms begin as legal firearms, measures to improve controls over sale, possession and transfer, as well as measures to improve accountability and enforcement, would make a major contribution to stemming the illegal supply. The recommendations of the 1997 UN Commission on Crime Prevention and Criminal Justice provide an excellent starting point. In addition, consideration should be given to measures to reduce proliferation of weapons where the risks to society outweigh the utility—for example, a ban on the sale to civilians of military assault weapons and large capacity magazines, as well as some types of handguns.

Norms regarding stricter controls should also be reinforced, and the efforts of countries such as South Africa and Brazil to tighten their domestic regulations should be supported. More recognition should be accorded to the importance of firearm legislation to the general establishment of effective governance and justice, as well as to economic development.

Marking firearms

Both domestic regulation of firearms and the control of the international trade require that authorities be able to track individual firearms. As police agencies cooperate to combat transnational organised crime, the establishment of consistent standards for information becomes increasingly important to assist in criminal investigations and reduce the illicit trade in firearms. Efforts to develop appropriate international standards for marking weapons are currently underway. These standards are essential to tracing weapons back around the globe to their source, and they should be given high priority. (Individual countries may, of course, implement a higher national standard in terms of marking procedures than the international standard eventually adopted.)

Several components must be included. First is the development of an international nomenclature, or coding system, that provides unique identification for each firearm, as well as essential information on the manufacturer and place of origin. Second are international standards for actually placing the unique identifying marks on the firearms in ways that cannot be removed. New firearms must be marked at the point of manufacture, and existent stocks at the point of import, so that firearms recovered in crime can be traced back to their source. Third are standards for the identification of firearms. And finally, standards for record keeping among manufacturers, importers and exporters must be established. Since firearm manufacturers often serve both commercial and military markets, cost-effective efforts should be made to coordinate marking efforts among all relevant UN initiatives.[59]

Rigorous controls on state-owned weapons

In many countries police and state-owned weapons are targets for theft and illegal trading on a much larger scale than are civilian weapons. Just as standards for controlling civilian possession, use and storage—and the means to enforce them—are needed, so are controls on weapons used by the police and military. Strict standards should be established for possession, use and storage. In addition, meticulous record keeping and auditing processes are needed. Serious consideration should also be given to policies mandating destruction of surplus and seized weapons, rather than permitting 'recycling' of these weapons.

Control of international movement of weapons

Effective regulation of import, export and transit of weapons is necessary to stem global firearms trafficking and to reduce misuse. A number of international agreements have been or are currently being negotiated to address aspects of illicit trafficking on a regional and/or global basis (see chapter 8). Central to effective international regulation are general requirements for domestic authorisation of imports and exports and systems for record keeping and verification of imports and exports.[60]

Enforcement and implementation

While many countries have strict domestic firearm regulations on the books, they lack the infrastructure and resources necessary to effectively implement them. Cooperative and targeted enforcement strategies linking police agencies, customs officials and others on a national, regional and international basis are critical (see chapter 9). Currently, many donor countries have not emphasised support for crime prevention, policing and the administration of justice as priorities for aid. Many states are willing to support UN and other anti-trafficking initiatives, but they lack adequate resources to do so. Given the huge costs of crime and violence, and the impediment they present to development and the attainment of human rights, donor states should give increased priority to compliance with anti-trafficking standards when providing assistance.

In this regard, some governments have undertaken unilateral or bilateral initiatives to strengthen border controls. For instance, the illegal flow of weapons from Mozambique has made border control a key part of South Africa's national crime prevention strategy. Export controls are as critical as import controls in terms of reducing illicit firearms trafficking. Governments must become more accountable for what they allow to leave their territory.

Measures to counter demand

The complex of factors shaping demand cannot be ignored. Efforts to market guns and create demand in the industrialised countries have been well documented.[61] Not only do firearm manufacturers seek new markets—women and children, for example—but technological changes to guns are often introduced to expand sales. These efforts are reinforced by aggressive advertising campaigns proposing that guns are an effective crime prevention strategy, and they are supported by trade associations and gun owner lobby groups and reinforced by violent entertainment media. Given the links between the licit and illicit gun markets, efforts should be directed at reducing primary demand, discouraging casual gun ownership and countering the glorification of violence.

Research and education

Documenting and publicising the widespread and diffuse consequences of the misuse of firearms is critical to shaping public policy in domestic and international contexts. In addition, efforts to better communicate the rationale for improved regulation of firearms are critical. In discussions of firearm regulation, opponents often argue that 'criminals will always get guns.' This truism begs the question of where these criminals get their guns. More effort to increase awareness of the links between licit and illicit markets and of the rationales for regulating firearms is essential. In addition, making governments and their publics aware and accountable not only for the way guns are managed within their borders but also for those flowing out is consistent with approaches taken toward other hazardous commodities.

Marketing efforts of gun manufacturers are a major impediment to efforts to reduce the misuse of firearms. Ad campaigns promote weapons as solutions and target vulnerable populations.[62] Another impediment is the National Rifle Association (NRA), which aggressively opposes all efforts to strengthen firearm legislation in the United States and abroad. The NRA reinforces the manufacturers' message by promoting the notion that guns are an effective means of civilian protection. Further research and dissemination of the wealth of existing information regarding the risks associated with firearms, the extent of the problem and the measures that improve public safety are essential. In particular, emphasis should be placed on the importance of firearm regulation in the context of international human rights. Freedom from fear is a fundamental right.

Conclusions

Historically, discussions on domestic firearm regulation and on international arms trafficking and conflict prevention have tended to run on separate tracks. However, the illicit firearms market does not recognise distinctions between 'criminals,' 'warring factions,' 'insurgents' or 'freedom fighters.' Nor does it observe national borders. Inadequate domestic gun control procedures, gaps in import/export control regimes and insufficient enforcement all fuel illegal firearms markets.

Many countries allow civilian possession of firearms for purposes defined as legitimate, such as hunting, target shooting, collection and, in a few cases, self-protection. Gun possession is subject to varying degrees of regulation in such countries. Levels of regulation, enforcement and ownership have a significant impact on the ease with which firearms can be diverted from these legal purposes to illegal markets, either domestically or internationally. In addition, most states have police and armed forces possessing large quantities of firearms. Experience has shown that these weapons are also frequently diverted to illegal markets. Finally, while countries have different challenges with respect to border controls, most place greater emphasis on controlling what comes in rather than what goes out. With globalisation and growing emphasis on free trade, the obstacles to detecting and stopping illicit arms trafficking are increasing.

Complex problems require complex solutions, and there are no easy answers to curtailing the illicit trafficking of firearms. However, there is considerable evidence to suggest that efforts to strengthen controls over legal firearm possession and use do have an impact on illegal markets and on misuse. Individual countries should accept more responsibility for how they manage state-owned and civilian supplies of firearms, as well as their border controls. In addition, measures aimed at supporting international standards, cooperative enforcement and capacity building are imperative.

Notes

[1] See Philip Cook and James Leitzel, 'Perversity, Futility and Jeopardy: An Economic Analysis of the Attack on Gun Control,' *Law and Contemporary Problems*, Vol. 59, No. 1.

[2] United Nations, General Assembly, Ad Hoc Committee on the Elaboration of a Convention against Transnational Organised Crime, Draft Report: Revised Draft Protocol against the Illicit Manufacturing of and Trafficking in Firearms, their parts and Components and Ammunition, Vienna: United Nations, 17-18 January 2000.

[3] The US government now provides some data on firearm imports and exports it authorises. For good analysis of the former, see Tom Diaz, *Making a Killing: The Business of Guns in America* (New York: The New Press, 1999).

[4] United Nations, *International Study on Firearm Regulation* (New York: UN, 1998), pp. 73-102.

[5] Joseph Vince, 'Disarming the Criminal,' Firearms Enforcement Division, Department of the Treasury, Washington, DC, 1996.

[6] Shannon McCaffrey, 'Report Traces Gun Sales,' Associated Press, 20 December 1999; Philip J. Cook et al., 'Regulating Gun Markets,' *The Journal of Criminal Law and Criminology*, Vol. 86, No. 1 (1995), pp. 59-91.

[7] Justice Canada, Smuggling Work Group, 'Report of the Smuggling Work Group,' 1995; Daniel Antonowicz Consulting, 'Firearms Recovered by Police: A Multi-Site Study,' for Justice Canada, July 1997.

[8] John Thompson, 'Misfire,' McKenzie Institute, Toronto, 1995.

[9] Smuggling Work Group, 'Report of the Smuggling Work Group'; Daniel Antonowicz Consulting, 'Firearms Recovered by Police.'

[10] National Police Agency [Japan] Firearms Division, Firearms Control in Japan, 1996.

[11] 'Brazil to Push for Gun Control within Mercosur,' FBIS Daily Report, 3 August 1999.

[12] G. Khatchik and L. Carneiro, *Connecting Weapons with Violence: The South American Experience*, Institute for Security Studies, monograph No. 25, 1998.

[13] Robert Chetty, ed., *Firearm Use and Distribution in South Africa*, National Crime Prevention Centre, for the Secretariat of Safety and Security, Government of South Africa, 2000.

[14] Cook et al., 'Regulating Gun Markets,' notes that the absence of reporting requirements make this figure of 12,000 an inadequate measure of the level of theft. Given that over 40% of US households have firearms, a burglar has a good chance of finding a gun in a break-in. The FBI compiles national data only on the value of the firearms reported to the police department, not on the number of firearms. Depending on the assumptions regarding the average value of guns, the Police Foundation estimated that in 1991 between 300,000 and 600,000 guns were stolen. And, according to the National Crime Victimization Study the average number of incidents in which at least one gun was stolen during the period 1987-1992 was 340,700 per year.

[15] Adam Graycar, CSCAP Working Group on Transnational Crime, 'Small Arms Project: An Australian Perspective,' 1998.

[16] Craig Whitlock, 'Gun Thefts Put UPS in the Cross Hairs,' *Washington Post*, 24 December 1999.

[17] Holly Woolcott, 'UPS is Taking Aim at Gun Thefts,' *Los Angeles Times*, 8 November 1999.

[18] Graycar, 'Small Arms Project: An Australian Perspective.'

[19] Chetty, *Firearm Use and Distribution in South Africa*. See also '200,000 State-owned Firearms Missing,' ANC Daily News Briefing, 23 November 1999.

[20] Barbara Vobejda, David Ottaway and Sarah Cohen, 'Recycled DC Police Guns Tied to Crimes,' *Washington Post*, 12 November 1999.

[21] US General Accounting Office, 'Small Arms Parts: Poor Controls Invite Widespread Theft,' Report GAO/NSIAD-94-21 (1994).

[22] *Washington Post*, 18 October 1997.

[23] 'Mexico Drug Trafficking Groups "Promoting" Arms Trafficking,' *La Jornada*, 27 September 1996, as translated in *FBIS Daily Report*.

[24] John Duncanson and Jim Rankin, 'Officer is Jailed in Gun Scandal,' *Toronto Star*, 15 April 1998; John Duncanson and Jim Rankin, '3000 Guns Go "Missing" from Police,' *Toronto Star*, 10 September 1997.

[25] Natalie Goldring, 'Domestic Laws and International Controls,' in Jeffrey Boutwell and Michael T. Klare, eds., *Light Weapons and Civil Conflict: Controlling the Tools of Violence* (Lanham, MD: Rowman & Littlefield, 1999).

[26] Geoffrey A. Francis, 'Illicit Firearms in Canada: Sources, Smuggling and Trends,' *RCMP Gazette*, Vol. 57, No. 2 (1995), pp. 22-24.

[27] In 1991 the BATF reported that three Arizona residents had previously purchased 93 assault rifles and 22 handguns for resale to a Mexican drug

baron who then smuggled the guns into Mexico (US Department of the
Treasury, Bureau of Alcohol, Tobacco and Firearms, Firearms Division, *International Traffic in Arms, Report to Congress*, 1991). See also Lora Lumpe,
'The US Arms Both Sides of Mexico's Drug War,' *Covert Action Quarterly*,
Vol. 61 (Summer 1998).

[28] Daniel Garcia-Peña Jaramillo, 'Linkages between Drugs and Illicit Arms
Trafficking: Issues of Current Concern to Colombia,' 1998.

[29] United Nations database, 1999.

[30] US Department of Justice, Export Control Enforcement Unit, computer
printout of 'Significant Export Control Cases,' 5 September 1997.

[31] United Nations database, 1999.

[32] *Ibid.*

[33] *San Diego Union-Tribune*, 14 March 1997.

[34] Wendy Cukier, 'The Case for Registration,' a submission to *Review of
Firearms Control*, New Zealand, February 1997.

[35] See Phillip, et al., 'Regulating Gun Markets.'

[36] Glenn Pierce et al., 'The Identification of Patterns in Firearms Trafficking,
Implications for Focused Enforcement Strategy,' US Department of the
Treasury, Bureau of Alcohol, Tobacco and Firearms, 1995.

[37] Michael Hallowes, Directorate of Intelligence, Operation ABONAR, unpublished report, London, Scotland Yard, 1999.

[38] Chetty, *Firearm Use and Distribution in South Africa*.

[39] 'Illegal Weapon Producing Shops Discovered in Kazanluk,' as translated
in *FBIS Daily Report*, 3 April 1998.

[40] United Nations database, 1999.

[41] 'Gangland Armourer Facing Long Jail Term,' *The Times* (London), 21
January 1999.

[42] Wendy Cukier, 'Firearms Regulation: Canada in the International Context,' *Chronic Diseases in Canada*, No. 19, 1998.

[43] A wide range of researchers have examined aspects of this relationship,
among them: D. Hemenway *et al.*, 'Firearm training and storage,' *Journal of
the American Medical Association*, Vol. 273, No. 1, pp. 46-50; L.E. Saltzman et
al., 'Weapon involvement and injury outcomes in family and intimate assaults, *Journal of the American Medical Association*, Vol. 267, No. 22, pp. 3043-
3047; C. Loftin et al., 'Effects of restrictive licensing of handguns on homicide and suicides in the District of Colombia,' *New England Journal of Medicine*, Vol. 325, No. 23, pp. 1615-1620. P.E. Pepe et al., 'The effect of a municipal gun responsibility ordinance on firearm injury deaths in minors,'
Academic Emergency Medicine, Houston, TX, March/April 1994; A.L. Kellermann et al., 'The epidemiological basis for the prevention of firearms
injuries,' *Annual Review of Public Health*, 1991, No. 12, pp. 17-40; A.L. Kellermann et al., 'Gun ownership as a risk factor for homicide in the home,'
New England Journal of Medicine, Vol. 329, No. 15, pp. 1084-1091; Thomas
Gabor, 'The impact of the availability of firearms on violent crime, suicide,

and accidental death,' Department of Justice, 1994; Martin Killias, 'Gun ownership, suicide and homicide: An international perspective,' *Canadian Medical Association Journal*, April 1993.

44 D. Meddings, 'Weapons injuries during and after periods of conflict,' *British Medical Journal*, November 1997.

45 Centre to Prevent Handgun Violence Legal Action Project, Outline of Gun Manufacture and Seller Liability Issues, Washington, DC, 1995.

46 David Kennedy et al., 'Youth Violence in Boston,' *Law and Contemporary Problems*, Vol. 59, No. 1, pp. 173-174.

47 G. J. Wintemute, 'The Relationship between Firearm Design and Firearm Violence: Handguns in the 1990s,' *Journal of the American Medical Association*, Vol. 225, pp. 1749-1753.

48 R. J. Flinn and L.G. Allen, 'Trigger Locks and Firearm Safety: One Trauma Centre's Prevention Campaign,' *Journal of Emergency Nursing*, 1995 (No. 21), pp. 296-298.

49 Douglas S. Weil and Rebecca Knox, 'Effects of Limiting Handgun Purchases on Interstate Transfer of Firearms,' *Journal of the American Medical Association*, Vol. 275, No. 22, pp. 1759-1761.

50 See C.M. Callahan et al., 'Money for Guns: Evaluation of the Seattle Buyback Program,' *Public Health Reports*, 1994, No. 109, pp. 472-77; M.T. Plotkin, ed., *Under Fire: Gun Buy-backs, Exchanges and Amnesty Programs* (Washington: Police Executive Research Forum, 1996); Sarah Meek, *Buy or Barter: History and Prospects for Voluntary Weapons Collection Programmes*, Institute for Security Studies, Monograph No. 22, March 1998.

51 Rosemary Gartner et al., 'Homicide and the Death Penalty: A Cross National Test of a Deterrence Hypothesis,' *Journal of Criminal Law and Criminology*, 1984, No. 75; Rosemary Gartner, Affidavit of Rosemary Gartner, Court of Appeal of Alberta, Vol. 39.

52 Cukier, 'The Case for Registration.'

53 For example, R. v. Hasselwander (1993), 81 C.C.C.(3d) 471 (S.C.C.); Police v. Goodwin (1993, unreported AP 107/93) (New Zealand High Court). Also, see the references to boards of inquiry in Great Britain, New Zealand and South Africa in W. Cukier and T. Sarkar, 'Firearm regulation and human rights in the Commonwealth,' in Abdel F. Musah and Niobe Thompson, eds., *Over a Barrel: Light Weapons and Human Rights in the Commonwealth* (London/New Delhi: Commonwealth Human Rights Initiatives, 1999).

54 See, for example, International Committee of the Red Cross, *Arms Availability and the Situation of Civilians in Armed Conflict* (Geneva: ICRC, June 1999).

55 See, for example, Cukier, 'Firearms Regulation'; Cukier and Sarkar, 'Firearm Regulation and Human Rights in the Commonwealth.'

56 United Nations Commission on Crime Prevention and Criminal Justice, Sixth Session, Criminal Justice Reform and Strengthening of Legal Institu-

tions Measures to Regulate Firearms, Resolution L.19 (E/CN.15/1997/L.19/Rev.1), Vienna: United Nations, 1997.

[57] Although fully automatic weapons are in many homes in Switzerland, they are strictly controlled. Austria is the only other industrialised country with relatively loose restrictions on civilian handgun possession, but its rules are much tighter than those of the United States.

[58] United Nations, *International Study on Firearm Regulation*.

[59] Canada, Department of Foreign Affairs and International Trade, 'Marking Small Arms: An Examination of Methodologies,' February 1999.

[60] This is covered in Article 11 of the draft protocol.

[61] Diaz, *Making a Killing*.

[62] *Ibid.*

part 3
MECHANICS
OF THE
TRADE

6/Making the Deal and
Moving the Goods —
the role of brokers and shippers

by Brian Wood and Johan Peleman

This chapter casts light on the techniques used to traffic arms to regions of violent conflict and serious human rights abuse via 'third countries.' It describes the main methods arms brokers and transport agents employ to circumvent the existing national and international laws and procedures that regulate the arms trade. It also examines what effective measures governments can take to prevent such activities.[1]

Brokers are middlemen who organise arms transfers between two or more parties. Essentially, they bring together buyers, sellers, transporters, financiers and insurers to make a deal, especially where the players are divided by culture, politics and/or geography. They do so for financial consideration, taking a commission from the arms supplier, the arms recipient or both.

Experienced transport agents — shipping brokers, freight forwarders and charterers — are central to the arms brokering business. They contract transport facilities, carriers and crews to move arms cargoes by sea, air or road, and they ensure that storage, ports and routes are all in order.

These dealers usually do not actually own the arms that they arrange to sell and ship. Because they are not arms traders in the strict sense of being retailers and wholesalers, they frequently are not defined as a specific category under states' national arms export laws, and their activities, therefore, go unregulated.

Not all arms brokers are involved in illegal or shadowy activities. In fact, in an era of increasing 'privatisation' of state functions, many governments today rely on private brokers when they need a specialist to negotiate military or police equipment contracts and take care of the complex procedures required for the shipment of strategic equipment across several borders.

Unfortunately, however, many brokers are at the core of shadowy networks arming rebels, death squads, mercenaries, criminal gangs and even pirates. As few state governments will openly supply arms to such groups, they have to rely on private dealers who can organise illicit and secretive supplies, including into hot war zones. Growing public awareness of human rights and humanitarian standards has also caused many pariah governments to rely on arms brokers to secure clandestine supplies.

Modus Operandi

A major source of the very high profits made by some arms brokers are the surplus stocks from former Soviet military bases all over Eastern Europe, which have been turned into warehouses for weapons. Shopping lists circulate between traders and suppliers; when a recipient who cannot buy in the mainstream government markets is found, the weaponry is shipped by civilian cargo companies to a transit point, from where it is transported to a final destination in a war zone. Once the war is over, large quantities of weapons are stockpiled or exported, often through the same brokering channels that were used as supply channels during the war.

To cover up their trail—for legal or ethical reasons, but also to secure their future business prospects—shipping agents and arms brokers go to considerable lengths to establish intricate international webs involving multiple subcontractors, front companies and circuitous transport routes.

If domestic arms export, transit or import controls would prevent the execution of a controversial, but profitable, international arms deal, brokers and shippers can often arrange the deliveries so that the arms never enter the territory or jurisdiction where they live or base their companies. Such practice is called 'third-country' arms brokering. (In practice, deals often extend to fourth, fifth and even more state jurisdictions.) Client confidentiality and the organisation of transactions for clients in different jurisdictions for third parties are core functions of brokers. The use of such techniques makes it difficult to regulate and monitor their activities.

In general, arms brokers operating outside their home countries on behalf of customers of dubious legitimacy will try to locate

cheap supplies of arms in states that lack the capacity to control
surplus stocks and arms exports properly. Alternatively, they will
operate where governance is so weak that there is no manifest political will to exercise proper control.

The physical transportation of weapons, ammunition or other
sensitive equipment to warring parties is usually the most vulnerable aspect of a clandestine or illegal arms transaction. From a law
enforcement point of view, transport is the most visible stage of the
transaction. For every movement of a cargo vessel or aircraft, paperwork is needed. Loading and unloading cargo, clearance at borders, registration of the plane or ship, insurance, landing rights at
international ports or airports and the paperwork required to
transport military equipment, all constitute physical or documentary evidence that can be used to reconstruct suspect transactions.

International conventions exist to regulate the aviation and
shipping industries, and national authorities are supposed to implement and enforce these regulations. However, a lack of international cooperation and coordination between different national
authorities and legislation, and the ever growing volumes of goods
that are traded and shipped across borders, make it increasingly
difficult for under-resourced agencies to regulate the transport
market. In addition, in recent years the aviation industry increasingly has moved away from traditional public ownership.[2] Cross-
border mergers between airlines, marketing alliances, leasing,
chartering, franchising and offshore registration of fleets, crews and
companies all make it even more difficult to monitor and regulate
the airspace and freighting industry. Shipping agents, in partnership with arms brokers, have become skilled exploiters of these new
market realities.

Brokering arms deals is not a new phenomenon. Throughout the
Cold War, networks of brokers and shippers developed with close
ties to competing national security agencies, and the major military
powers used them to make covert arms transfers to politically favoured recipients (see chapter 3). What is new, however, is that
many of these state-affiliated private brokers have shed the (ad-
mittedly loose) reins of their former state partners. In addition, as
the Cold War began to wane and many former military or intelligence officers left government service, it was inevitable that some
of the pilots and operators of secret arms supply missions would
apply their trade independently in the private sector.

It is estimated that most European countries now have hundreds
if not thousands of private brokering agents and companies that are

allowed to trade internationally in military and security equipment. Very few states register arms brokers, however, and none report on them publicly, so the exact numbers are not known.[3] Moreover, a new wave of deal makers emerged in the 1990s, expanding with the pace of privatisation in the former Soviet Union. And while brokers generally still prefer to live in luxury in North America or Europe, more today are originating or locating in less developed countries. Learning the tricks of the trade from their counterparts in the North, brokers and shippers in the South have the comparative advantage of being closer to the zones of violent conflict and hence to the demand side of the market for arms.

Laws and Loopholes

There is a general absence of laws and regulations governing the brokering of arms transfers using routes through foreign countries. When challenged, several powerful Western governments have retorted that the lack of strict regulation of third country brokering and transport is not primarily their problem: Export cargoes *should* be checked and approved by the authorities in the originating country, as well as by authorities in trans-shipment or transit states and finally in the recipient country. However, these same officials acknowledge that, in the real world, senders and recipients of arms in countries chosen for business by unscrupulous brokers may turn out to be corrupt officials, regimes that grossly violate human rights or even armed opposition or criminal groups.

Consider the following scenario: A Belgian resident, acting from a hotel room in Paris, brokers a deal between an arms sales agent in Lithuania, who is selling Russian weapons stocks, to a recipient in a war zone in Central Africa. This deal demonstrates how difficult it would be to control such activities without active, integrated cooperation between all of the individual states and national authorities concerned. Very often the transactions will be even more complex, including a chain of interlinking brokers, companies, bank accounts and shipping agents, so as to camouflage the true nature of the transaction or identity of the players involved.

The difficulty of capturing the varied and complex activities of brokers in distinct definitions, in order to distinguish legal from illegal transactions, presents a serious challenge. A discussion is emerging among some governments, prompted by pressure from nongovernmental organisations, to consider how it might be possible to strictly regulate third-country arms brokering. However, such strict regulation will only succeed if a sufficient number of states agree to join a coordinated initiative.

Only a few states currently have laws requiring brokers to register and receive explicit authorisation by state officials before a brokered deal involving the shipment of arms entirely through foreign countries can be concluded and the weapons delivered.[4] Such approval would be in addition to the necessary export, import and transit authorisations from the relevant foreign authorities in the countries where the consignment is transported. Close coordination between the licensing and customs authorities of the sending, transit and receiving states would be a necessary condition for the success of any control regime.

Descriptions of several states' legal and regulatory frameworks in this area follow, along with an examination of how brokers currently exploit loopholes and differences in these frameworks.

The United States

A relatively tough new US law on international arms brokering was introduced in March 1998. It requires any US citizen, wherever located, and any foreign person located in the United States or subject to US jurisdiction engaged in the brokering of arms to first register as a broker and then to obtain prior written approval for each proposed transaction. Registration and licence approval must be obtained from the State Department's Office of Defense Trade Controls. These requirements are set out in the Arms Export Control Act and in the International Traffic in Arms Regulations. The latter defines a broker as:

> any person who acts as an agent for others in negotiating or arranging contracts, purchases, sales or transfers of defense articles or defense services in return for a fee, commission or other consideration...[and] brokering activities include the financing, transportation, freight forwarding, or taking of any other action that facilitates the manufacture, export, or import of a defense article or defense service, irrespective of its origin. ... [T]his includes, but is not limited to, activities by US persons who are located outside the United States or foreign persons subject to US jurisdiction involving defense articles or defense services of US or foreign origin which are located inside or outside the United States. But this does not include activities by US persons that are limited exclusively to US domestic sales or transfers.[5]

The framing of this regulation is a major advance over what exists in other states. However, there remain three defects in the US law. First, arms brokers and shipping agents based in the United States use the privileged status of NATO partners as a weak link to forward arms to prohibited destinations. Foreign purchasers of US arms are required to sign a statement pledging that they will not re-export the items without prior authorisation by the State Department, but EU law does not recognise this re-export ban as long as the re-export remains within the European Union.[6] Several EU states have porous borders, however, making such 'control' difficult to ensure. Secondly, third-country deals are not controlled by this regulation for some police equipment that is regulated by the Commerce Department, as opposed to those items controlled by the State Department. Thirdly, a general weakness of US arms export law is that strong human rights and conflict criteria for determining export licence approvals are not elaborated or binding.[7]

Sweden, Norway and the Netherlands

In Sweden, all tax-paying residents must register and receive a permit to engage in arms brokering activities. Once a brokerage permit has been issued, the individual transactions are judged according to the same rules as arms exports from Sweden. Brokers must obtain a licence from the government to fix a deal even where the transfers take place entirely outside Swedish territory.

Under the Norwegian arms control law and regulations, it is prohibited for persons domiciled in Norway and for Norwegian companies, foundations or associations to engage in trade or negotiations to assist in the sale of controlled military products from one foreign country to another without the consent of the Norwegian Ministry of Foreign Affairs. The list of controlled goods, services and technology includes weapons, ammunition and other military goods, as well as services connected with such products and technology. Where there is a war or threat of war, all goods, assistance and services require a licence — even if they are non-military items. The law places strict responsibilities on the licensee to report on the delivery of items.[8] It is not known whether the law would cover Norwegian nationals domiciled abroad who broker or arrange shipping of arms and other security equipment.

The Netherlands has ambiguous legislation on arms brokering, but Dutch officials claim that it is more or less legally covered by a procedure called the 'arrangement [on] financial movement of strategic goods.' This October 1994 amendment to the law on financial relations abroad enables the Dutch authorities to request a full licensing procedure for anyone 'financially involved' in transactions or cross-border transport of military goods taking place outside the territory of the European Union. However, this law does not apply to overseas dependent territories such as the Dutch Antilles and Aruba, from where arms brokers have been reported to operate.[9]

The United Kingdom

In the United Kingdom, third-country arms brokering is unregulated unless it is specifically prohibited to certain destinations when a United Nations or European Union arms embargo is imposed. The absence of a regulatory system, coupled with the modern infrastructure and low-tax banking facilities, has made the United Kingdom a prime site for arms brokering activities. Although large firms are known to conduct third-country arms brokering, most of it is carried out by small, itinerant operators who usually work with several agents and subcontractors.

Even where a UN arms embargo was in place, UK-based arms brokers have been able to circumvent it. On 17 May 1994, one month after the genocide began in Rwanda, the UN Security Council imposed an international arms embargo.[10] However, documents found in late 1996 near a refugee camp in eastern Zaire—on a lorry belonging to the exiled Rwandan Ministry of Defence—corroborated previous confessions by UK aircrew regarding a secret series of arms flights from Albania and Israel into Goma and Kinshasa airports (in Zaire), brokered by agents in West Europe, particularly in the United Kingdom.[11] Kenyans based in London brokered the delivery of seven large cargoes of small arms worth $6.5 million, using an offshore company, Mil-Tec Corporation. They worked with another UK air cargo broker in Windsor to arrange secret charter flights from Tirana and Tel Aviv between mid-April and mid-July 1994. The arms deliveries to the now-exiled Rwandan armed forces arrived as they were then carrying out the genocide in Rwanda, even during the time when the mass killings were being reported daily by the international news media.[12]

Deliveries reportedly continued in the aftermath of the genocide as well. The Russian-Israeli owner of TIG Bulgaria and Phoenix Air Bulgaria later admitted in a UK news programme that a British company based at Gatwick had also chartered his aircraft to fly

arms to Goma in 1995. He said that he assumed it was a government-to-government delivery: 'We fly if the documents are right.
We don't check the papers. ... [W]e just check the export certificates.'[13]

It was generally agreed that the UN arms embargo imposed
during the mass killing also applied to the ousted Hutu Rwandan
regime-in-exile. However, the UK government later denied this
common interpretation. In answer to a letter from the United Nations asking what action the UK government was taking on Mil-
Tec, the Minister of State for Foreign Affairs replied on 9 October
1998 that there had been in 1994 'delays and omissions in implementing the United Nations arms embargo.' He concluded that 'because the legislation imposing the embargo in the United Kingdom
did not fully cover the supply of arms to neighbouring countries,
the Customs and Excise investigation was unable to take forward
criminal proceedings against Mil-Tec.'[14] It should be recalled that,
by the last week of April 1994, humanitarian organisations were estimating that over 300,000 Rwandans had been killed. The UK government made no mention in its reply to the United Nations of the
possibility of a prosecution of Mil-Tec under the 1948 Genocide
Convention, to which it is a party.[15]

It was not only UK arms brokers and shippers who were involved in supplying the perpetrators of the genocide. After the
United Nations established the International Commission of Inquiry into the arms supplies in 1995, the Commission's reports alleged that arms suppliers, brokers and shippers in many countries
were involved in similar supply operations.

France

Arms brokers in France must, by law, be registered like other
arms exporters, and they must obtain prior authorisation for ar-
ranging transfers from French territory. They remain unregulated,
however, if the deals and deliveries are conducted outside of
France.

In 1991, Dominique Lemonnier began working with arms
sources in Poland to supply Burkina Faso. Then, in May 1993, he
managed to secure a $12.16 million contract with the Kigali (Hutu)
regime in Rwanda to supply a large array of arms.[16] Lemonnier
registered his company, DYL, in the Turks and Caicos Islands in
May after getting the Rwandan contract.[17] Nevertheless, he continued to operate from Cran-Gevrier, Haute-Savoie, in France, and

used a cover address in Geneva, where he opened an account with the Banque Internationale de Commerce. Between May and September 1993, DYL received four payments from Kigali into the Geneva account, each for about one million dollars. Deliveries of arms to Kigali were made from Poland and from an Israeli company, Universal, using East Africa Cargo airlines.[18]

However, Lemonnier made the mistake of including DYL's French address on the contract instead of only the British offshore tax haven.[19] Unlike the situation faced by Mil-Tec in the UK, DYL was supposed to have obtained prior authorisation from the French Ministry of Defence. When his Polish weapons source dried up, Lemonnier tried to re-activate the Israeli one, but he was unable to secure an air shipping agent or carrier with the right to over-fly countries between Tel Aviv and Kigali. When DYL failed to make two thirds of the arms deliveries, Lemonnier faced legal action in France from his Rwandan paymasters to recover a large portion of what he had been paid.[20] By early May 1994, the authorities commanding the genocide pressured DYL to pay $450,000 to Mil Tec, the UK brokering company that apparently had taken over part of the supply operation.[21]

According to Mil-Tec records, this DYL payment to the UK company met costs for the third arms shipment to Goma. It also brought into play the services of an Afghan agent in Rome, Dr Ghazi Tamiz Ud Din Khan, who signed himself 'Consulate General, Rwanda in Rome.' Italian law did not require him to be registered as an arms broker or for his transaction to be licensed. After meeting Colonel Kuyumba, of the Rwandan Ministry of Defence, in Paris, Dr Khan promised that the $970,000 order of ammunition and grenades was 'ready ... please wait tomorrow for the next fax.'[22]

This example illustrates how interconnecting networks of brokers, shippers and suppliers in different countries can conspire to swiftly shift their operational base to another national jurisdiction whenever facing legal or contractual difficulties, even in the case where they are equipping ongoing acts of genocide.

Germany

Some large German companies broker arms deals from their headquarters with the items flowing entirely through foreign countries and never crossing German soil. Such deals are negotiated while the firm is fulfilling an international supply contract, and it is found that additional items are needed from other countries. The German companies seek permission from the German government for such activity, since German law requires arms brokering deals to be licensed if the deal is fixed on German territory. However, German arms brokers are able to exploit this law by simply crossing the border to conduct their deals and avoid seeking the government's permission.

The following case shows the complexities of the brokering activities of a German broker in South Africa, who set up an almost global network of companies and bank accounts to supply the war in Congo-Brazzaville in 1997.

Documents found in the offices of the ousted government of Congo-Brazzaville show that, between June and September 1997, a German arms broker and an arms trader reportedly of Belgian nationality supplied millions of dollars worth of military equipment to the forces of the beleaguered President Lissouba.[23] Both dealers operated from South Africa using several companies registered in various countries, including Germany and the UK, as well as French, Belgian and UK bank accounts.[24] The weapons originated in Central Asia and the shipments were negotiated at a time when the rivalry between political militias in the Congo was increasing. Observers were warning of an outbreak of fighting and the probable slaughter of many civilians. The deliveries took place when the war had already started.

Among the documents seized from the presidential palace by the militia of the new head of state, Sassou-Nguesso, was a letter dated 8 December 1997 from the former Congolese Prime Minister to the Director of Ebar Management & Trading Ltd in Pretoria, South Africa. The letter informs him about the visit of a mission on behalf of the Congolese Prime Minister, Bernard Kolelas, to discuss the purchase of planes, helicopters and trucks and an oil contract between the company in Pretoria and the Congolese government. The announced mission included the son of the Prime Minister and two other officials of the Prime Minister's cabinet.[25]

The German director of Ebar signed all but one of the invoices sent to the Congo government between 1 June and 19 September 1997. One pro forma invoice from Ebar requested payment for the air transport in a luxury jet of several officials from Brazzaville to Paris. Another was issued by and Exotek.'[26] It mentions an amount of $19.9 million for the supply of four Puma transport helicopters. It specifies that the aerospace corporation Denel Aviation of South Africa would 'recondition' these helicopters prior to delivery, after payment of half the price. In September, the director of President Lissouba's cabinet, Claudine Munari, wrote that $10 million had been transferred to Ebar and a further $9 million to Ingwe Traders, another company linked to the German dealer.[27] Although the German reportedly took up residence in South Africa in 1994, he maintained a company called CED in Frankfurt and a branch in Aalen, Germany.

Other companies used by the German dealer were based in Namibia and apparently in Zambia. For example, Caprivi Cargo was a South African freight company based in Namibia that was allegedly used for shipment to Pointe Noire in Congo-Brazzaville.[28] Other invoices relate to the registration of Antonov AN-24 and AN-26 aircraft, to the costs of the crews required to pilot them and to the supply of military trucks. One invoice states that, 'all items are sourced, shipped and delivered via SAPROD Namibia,' apparently a Namibia-registered transport company. Arms appear also to have been shipped from South Africa and from Central Asia using large Ukrainian-registered Ilyushin-76 cargo aircraft which flew via airports in Namibia and Egypt.[29]

Another document dated 27 June 1997 and signed by the German broker as chairman of CED Marketing acknowledged an order from the Congo-Brazzaville government for the purchase of two MI-17 IV transport helicopters. This deal was reportedly made through the Belgian manager of a company called Sablon Trading, which had an account at the First National Bank in Johannesburg.[30] According to the letter, the helicopters were ordered from an 'East European' supplier. Other documents show that a contract existed between the Kirghiz Republic (Kyrgyzstan) and the Brazzaville government for the purchase of five MI-8 and three MI-24 attack helicopters.[31]

Combat helicopters piloted by East European mercenaries reportedly began firing indiscriminately on civilian areas in Brazzaville on 19 August and were allegedly used to bomb civilians in the Mpila and Poto-Poto district of Brazzaville on 26 August 1997, and again on 10 September.[32] The new Congo-Brazzaville government declared the bombings a crime against humanity and submitted evidence to the United Nations, as well as to the French, Belgian, German and US governments.[33]

Air Transport

Experienced arms brokers and their agents disguise their routes, and official regulatory systems are simply not capable of detecting dubious air cargo. According to the US International Air Cargo Association, the international rules governing cargo planes are archaic and inconsistent.[34] Air freight businesses want faster procedures and simpler regulations, but many countries lack the resources for stringent airport monitoring of dangerous cargoes. Electronic tagging systems akin to those for international passenger baggage would be fast, but costly.

Currently, air freight documents such as air waybills and cargo manifests do not require detailed descriptions or cross-referencing of the goods described in arms export and import licences. The routes, names of subcontractors, the ultimate supplier and customer do not need to be specified. Arms have been found described as agricultural equipment, mining equipment, spare parts, fish, tents and second-hand clothing, so it is easy to see how the absence of comprehensive records makes it exceedingly difficult for law enforcers to quickly identify all those who might be involved. Moreover, as a leading traffic control company manager explained, the commercial interests of a rapidly expanding and competitive industry make it difficult for national aviation or navigation controllers to insist on sufficient manpower and safe but expensive navigation and radar capacity.[35]

It is not only cargo that needs international monitoring. An aircraft registration number and the name of the airline leasing or operating the plane can readily be switched to conceal an operation. A cargo aircraft might typically be registered in one country, then leased and chartered by companies registered in another, while their crews can be hired in yet other countries. In addition, the plane might be serviced and based for practical purposes somewhere else, with the main operating offices of the airline or the handling agency based in yet another country or countries. The sub-leasing of international over-flight permissions means that one air carrier can use another carrier's call sign—a practice has been used to obfuscate arms deliveries.

The more complex the arrangements, and the less capacity there is to monitor them, the easier it is for operators, agents and subcontractors to find ways of denying their involvement in illicit trafficking. A national authority that registers an aircraft to fly under its flag may fail to ensure the air-worthiness and safety of that plane. Airlines, planes and aircrew may not be required to register at all, and foreign operator permits may carry minimal responsibilities. Even where several aviation authorities try to carry out routine checks on an aircraft's filed flight plan, they will usually not have legal powers to act decisively against serious abuse. This reality, in turn, serves to discourage such checking.

Conversations with pilots, loadmasters and aviation inspectors show how easy it is to evade existing controls in countries that lack regulatory resources. A cargo plane was named as flying in at an airport with one registration number and then flying out with a different one. Another airline was said to have changed its corporate structure and name overnight when its name became linked to illicit activities. One operator used an old licence that had been cancelled by aviation authorities to fly several 'ghost planes' to hot spots in Africa.[36] Another corporate owner used the logo and colours of a licensed company to fly non-licensed planes. Yet another abusive practice reported is for a cargo plane using a certain flight schedule to arrive very late at its stated destination: the plane has in fact made an illegal landing on the way to its destination, unloading illicit cargo without reporting it. More often, non-scheduled landings are used to load illicit cargo *en route*, and then ship the additional load under cover of the legal cargo.

Sub-Saharan Africa, in particular, lacks sufficient skilled air traffic controllers, radar equipment and trained personnel to monitor the vast air space between the southern border of Egypt and the northern borders of South Africa.[37] Smaller freight operators often use older aircraft that can evade long-range radar. Moreover, the communications systems of ex-Soviet aircraft are not always compatible with those of other aircraft, making it necessary for pilots to be able to guide themselves.[38] (Thus, pilots with military training are in demand.) Sub-Saharan air traffic control has been highly dependent on the selective intelligence and satellite capacity of the former colonial and major world powers and on the alertness of thinly spread airport inspectors and customs agents.[39] In such an environment, arms smuggling thrives.

In 1997, the Liberian Minister of Transport appointed a Belgian pilot, who had flown for the Saudi royal family, as Chairman of the Liberian Aviation Authority's agency in the United Kingdom.[40] Liberia has been a flag of convenience for the fringe air-cargo industry because of its lax licence and tax laws. A company incorporated there can locate its executive offices in another country, conducting business activities at any location. Names of corporate officers or shareholders need not be filed or listed, and there is no minimum capital requirement. A legal existence can be obtained in one day. The country also has lax maritime and aviation laws and regulations that provide owners of ships and aircraft maximum discretion and cover, with minimal regulatory interference. Aviation officers and pilots have suggested that aircraft registered in Liberia should not be allowed landing or operating rights, as they doubt the credibility of air-worthiness and air-safety inspections of the Liberian aviation registry.[41] The UK agency lasted for about two years, after which time arms pilots were looking for other 'flags of convenience' under which to fly.

In August 1997, Air Cess Swaziland (Ply) Ltd, was granted a two-year licence by the Swaziland Civil Aviation Authorities.[42] The following year, the government of Swaziland ordered an independent investigation into the registration of certain aircraft in the country suspected of involvement in illegal acts. As a result, 47 aircraft operated mostly by former East European businesses were grounded and later de-registered. None of them had been able to show the necessary documentation covering the requirements to register aircraft in Swaziland. The licences had reportedly been obtained through a corrupt official, later suspended on charges of bribery.[43] In January 1999, the former Minster of Transport of Swaziland said in an interview that the grounded aircraft had been ex-Liberian or ex-Russian aircraft, and some of the planes were known to be involved in weapons trafficking to Angola and the Democratic Republic of Congo. Abandoned cargo in one of the grounded aircraft included two Russian-made military helicopters labelled as 'machine spare parts.'[44] The investigating authorities suspected that the helicopters were destined for a country in Central Africa, and Rwandan officials arrived later to inspect them.[45]

Air Cess was one of the companies de-registered in 1998.[46] It was accused in Swaziland of being involved in gun-running between Mozambique and Angola, using the revoked licence.[47] A confidential monitoring report in the possession of the United Nations recorded an Air Cess freighter landing in UNITA territory in Angola in mid-1997. It also listed an Antonov freighter belonging to Flying Dolphin, a Russian-operated cargo company, registered in Liberia and using Southern African airfields. The Air Cess plane was an Antonov-12 with registration number EL-RDL.[48] Although registered in Liberia, the aircraft was found based at the Pietersburg and Lanseria airports in South Africa. Soon after the UN had spotted the Air Cess and the Flying Dolphin Antonovs in UNITA territory, the Flying Dolphin plane was re-registered in Liberia as a division of another company, Santa Cruz Imperial Airlines, while the Air Cess plane was re-registered first in Swaziland, then in the Central African Republic with a new registration number — TL-ACR.[49] Ten other aircraft operated by one of several other companies run by the former Russian KGB officer who owned Air Cess were also registered in the Central African Republic, where many former members of the Mobutu regime have fled. In addition, four of the planes in the Russian's fleet were registered in Equatorial Guinea.[50]

Some of the other UN-inspected Russian- or Ukrainian-built aircraft using the Swazi register as a flag of convenience were reportedly operating from airports in South Africa, Lesotho, Malawi, Rwanda, Uganda and the UAE. Several planes that had fraudulently obtained a licence in Swaziland could not even land at the Swazi national airport and be inspected for air worthiness, as every aircraft should.[51] Air Cess Swaziland was supposedly shut down after the scandal, but the 'company' was still operating freighters that were not registered anywhere. Several Air Cess planes were subsequently grounded in South Africa, and by mid-1999 the company appeared to have moved the base of its Africa operations to the north and east of the Central African crisis zone.[52]

In 1999, the main operating office of Air Cess continued to be Sharjah in the United Arab Emirates, even though the aircraft were based in several other African countries.[53] The former KGB officer owning most of the companies involved was living in Europe and appeared to be using a last name in Sharjah that differed slightly from the one he used for his registration in Belgium.[54] According to officials in southern Africa, this man, Viktor Bout, uses five different passports, two of which are Russian.[55] In late 1998, the aircraft operated by his trading and handling agency in Sharjah were reportedly using Russian or Ukrainian crews based at Kigali airport, in Rwanda, and were accused of loading supplies for the armed opposition groups in war-torn eastern Congo and Angola.[56] An Angolan news source also refers to this Viktor Bout as 'the current spearhead' in the sale of weapons for Jonas Savimbi, UNITA's leader.[57] In 1999, 'a man whose name resembles one of Viktor Bout's many aliases' was also reported to be involved with a Ugandan airforce training operation.[58]

A human rights researcher also reported on Viktor Bout's sanctions-busting activities from South Africa to UNITA.[59] According to his report, aviation authorities at South Africa's Pietersburg Airport visited AirPass, a subsidiary of Air Cess, in April 1998 and, after assessing its documentation, issued '200 charges for violations of the Civil Aviation Act,' including transporting 'fuel tanks, tow trucks, boots, ponchos, food and mining equipment' to UNITA-held areas.[60] AirPass is run by Viktor Bout and a Russian business partner.[61] No arrests or confiscations in the case were made, this report goes on, because 'individuals involved in sanctions-busting operations via South Africa use foreign-registered companies' and 'they can not easily be touched as these fall outside South Africa's legal jurisdiction.'[62] AirPass has since moved some of its planes to other national registers.

Sea Freight

Ninety percent of world trade is maritime trade, and considerable quantities of arms are ferried by sea.[63] If an illegal shipment is found it can reveal a great deal about international brokering networks, but the sheer quantity of cargo makes checking very difficult. To varying degrees, all countries are faced with the same enforcement problems: lack of resources for customs officials at ports to check paperwork sufficiently against cargo and for port authorities to ensure that safety rules are followed. Resources are limited, and investigating suspected cargoes and traffickers who use evermore circuitous routes requires a great deal of time and effort.

At the busiest US port, Long Beach in California, an average of 8,400 cargo containers in port area could be checked every day, but US Customs has fewer than 135 inspectors there. It was therefore by accident that, in March 1997, federal agents at the US-Mexico border opened two suspect sealed containers that had entered the United States in Long Beach. This happenstance led to the largest illicit arms shipment ever intercepted *en route* from the United States to Mexico. The arms, including M-2 automatic rifle parts, had originally been left behind in Vietnam by the US armed forces. They had been shipped from Ho Chi Minh City to Singapore, then to Bremerhaven in Germany, then back through the Panama Canal and up to Long Beach for transit to Mexico.[64]

It is not only aircraft operators who can hide or camouflage their logos and airline name. Several shipowners or crews are also known to have changed the name of the vessel on the open sea. In 1993, an international warrant was issued for a cargo of arms aboard a vessel registered in Greece. While authorities were

searching for a ship called the *Maria*, the ship's name had been illegally changed to *Malo*. The *Malo* was finally held in the Indian
Ocean by the Seychelles authorities.[65]

Another vessel shipping 38,000 high-explosive mortar grenades
to apartheid South Africa in 1985, in breach of the arms embargo,
was actually sold on the open sea to a new owner. The new
shipowner was an agent of the former one, but the original owner
could apparently no longer be held accountable for the illegal
cargo. In this case, the ship's name, *Otter*, had been changed to *Reef
Moon* by the time it arrived in the port of Durban.[66]

Profits and Finance

Some brokers have found customers desperate enough to barter or
mortgage future national production in return for arms. The documents found in President Lissouba's office when he was overthrown indicate that his government concluded an oil-for-arms deal
with the German broker described above. On 2 October 1997 the
German broker signed a contract for a loan of $100 million with the
then ministers of economics and oil of the Congo. In this contract,
the Congo government committed itself to provide Ebar Management and Trading with 160,000 barrels of crude oil per month over
five years from 1 November 1997. The first disbursement of $50
million should have been made on 17 October, two days after Lissouba was overthrown.[67]

In order to transfer the large profits into accessible accounts, the
banking arrangements used by arms brokers for controversial
deals, even when the transactions may be considered 'legal' by the
exporting and importing authorities, can be extremely complex.

Mil-Tec Corporation used a North London branch of the National Westminster Bank to receive payments.[68] Rwandan officials
of the genocidal regime had facilitated payments to Mil-Tec initially
from Kigali in mid-April, then from the Cairo embassy and from
two Belgian banks in May, and finally from the Paris embassy in
mid-July. Lt.-Colonel Cyprien Kayumba, director of financial services in the Rwandan Ministry of Defence, wrote that he had left Kigali on 17 June 1994 to supervise the unloading of the first arms delivery in Goma; then, until the last delivery on 18 July, he had
toured Nairobi, Cairo, Paris (where he stayed for 27 days), Nairobi,
Kinshasa, Cairo, Tunis, Tripoli, Paris, Cairo and Nairobi in order to
facilitate the purchases and payments.[69]

Other arms shipments to the exiled Hutu armed forces in June 1994, arranged by a South African, 'Ters' Willem Ehlers, were purchased with two separate payments into the account of the Central Bank of Seychelles in the Federal Reserve Bank in New York.[70] Two amounts of $179,965 and $149,982.50 were sent to the Seychelles account from an account at the Union Bancaire Privée in Geneva.[71] The Swiss government acknowledged after a period of questioning by UN investigators[72] that Ehlers was the holder of numbered account 82-113 CHEATA at the Lugano office of Union Bancaire. The Swiss Prosecutor General confirmed that the two separate payments, $179,965 and $149,982.50 respectively, had been made from the account on 15 to 17 June 1994. Moreover, he stated that on 14 June and 16 June 1994, Ehlers' account had been credited with $592,784 and $734,099 respectively. In other words, almost $1 million more had been received into Ehlers account than had been paid to the Seychelles Central Bank in New York. The Prosecutor General told UNICOI that the large funds entering Ehlers' account had originated from an account at the Banque nationale de Paris in Paris, which had in turn been acting on behalf of the Banque nationale du Rwanda, Kigali. It was unclear where the money had really come from originally. The French newspaper Le Figaro tried to reconstruct these transactions in April 1998, but both the Banque national de Paris and the Union Bancaire Privée in Switzerland declined to comment. Representatives of the Federal Reserve Bank in New York referred Le Figaro's journalists back to the Swiss bank.[73]

Regulating Brokers and Transport Agents

It is important to note a distinction between arms brokers and shippers based in West Europe versus those based in East Europe. Within the European Union, brokering represents a cynical failure of rule of law to constrain commercial activity in keeping with domestic obligations. In the former Soviet Union, the sale of weapons, through brokers who are often from EU countries, reflects the general lack of standards in the state, corruption and the lack of control by the state over increasingly autonomous actors who once were state owned but are now effectively privatised and unregulated.

In December 1999 officials of 18 'like-minded' states met in Oslo to consider the problem of brokering as a principal contributing factor to the dangerous proliferation of small arms and light weapons. The assembled governments agreed to conduct a policy review

and to develop a set of appropriate measures to tackle the problem.
Among the measures, they agreed to:

> Develop model brokering legislation and regulations, including
> comprehensive definitions, in order to achieve more effective na-
> tional control on brokering in all its aspects as well as related ac-
> tivities. These could constitute international standards against
> which implementation could be measured.[74]

If they are serious about tackling illegal and/or unregulated trafficking in small arms, these most sympathetic of governments will
have to design a legal system that can close the gaps between various national systems. Removing the grey zones that lie outside the
reach of today's national laws is imperative. For a truly effective legal and regulatory system to exist, each government will have to set
up complementary mechanisms that cover the arms brokering and
shipping activities of:

- its own nationals and passport-holders, wherever located;
- all foreign nationals who are permanently resident in the country; and
- all companies incorporated or registered in that country.

When serving illegitimate customers, arms brokers and transport
agents usually use third countries. If there is to be effective regulation, national legislation with an extraterritorial dimension cannot
be avoided. Without tackling the third- (and fourth-, and fifth-)
country loophole, any attempt to control arms brokers and traffickers is bound to fail.

The Swedish approach: A first step

According to a thus far unpublished German government proposal made in the European Union in late 1999, an immediate first
step for international agreement could be for each state to adopt a
strong version of the Swedish government's practice in this area.
EU officials are still discussing this proposal, which may have an
unduly restricted definition of 'arms,' but it is possible that provisions from similar laws on brokering, such as those in Norway and
the Netherlands, could be added to strengthen the agreement. This
approach would mean that arms brokers and transport agents
domiciled in any of those states parties to the agreement would be

covered by the national laws and regulations where they pay taxes and where they are resident.

Under such a system, brokers would first have to obtain official written permission to operate. Then each proposed transaction would be subject to case-by-case consideration by the national government, which would grant a licence for deals it approves. The criteria used for deciding whether to register dealers as bona fide would be set at a high level, and the criteria used for considering each transaction would be those contained in the EU Code of Conduct, the EU Joint Action and other relevant international agreements. These criteria would also apply in cases where the proposed brokering and shipping operations were to be conducted abroad.

The home government, the third-country government and the recipient government would each need to consult the other about the proposed deal, and they would need to issue relevant documents to each other if the deal was approved. Clearly, the more states joining such a system, the more effective it would be, as unscrupulous brokers and traffickers would continue to operate out of tax havens and irresponsible states.

Strengthening the US approach

An even more effective approach would be for all states to adopt a stronger version of the existing US law on arms brokers and traffickers. This law would operate in a similar way to the Swedish one. First, bona fide operators would be registered. This registration would extend not only to residents but to all nationals of the home state, wherever they are based. Secondly, each transaction would be considered on its merits and only given a licence on the basis of internationally agreed criteria. Other governments affected by the proposed deal would be consulted.

This approach would be more consistent and comprehensive, because it would cover the arms brokering and trafficking activities of all citizens at home and abroad, regardless of their shifting residences or company registrations. Such a law, if accompanied by criminal sanctions, would act as a stronger deterrent to arms brokers and traffickers who migrate from country to country to escape proper regulation.

Some weaknesses in the US law would, however, need to be addressed:

• exemptions for NATO or other groupings could not apply;

- internationally agreed criteria for properly registering brokers and shippers, as well as for considering permits and licences, would have to be made explicit and binding; and
- transparent reporting requirements would need to be put in place, including the publication of lists of convicted arms brokers and perhaps some confidential exchange of information on those under investigation or who are being prosecuted for defying arms embargoes or other export restrictions.

Brokers need to be registered both in their country of nationality as well as in the country where they wish to fix a deal or maintain their residence. The US government has proposed such a scheme in the multinational negotiations in Vienna on the UN Firearms Protocol. If a broker has been convicted of smuggling, fraud, violent crime or a breach of arms control regulations in any country, that person or corporation should be denied registration.

Some provisions from the laws and guidelines of other states could help define the criteria and scope of an international agreement based on the US model. Some text consistent with international law from the EU Code of Conduct and Joint Action (see chapter 2), and similar language from US arms export legislation could be used to reach agreement on the best criteria for approving licences. The draft South African provisions to control brokering of firearms and the new law to control the export of military services from South Africa could also provide concepts helpful in defining the scope of the agreement.

The success of any agreement would depend not only on design, but on its implementation at the national level and on law enforcement. If loopholes or weaknesses remained at the national level, of course arms brokers and traffickers would continue to exploit them. And equally imperative is a need to move beyond cleaning up the practices of the liberal Western democracies, to bring China, Russia, East European countries, Israel and other states into such practice as well.

While the challenges are manifold, perhaps the interests of legitimate, non-weapons businesses—which stand to lose so much investment and profit around the world to armed conflict and violence—can be leveraged to press governments to increase their political will to end deadly arms brokering.

Notes

1 This chapter draws from a more extended study by the authors. See Brian Wood and Johan Peleman, *The Arms Fixers: Controlling the Brokers and Shipping Agents* (Oslo: PRIO/NISAT/BASIC, 1999).

2 The shipping industry went through this transformation much earlier. The more high-tech aviation industry, however, is only now loosening its traditional association with national sovereignty and strategic interest.

3 According to US State Department officials, since the United States implemented a new brokering registration requirement in 1998, less than 200 individuals or corporations have registered.

4 The Norwegian government initiated a survey in 1999 of national export laws concerning brokering through the 'Wassenaar Arrangement' group of 33 arms exporters. Responses from participants were due back to the Wassenaar secretariat by 15 April 2000.

5 Title 22, *US Code of Federal Regulations*, Section 129.2.

6 In 1998 the US State Department barred further commercial firearms exports to the United Kingdom to prevent exploitation of this loophole. The UK government had, in 1997, banned civilian firearms possession, meaning that any export licenses for the commercial market in the UK would result in illegal ownership or re-export.

7 Section 502B of the US Foreign Assistance Act bans security aid to any government which 'engages in a consistent pattern of gross violations of internationally recognised human rights,' unless the US President deems there are 'extraordinary circumstances.' The government has never used this section of the Act, which dates back to the mid-1970s, against a repressive foreign government. In an effort to enact relevant law that will be enforced, the US Congress recently passed a more limited provision prohibiting military aid to particular units of foreign security forces implicated in gross human rights violations until the perpetrators are brought to justice.

8 Norwegian Royal Decree Number 967 of 18 December 1987, and Regulations of 10 January 1989, as amended.

9 Dutch Royal Decision, 1994.

10 UN Security Council resolution 918, 17 May 1994.

11 Interviews with journalists from *Corriere Della Sera*, November 1996 and June 1998.

12 According to documents from the former Rwandan Ministry of Defence, the details of arms shipments arranged by Mil-Tec Corporation were as follows: 6 June 1993 ($549,503 of ammunition from Tel Aviv to Kigali, Rwanda); 17-18 April 1994 ($853,731 of ammunition from Tel Aviv to Goma, Zaire); 22-25 April 1994 ($681,200 of ammunition and grenades from Tel Aviv to Goma); 29 April-3 May 1994 ($942,680 of ammunition, grenades, mortars and rifles from Tirana to Goma); 9 May 1994 ($1,023,840 of rifles, ammunition, mortars and other items from Tirana to Goma); 18-20 May 1994 ($1,074,549 of rifles, ammunition, mortars, RPG rockets and

other items from Tirana to Goma); 13-18 July 1994 ($753,645 of ammunition and rockets from Tirana to Kinshasa, Zaire). The additional costs of delivering batteries ($511,415 in 1993 and $56,000 in 1994) and of airport delay at Kinshasa were added to the above by Mil-Tec, yielding a total sales figure of $6,615,313. To this total, Mil-Tec added bank interest charges of $254,062 due in December 1994 for the failure of the Rwandan MOD to pay $1,708,313 for deliveries in 1993.

[13] HTV Bristol, news team interview with Simon Spitz, 30 April 1998.

[14] The UK government's claim requires further examination of the Order in Council on Rwanda, Statutory Instrument 1994 No. 1637, United Nations (amending Statutory Instrument 1993 No. 1787), which came into force on 24 June 1994. The UK government also indicated that the previous government had not acted promptly in May 1994 to implement the UN arms embargo on Rwanda in the many UK dependent territories and the three Crown dependencies of Jersey, Guernsey and the Isle of Man.

[15] Article 3e of the 1951 Convention on the Prevention and Punishment of the Crime of Genocide defines 'complicity in genocide' as a punishable act.

[16] 'Un Français est écroué pour trafic d'armes de guerre avec le Rwanda,' *Le Monde*, 2 February 1995.

[17] *Ibid.*

[18] *Ibid.*

[19] *Ibid.*

[20] In April 1995, A CNN television crew filmed a meeting in a Nairobi hotel between an alleged foreign arms trafficker and persons purported to be the exiled Rwandan Ministers of Foreign Affairs and Finance, and a Lt.-Colonel of the ex-FAR. CNN could not identify the arms trafficker, but linked the meeting to a letter concerning the DYL legal case in France.

[21] The DYL payment to Mil-Tec was also recorded in an annex to a letter from Mil-Tec to the former Minster of Defence of Rwanda, 7 December 1994, and in a report by Lt.-Colonel Kayumba on his travels in 1994, quoted in *Le Figaro*, 14 January 1998.

[22] Copy of correspondence between Dr G. T. Khan in Rome and Lt.-Colonel Kayumba of the Rwanda Ministry of Defence, 19 May 1994, concerning the 'urgent' supply of arms.

[23] Government of the Republic of Congo, 'The civil wars of Congo Brazzaville, Documents for History,' November 1993-January 1994, 5 June-15 October 1977. The Nguesso government in Brazzaville compiled the documents and published this three-volume 'White Paper' on the wrongdoings of former President Lissouba. President Nguesso and his Cobra militia had their own networks of arms suppliers, some of whom seem to overlap with those in Lissouba's supply network accused in the White Paper (hereafter, WhP). We have used the documents reproduced in the White Paper, not the annotations.

[24] FIBA, Belgolaise and Barclays Bank.

25 WhP, Vol. 1, copy of letter reproduced on p. 107

26 WhP, Vol. 1, copy of document reproduced on p. 124.

27 Copy of document reproduced in Jean-Philippe Remy & Stephen Smith, 'Professeur Folamour et les vendeurs d'armes,'*L'Autre Afrique*, 18-24 February 1998, p. 30.

28 Remy & Smith, 'Professeur Folamour et les vendeurs d'armes,' pp. 28-31.

29 EBAR Management and Trading, Pro forma Invoice, 5 August 1997. Copy of letter reproduced in WhP, Vol. 3, p. 796.

30 An invoice from his company was sent to the Presidential cabinet on 12 June 1997, including 'Bank Details' with a request to transfer $1.8 million to the account of Sablon Trading at the First National Bank in Johannesburg. A copy of the document is in WhP, Vol. 1, p. 48.

31 'Congo-Brazza: Les vraies questions,' *Jeune Afrique*, No. 1915, 17-23 September 1997, p. 15. The 'Belgian' dealer we refer to is the one called 'French' by *Jeune Afrique*.

32 'Ukrainian Helicopters Make Brazzaville More Dangerous,' APS, 1 September 1997; Communiqué issued by the office of Denis Sassou-Nguesso, Paris, 28 August 1997; 'Many Casualties Reported in Congolese Army Raid North of Brazzaville,' *Radio France International*, 12 September 1997; Amnesty International, *Republic of Congo...*, 25 March 1999.

33 Most of the documents referred to in this case-study are included in the first three volumes of evidence that were distributed by the new Congo government.

34 *TIACA Times*, Fall 1998. The President claimed that 'Practices, policies and nomenclature keyed to the sailing ship still dominate' the air freight industry. The International Air Transport Association agreements, and hence the documentation, for cargo are viewed as being out of date because they assume that freight forwarders are simply the appointed agents of air cargo carriers, rather than independent brokers, charterers and sales agents.

35 Interview with air traffic control manager in South Africa, February 2000.

36 Correspondence with Dr John E. Tambi, Director Civil Aviation Department, Ministry of Public Works and Transport, Swaziland, 12 August 1999.

37 Even South Africa in 1997 had far too few resources to monitor the 36 airports used for international traffic. After much international criticism, the government reduced the number of such airports to eight and promised to increase customs, immigration, police and air traffic control. See Alex Vines, *Angola Unravels: The Rise and Fall of the Lusaka Peace Process* (New York: Human Rights Watch, September 1999), pp. 116-117.

38 Christopher Bellamy & Elizabeth Wine, 'Fears Grow in a Bad Year for Aviation Safety,' *The Independent*, 14 November 1996.

[39] Vines, *Angola Unravels,* chapter 9; also authors' interviews with customs agents, police, aviation inspectors, pilots, airline owners and officials in Belgium, the UK, South Africa and Zambia.

[40] A letter to this effect was sent to other aviation authorities. The pilot's background was described in *La Lettre du Continent,* No. 334, 29 July 1999.

[41] An aviation officer in South Africa referred to 'highly irregular and illegal' practices. A spokesman of a Belgian pilots' association suggested that Liberian planes should not be allowed to land in Belgium or elsewhere.

[42] Licence number obtained: ASL/97009/37/02. The licence was valid until 19 August 1999. (Swaziland Licence Applications and Licences Granted, published 10 March 1998.)

[43] Interviews with the Swazi Embassy in Brussels; interview with P. Lott, a South African aviation expert who chaired the commission of enquiry probing the fraudulent registration of the aircraft, April and May 1999.

[44] 'Ex-minister Admits Registering "War" planes,' *The Swazi Observer,* 11 January 1999.

[45] 'Swaziland Seizes Helicopter Gunships,' *Mail & Guardian,* 10 July 1998; also *The Times of Swaziland,* 10 July 1998; and 'Rwanda Wants Govt to Release Military Planes,' *The Swazi Observer,* 12 January 1999.

[46] Interview and correspondence with Dr John E. Tambi, Director, Civil Aviation Department, Kingdom of Swaziland, August 1999.

[47] 'SD Being Used for Arms Smuggling to Angola?,' *The Swazi Observer,* 21 May 1999.

[48] Fax from the United Nations, September 1997.

[49] Interviews with aviation official in South Africa. Also: 'World Airline Directory 1995-1998,' *Flight International,* 30 March 1999; Ulrich Klee, *JP Airline Fleets International,* 1999-2000 (33rd edn), (Glattburg, Switzerland: Bucher & Co, March 1999).

[50] Interviews with aviation official in South Africa. Also: 'World Airline Directory 1995-1998'; *JP Airline Fleets International 1999-2000.*

[51] 'SD Being Used for Arms Smuggling to Angola?,' *The Swazi Observer,* 21 May 1999.

[52] Interview with aviation official, May 1999.

[53] Reflected on his business card and aviation registers, Klee, *JP Airline Fleets International*

[54] Comparison of documents from the Belgian trade registrar 1995-1996, a business card from Viktor Bout in Sharjah and his name mentioned in Klee, *JP Airline Fleets International*

[55] Interviews with officials, May 1999, copies of passport numbers disclosed.

[56] NCN (New Congo Net), News, 29 December 1998 (available on the Internet at www.marekinc.com/NCN/news12291.html).

[57] 'Ukraine Citizen Supplying Arms to UNITA,' FBIS translation from *Noticias da Angola,* 7 June 1999. Vines refers to a US intelligence assessment that

mentions Viktor Bout and Air Cess as being known to supply services to UNITA in exchange for diamonds (Vines, *Angola Unravels*). An Interpol report disclosed to the authors in 1999 concurs with this.

58 'Air Force in Formation,' *The Indian Ocean Newsletter*, 10 April 1999.

59 Vines, *Angola Unravels*.

60 *Ibid.*

61 *Ibid.*

62 *Ibid.*

63 *Worldwide Maritime Challenges 1997*, Office for Naval Intelligence, United States, March 1997, p. 20.

64 Valerie Alvord, 'Illegal Weapons Were well Travelled,' *San Diego Union Tribune*, 21 March 1997.

65 Arms from the *Malo* were later transferred from the Seychelles to the perpetrators of the Rwandan genocide.

66 Hugo Gijsels, 'Het schip dat in de mist verdween,' *Humo*, 1 June 1987.

67 'Contrat de Pret,' Copy of document reproduced in WhP, Vol. 1, p. 126.

68 Letter from National Westminster Bank of Kilburn, London, to Mil-Tec Corporation Ltd, c/o Isle of Man, dated 11 November 1994.

69 Lt.-Colonel Kayumba's report on his travels and payments is part of the ex-MOD papers, and is quoted by Patrick St Exupéry, 'France-Rwanda: Silence of State,' *Le Figaro*, 14 January 1998.

70 UNICOI Third Report, paras. 62-63.

71 UNICOI Third Report, para. 35.

72 UNICOI, or the UN International Commission of Inquiry, was established in 1995 pursuant to UN Security Council resolution 1013, to 'investigate, *inter alia*, reports relating to the sale or supply of arms and related-materiel to former Rwandan government forces in the Great Lakes region in violation of Council Resolutions 918, 997 and 1011.' The following reports were published: Interim Report (17 January 1996) UN Doc. S/1996/67; Second Report (13 March 1996) UN Doc. S/1996/195; Third Report (1November 1996) UN Doc. S/1997/1010; Addendum to the Third Report (22 January 1998) UN Doc. S/1998/63; Interim Report (18 August 1998) UN Doc. S/1998/777; and Final Report (18 November 1998) UN Doc. S/1998/1096.

73 'Quatre ans après la tragédie rwandaise (5): Les armes du génocide,' *Le Figaro*, 3 April 1998. The French daily produced a series of five articles on the alleged involvement of France in the 1994 genocide in Rwanda.

74 'Elements of a Common Understanding,' The Second Oslo Meeting on Small Arms and Light Weapons, 6-7 December 1999 (available at www.nisat.org). The meeting was attended by officials from Australia, Austria, Belgium, Brazil, Canada, Chile, Finland, Germany, Japan, Mali, Mexico, the Netherlands, Norway, South Africa, Sweden, Switzerland, United Kingdom and the United States.

7/Gunsmoke and Mirrors: Financing the Illegal Trade

by R. T. Naylor

Prospects today for curbing violent conflict run afoul of a simple but powerful contradiction between the enormous damage weapons do and the almost trivial process by which they are acquired. The compelling question becomes how that contradiction can be resolved. To answer it requires a real understanding of the operation of the modern black market in arms—including the sources of money used to finance the deals, and the convoluted mechanisms used to hide the payment flows.[1]

The first section of this chapter describes the factors that go into determining the cost of arms shipments, legal and illegal. The second part explains the complex means gun-runners use to accept and make clandestine payments. The chapter then dissects the various roles that banks play in black-market deals, including 'offshore' banks and bank secrecy laws. Next, fund-raising mechanisms used by insurgents are examined. The final section critiques supply-side approaches in general, and targeting financial flows in particular, to curb gun trafficking.

Setting the Price

In a legal arms deal, the most important element of cost is the acquisition of the basic material. The purchaser pays a sum sufficient to cover the manufacturers' costs and profit, plus fairly standard charges for shipping and insurance. If kickbacks for personal or political expenses must be included, the manufacturer might submit two invoices—one, for public consumption, specifying the original sum, and the second artificially inflated to cover the amount of graft required.

Corruption payments generally take one of three forms. One is, or rather used to be, direct cash transfers. Back in the 1970s, Northrop's Paris-based agent wore a double-lined raincoat specially designed to conceal the wads of money he had to dish out.[2] However, by the late 1980s, this crude method was largely gone, at least for major deals. Instead payments came to be transferred through phoney subcontracting, 'offset' or 'consultancy' arrangements, or disguised as payments for after-sales services.[3]

Alternatively, corruption payments could work through brokers' commissions. In state-to-state arms deals there is generally no real need for brokers; nevertheless, sometimes one or both sides insist on using them.[4] The seller might require the broker to kick back a certain percentage into a political slush fund, and the buyer might require the broker to deposit some money into an offshore retirement account. Working through a broker rather than a manufacturer has certain advantages in disguising the trail of corruption payments. A manufacturer's books are subject to audit by the home government, while brokers' payments are likely to go into and through foreign accounts protected by bank secrecy laws.[5] On the other hand, running corruption payments through subcontracts or consultancy arrangements created by the manufacturer confers a certain apparent legitimacy that may throw investigators off the trail. And with a bribe properly hidden in an offset deal it is virtually impossible to unscramble the money flow.[6]

Whether corruption payments are added to manufacturers' costs or to brokers' commissions, they simply represent a mark-up on the base price. The deal remains a bilateral transaction, and the pricing formula is essentially unaffected. In a black-market transaction, however, acquisition of the basic material is only the first step of a long and complex commercial chain that adds 'service' charges at each stage.

First, the gun-runner is often a merchant, rather than a broker. If this is the case, he will have to either front the money or provide a letter of credit to purchase the weapons stock before resale. Doing so will add to the total acquisition cost interest paid or foregone and, perhaps, bank charges for issuing letters of credit.

Second, if the weapons are to come from existing state-controlled stocks, there will be charges incurred to free them up. These charges will include the cost of acquiring and using phoney end-user certificates. The party providing the certificate will have to be squared away, with either a fixed fee (typical for poor quality fakes) or a percentage of the total deal (for genuine paper issued by a complicit official). The costs may also include payments for electoral or personal expenses to assure the seller accepts the end-user certificate and issues the export license. In addition, obstructionist customs officials in the exporting country may have to be paid off.

Third, there are costs associated with the use of cut-outs, frontmen and subcontractors. Multiple intermediators act for commercial transactions like multiple transfers through offshore banks do for financial transactions—that is, they hide the trail. But each layer of the intermediation process requires a fee for service.[7]

Fourth come elevated costs of transportation. Sometimes general cargo carriers are employed, but in other cases the job is turned over to specialised shipping companies. A ship may require particular equipment—on-board derricks, for example—if cargo is to be off-loaded at a small fishing village or beside a mangrove swamp rather than at a modern port. However shipped, the load must be carefully packaged, usually with legitimate merchandise as cover.[8]

Shipping frequently also requires hiding the destination by re-routing at sea or trans-shipping via third countries, either of which deepens the cover while increasing operating expenses. While customs *normally* will not inspect cargoes being trans-shipped, it is still best for a stopover to be kept as brief as possible, and nothing should be done to attract attention. Otherwise, further expenses may be entailed in the form of hush payments to port officials. And, not least of the extra shipping costs, the crew must be well paid to assure silence.

Fifth, if the deal is being monitored by one or possibly several intelligence services, each agency may demand a sort-of 'covert action tax.' Despite all the attention to the Iran-*contra* scandal, the United States is certainly not the only country where the intelligence agencies have taxed contraband, particularly arms deals, to top up a 'black budget.'

Sixth, at the port of disembarkation there may be additional payoffs to Customs or police officials, kickbacks to purchasing officials and payoffs to 'skimmers' who catch wind of what is happening and muscle in on the deal. Under normal circumstances, these fees would be expected to be less onerous than the equivalents demanded in regular state-to-state arms deals.

Even after taking care of all officials at both ends, the gun-runner is far from being in a position to simply pick up his cash, deduct his expenses and bank his profit. Seventh are additional, possibly quite substantial costs, in the form of such things as exchange discounts and commodity brokers' fees. These result from the fact that payments for a black-market deal are often made in non-conventional forms—soft currency, precious commodities like diamonds and ivory or counter-trade deals for items like oil, drugs or other weapons.

Once all of the elements of price are factored in, then a profit percentage (including risk premium) must be added. The profit rate will also reflect the nature of the customer. A state under embargo because the international community has chosen to protest its human rights record or its secret nuclear acquisition strategy is an excellent customer. But even better—from a profit point of view—is one placed under embargo in an effort to stop an ongoing war. In such a situation, a gun-runner can pick up stocks of arms at bargain prices on the glutted black market, then resell them at a hefty mark-up to a desperate belligerent.

It was precisely because of these additional service charges that black-market weapons historically tended to be more expensive than their legal equivalents, sometimes considerably more so. For certain types of specialised equipment, this price difference undoubtedly still holds. But for more mundane items, it does not. Today, with the second-hand markets in weapons glutted, base acquisition costs for ordinary equipment have fallen so far that there is no longer much, if any, of a cost deterrent to bypassing legal channels altogether.

In fact, the price differential contains its own unstable dynamic. An army reckons its cost of acquisition not simply according to the price tag attached to the equipment, but also by estimating what that material will eventually fetch on the second-hand market when the time comes to upgrade. The lower the price on the second-hand market, the higher the effective cost of purchasing new material, therefore increasing the temptation to buy old stocks, including those available illegally. Indeed, the former Minister of Defence of Croatia (who was in a position to know on both counts), complained during the recent Balkan wars that prices on the legal market were three times as high as those on the illegal one.

This situation, in which the terms of trade turn progressively against the legal market, will persist until illegally available second-hand stocks approach exhaustion, a point that is today nowhere in sight. When the phenomenon of lower cost is added to the traditional black-market advantages of anonymity and rapid delivery, the competitive balance shifts decisively in favour of the black market. Furthermore, unlike in the past when the black market dealt mainly in 'light' material, today it can deliver virtually everything, from assault rifles to nuclear precursors. The key question is not whether weapons are 'light' or 'heavy,' but whether or not the would-be buyer can afford to pay for them, and whether or not the seller will accept the particular currency in which the payment can be made.

Getting Paid

The stereotypical view is that a legal arms sale is financed by bowler-hatted bankers who settle the accounts after smirking arms company executives have struck a deal with generals embellished with self-awarded decorations. By contrast, an illegal deal involves men with black eye-patches exchanging valises stuffed with $100 bills in a smoky bar. In reality, payment mechanics are usually a little more complex.

When one country openly sells weapons to another, payment can take political, commercial or financial forms. Political payment takes the form of favours or concessions—for example, permitting the use of military bases or voting a particular way on a UN resolution. If commercial, the deal is settled through a counter-trade arrangement involving the purchasing country's export goods.[9] If financial, the supplier is paid via regular bank transfers, with the buyer drawing down an official bank balance, likely from its hard-currency reserves held in an American or British bank.

Many deals, perhaps the majority, involve a blended payment mechanism. In an apparently financial arrangement, payment might be made over time with easy credits arranged by the supplier state—at which point financial considerations begin to shade into political concessions. As the terms get softer and the delays longer, sometimes the loans are quietly written off. Similarly, many major deals involve a mixture of commercial and financial aspects. They require the negotiation of complex offset packages, which may require the seller to arrange investments in the buyer country in sec-

tors totally unrelated to arms, or to purchase from the buyer and
resell completely unrelated goods.[10]

If a sale is made by a country's private (but regulated) arms
manufacturers, the terms of agreement may still be commercial.
Unlike the case of straight state-to-state deals, if a corporation-to-
government transaction involves counter-trade, the arrangements
tend to be multilateral and therefore as much financial as commercial in nature. The seller's government may assist through credit
guarantees to permit lower than market interest rates. At this point
banks enter to handle the arrangements, much as they do with any
form of trade finance. The would-be buyer opens a letter of credit
(LC) at his bank, presents the LC to the seller and the seller cashes
the LC at the seller's bank when and if the terms of the contract are
fulfilled. The seller's bank, in turn, collects from the buyer's bank
according to standard inter-bank settlement procedures. The circle
is closed when the buyer settles accounts with his bank.

When a country (or one of its regulated manufacturers) makes a
covert sale to another state, perhaps in violation of an international
arms embargo, payment may still take commercial form. For example, secret South African oil-for-arms deals with both belligerents
were commonplace during the Iran-Iraq war. Two oil-rich countries, one of which was under an arms embargo, formed natural
covert counter-trade partners for arms-rich South Africa, then under an oil embargo. While legal counter-trade deals often involve
brokers to sell the merchandise, in covert ones, particularly those
involving strategic commodities like oil, the swap is more likely
strictly bilateral. Therefore, there will be no need for bank instruments to change hands.

However, in most covert state-to-state deals financial arrangements predominate, mainly because such payments are easier to
hide. The seller may require secrecy to build up an underground
treasury that can finance future political or military adventures, to
try to hide its assets from international creditors or to attempt to
disguise violations of end-user certification pledges made to its
original arms suppliers. The buyer may need secrecy because it is
violating an embargo or because it wants to keep its neighbours
blissfully unaware of its intentions. In such cases, the payment
flows usually take the form of drawing down a secret foreign bank
balance kept for such purposes or the secret pledge of national gold
reserves against supplier-provided or supplier-guaranteed loans.

The political form of payment used to be dominant, if not exclusive, when a country secretly supplied weapons to an insurgent group. Certainly today some such deals are still political in nature. But with the general commercialisation of the arms market, it is likely most states covertly supplying guerrilla groups will insist on a financial or commercial consideration. That is all the more true to the extent that their military forces run the arms business and have a high degree of autonomy. However, in such deals, the state, to maintain deniability, would usually choose to work through the intermediation of one or several gun-runners. At that point, the payment mechanics become identical to those in straightforward deals between private suppliers and sub-state buyers.[11]

The financial mechanics are more complicated when a manufacturing corporation sells to a black-market customer—usually an embargoed state. The currency will be conventional letters of credit, generally dollar denominated, issued by obliging banks. However, the money will require laundering to disguise the destination of the arms. A letter of credit might be issued by a third-country bank with a perhaps secret correspondent relationship with a bank in the receiving country. It will then be used as security for new letters of credit issued by yet another bank on behalf of a foreign subsidiary of the selling corporation. Such back-to-back letters of credit are often used to disguise the payment trail.[12]

When a private arms merchant sells to an embargoed state, political concessions will rarely, if ever, figure among the payment mechanisms. There may be some scope for counter-trade in basic commodities, but such deals produce additional complications. If a country is subject to international sanctions, it may have trouble raising foreign currency through exports or borrowing abroad. Sometimes it can get around the problem by drawing on secret credits provided by supporters abroad; sometimes it can smuggle some of its goods. In both cases the funds must be laundered and the resulting arms smuggled back. Even if it cannot draw on foreign earnings, all is not lost. The country can still collect revenues through taxation of domestic economic activity. Provided it can also exchange its national currency at a reasonable rate into the foreign exchange (usually US dollars) required for arms purchases, it is then set to use funds that are (by its definition) legitimate, for purposes that are (by other people's definition) illegitimate.

Most deals with embargoed governments, however, will be financial. Payment will therefore take the same form as when a state or primary supplier is the seller—that is, dollar-denominated letters of credit washed through accommodating banks.

If the customers are insurgent groups or warlords, the payment mechanism might well have to change. It is possible that a gun-runner would accept payment in the form of natural resource concessions. Concessions are promises of trade deals or of property and resource rights that can only be realised once the customers have achieved their political objectives.

There have been several instances when such deals might have occurred.[13] For example, when a rebellion ousted Sierra Leone's head of state in 1997, he hired Sandline, a British private security firm. Into Sandline's Gibraltar bank account came payments from a Thai banker who was reimbursed with the promise of mineral concessions when the old government was restored. Payments also came from two Canadian diamond-mining companies that had lost their rights when the government was overthrown. The money was used to buy arms and train paramilitary forces on behalf of the deposed government.[14] Although arms-for-future commercial concessions deals occasionally occur, they are a gamble as a means of payment. Usually a gun-runner will insist on being paid as quickly as possible and, whenever possible, through normal financial instruments.

The Role of Banks in the Black Market

International banks play a number of roles in the underground arms trade. They act as fiduciaries, depositories, fund transmitters, providers of personal and commercial credit and asset managers.

A bank's role in providing trustee services might be important in early negotiations. Sometimes a deal will have two distinct contracts. For security, the 'inner contract' that actually states the terms, including details of payoffs, is stashed in a safety deposit box of a bank, probably in a jurisdiction with tight secrecy laws. Meanwhile an 'outer contract' might, for example, stipulate conditions under which the parties can get access to the 'inner contract' to study its terms, but not to remove the contract from the custody of the bank without explicit authorisation of all of the other parties. It might permit photocopying of the contract, if the party first cuts off any letterheads and signatures. [15]

Another important role is the provision of deposit and transfer facilities for gun-runners and their customers. If a deal requires no credit, the role of the bank is passive. The buyer merely draws down a bank balance and remits payments to the seller's account, perhaps passing them through several intermediary institutions for additional cover.

The bank's role might be more active if the payment mechanics require that the buyer deposit the full sum in an account in advance. In this instance, payments to the seller will be made in instalments as the contract proceeds, with agreed neutral parties (perhaps officers of the bank) determining when sufficient progress has been made.

However, most private-sector arms deals seem to involve the bank actually advancing credit, which might take the form of an open line of credit that can be drawn upon at will. This offer will only be made to favoured customers, whose capacity to repay is unquestioned, as they either have a longstanding relationship with the bank or they have pledged assets to back up the full amount of the credit line. In this instance, the bank can claim no direct involvement with the transaction the customer wishes to finance. More commonly, though, arms deals involve dedicated letters of credit, issued by the buyer's bank and tied to a specific transaction.

Typically, in an underground arms deal, neither side trusts the other, and there is no possible recourse to any legitimate dispute resolution mechanism. It is difficult to take a delinquent gun-runner to court or for the gun-runner to sue the leader of a guerrilla group. A bank LC can be an essential guarantee for both sides. Arms merchants cannot sell unless they can first buy. And suppliers, though perhaps willing to extend credit to a state engaged in a clandestine arms buildup, will usually not provide a private gun trafficker with inventory unless he can show an irrevocable letter of credit to prove that he can back his bid. The gun-runner, in turn, will probably require a letter of credit from his would-be client.[16]

Therefore, the seller provides the potential purchaser with a quote. The buyer must then satisfy himself about the reliability of both product and seller. If satisfied, the buyer has his bank telex the seller's bank, stating that the buyer's bank is willing and able to open a letter of credit for a certain sum, provided certain conditions are met. Preliminary agreement made, the buyer's bank sends an irrevocable LC to the seller's bank. The LC will specify such things as delivery date, the date of manufacture of the material being supplied, the price of the merchandise, and the currency in which payment is being made. (In the arms trade, though the US dollar is the standard unit of account, actual payments might be made in other forms.) It might also stipulate penalties for late or incomplete delivery. In addition, it might require prior to payment signed certificates by approved examiners that the goods are as specified.[17] The seller's bank will cash the LC once certain documents are presented attesting to the existence and condition of the cargo, and its readiness for shipment.

Before that happens, the banks might be required to perform an additional service. The buyer may insist that the seller post a performance bond for a sum of money which is forfeited if the deal is not completed as stipulated in the contract. In this case, the telex sent by the buyer's bank will advise the seller's bank that it stands ready to open a letter of credit once it is in receipt of the performance bond for, say, 5-10% of the value of the deal. The two banks then exchange documents. Upon successful completion, the buyer's bank cashes the LC and the seller's bank voids the performance bond.

Sometimes the bank will be perfectly upfront about what it is doing. It will issue a letter of credit specifying the nature of the transaction, up to and including a price list for all the weapons being moved. In one notorious case in the early 1980s, an Austrian meat broker in league with a West German arms dealer arranged on behalf of South Africa a shipment of East Bloc arms to be transferred to UNITA and RENAMO guerrillas in Angola and Mozambique respectively. After the order was placed by an ARMSCOR (South Africa) front company in Liechtenstein, the Nigerian High Commission in London provided the end-user certificate, backed by a forged affidavit from the British Foreign Office attesting to its veracity. The International Bank of Luxembourg telexed Bulgaria confirming that it would open an irrevocable LC and actually listing the weapons and their prices. The profits, even after bribes and kickbacks, were up to 60%.[18]

In strict theory a letter of credit is not paid unless other documents—certificates of origin and of quality, cargo manifests, insurance policies and the like—are presented along with it. Of them all, the most important is the bill of lading, indicating that the merchandise specified in the LC has been loaded in good order aboard a commercial carrier (usually a merchant ship, though for small, highly specialised or rush orders sometimes a cargo plane). It will also attest that the goods are bound for the port specified by the buyer. Like the LC, the bill of lading in an arms deal will normally misrepresent the nature of the cargo. If the truth is eventually revealed, the misleading bill of lading gives the bank the same sort of alibi a phoney end-user certificate grants a primary supplier.

However a fake bill of lading creates an opportunity for the arms dealer to scam the buyer. The cargo may not exist at all; or it may get diverted *en route* and sold to another customer. The ship itself may be a fiction created by the gun-runner, or it might be sitting in dry dock at the time it is supposed to be chugging towards the port of delivery. In some cases the ship arrives with all documents in order, and the cargo, represented on the LC and bill of lading as bricks or Brylcream, turns out to be … bricks or Brylcream. Ultimately, the cost of such 'fraud' falls on the buyer. For, if the correct documents are presented with the letter of credit, the bank's legal responsibility ends.[19] The seller's bank cashes the LC, and demands payment from the buyer's bank, which must comply. The buyer's bank then seizes any collateral posted by the purchaser.[20]

Even a performance bond is not a full guarantee. It may help assure that proper merchandise is loaded, but it cannot suffice to guarantee that merchandise or ship will ever arrive. Nor will preshipment inspection by parties appointed by the buyer suffice. Hence buyers might insist that an agent of their selection, a 'supercargo,' accompany the shipment. The inclusion of such a person adds extra expense, as well as increasing the risks of information leaking out. Furthermore there is no guarantee that the supercargo will not hatch a deal with the seller to jump ship at the nearest port and head for a comfortable retirement on some tropical paradise. In the final analysis, the ultimate performance bond in the illegal arms business is the seller's own hide.

Offshore Banks and Secrecy Laws

Given the many services required, a gun trafficker must pick a bank carefully. In lurid novels or journalistic accounts, the banks of Switzerland are the sentimental favourites. In fact there are many other candidates. For Belgian companies, it has been common to divert the payment flows through the Luxembourg affiliates of Belgian banks. Bank secrecy laws in Luxembourg are so tight that a bank legally cannot reveal information even if the client requests a waiver. Serbia, anticipating an international freeze, moved the assets it required to bust an arms embargo and other sanctions behind the protective screen of bank and corporate secrecy laws in Cyprus. Liechtenstein is yet another prime choice.

Whether a country is chosen for the honour of having its banks finance an arms deal does *not* depend on that country hosting 'offshore' banks. An offshore bank exists in a regulatory vacuum. It is exempt from its host country's rules regarding interest rates, capital adequacy and liquidity. Offering offshore facilities is something quite different from offering bank secrecy. Bank secrecy laws make it a criminal offence for officials of the bank to reveal information about clients. Switzerland is often regarded as the model for bank secrecy, even though its secrecy laws have in recent years come to resemble Swiss cheese. It has signed memoranda of understanding for the exchange of information, criminalised insider trading and money laundering, abolished the old practice of letting lawyers front for their clients in setting up accounts and frozen the accounts of numerous high-profile depositors—from the Marcos family to Raul Salinas—at the request of foreign investigators. Still, Switzerland continues to offer sufficient secrecy to attract routine tax and exchange control evaders. Yet it is not an offshore centre.

On the other hand, the world's biggest offshore centre is the City of London, where transactions are *not* protected by bank secrecy law. At best, British banks used to offer confidentiality, backed only by the fact that a client could sue the bank in civil court if that confidentiality were breached. But even this degree of protection has been largely eroded by the hysteria over 'drug money' in the last few years.[21]

There are indeed places that offer the services of unregulated offshore banks, and in some cases their operations may also be protected by bank secrecy laws. But they operate largely, if not exclusively, in the wholesale sector. They exist mainly to transmit funds from bank to bank, or to act as artificial booking agents for loans actually made by their parent banks domiciled in major economic centres. Therefore, when a gun-runner needs to negotiate credits, he will normally do so with a domestic bank in a major financial centre, rather than some obscurely named insta-bank in an exotic setting. However, when it comes time to shift the resulting funds to avoid possible search and seizure, the offshore banking system becomes useful. It can zip money from place to place in a series of deposits and withdrawals conducted in the name of a series of shell companies to hide the trail behind multiple layers of banking and corporate secrecy.

One final service banks can provide is the solicitude of their 'private banking' departments, the departments whose job it is to manage the personal assets of what is euphemistically known in the trade as the 'high net-worth individual.' Once a gun-runner has paid off suppliers, settled accounts with the shipping companies and squared away all the officials, fixers and skimmers necessary to grease the deal, it is time to enjoy the profits. At that point the role of a bank is to act as fund manager, handling the gun-runner's balances no differently from those of the tax dodgers, stock-fraud artists, heroin traffickers and cigarette smugglers that make up so much of its private banking department's regular clientele.

Fund-Raising by Insurgents

Although gun-runners prefer to work through normal banking channels, sometimes it is impossible. This is particularly true if their customers are not states, even under embargo, but insurgent groups or warlords in control of bits and pieces of countries. Under these circumstances, the payment mechanism, and even the medium in which payment is made, might well have to change. That is because insurgent financing takes forms that are doubly underground – not only when money is spent, but also when it is raised. Precisely how insurgent groups raise money in turn reflects three things—their degree of international political support, their strategic position *vis-à-vis* the home government and their countries' national wealth endowment.[22]

During the Cold War, external sponsors were usually political in nature. A government would quietly (or not so quietly) provide financial and logistical support money to an insurgent group making trouble for a rival. Although there was a popular misconception, deliberately fed by Western intelligence agencies, that most anti-state insurgencies were a product of a Moscow-based conspiracy, in reality most of the covert financial support provided by the USSR to political dissidents went to Communist parties legally contesting elections.[23] Even China confined its sponsorship of insurgencies to a handful of groups operating in countries on its immediate borders. However, the United States, Britain, France and Saudi Arabia provided a veritable cornucopia of aid to insurgent forces opposing Soviet-backed regimes (see chapter 3). Today, the major powers provide little such aid, while the opportunities for independent fund-raising are far greater.

Even during the Cold War, guerrilla groups raised money independently. Political support for some insurgents, like El Salvador's FMLN, was so open that in Germany solidarity groups raising money actually bore such names as 'Arms for El Salvador.' Ethnic or religious solidarity could also play an important role, as with the Irish in the United States pumping arms and money to the IRA, or the Turkish diaspora in Germany sustaining the Grey Wolves, a proto-fascist pan-Turkic group, back home. As the 1980s wore on and the 1990s dawned, this phenomenon became more widespread. Sikhs in Canada, Croats in Chile, Kosovars in Switzerland, Armenians almost everywhere and many more all raise funds and arrange arms shipments to their co-religionists or ethnic kin.

They do so in two distinct ways. Some of the money is raised from legitimate donors using methods that are legal, even if the money is subsequently diverted to illegal uses. In many cases such donations are even tax deductible. Therefore, part of the burden of financing the insurgency falls on the taxpayers of the country hosting the exile community. In addition, some money is raised through extortion, racketeering and smuggling. Along with the unparalleled expansion of international migration in the last two decades has come the formation of underground trade networks of Kurds, Tamils, Algerians, Kosovars and many others. Spread throughout North America and Europe, these networks are well positioned to smuggle everything from diamonds to designer jeans and from cigarettes to heroin—with some of the profits recycled into arms.

Meanwhile, those on the home front usually evolve their own methods of financing, closely linked to the military stage an insurgency has reached and the resources available in the regions in which the guerrilla group is strongest. In the earliest stage, insurgent organisations usually engage in hit-and-run operations against individual symbols of the state, either officials or isolated institutions like police stations and army outposts. The group's expenditure requirements are relatively small and mainly military. Hence, it can rely on fund-raising activities based on similarly sporadic and predatory actions such as bank robbery and ransom kidnapping—actions that yield not only quick cash, but hard currency.

In the next stage the guerrilla group begins openly disputing the political power of the state, mainly through the conduct of low-intensity warfare against the infrastructure of the formal economy. Confrontations are more intense, and the logistical requirements heavier. The guerrilla group's expenditures are not only much greater in absolute amounts, but also include a rising social security component for the care of dependents of its militants, as well as providing some assistance to the population whose support it is attempting to win. Furthermore, by this point, the group is likely beginning to be concerned about its international standing, and predatory actions, particularly kidnapping, are bad for public relations. Fund-raising, therefore, shifts from predatory operations to parasitic ones that yield a steadier and more dependable flow of income at the expense of the formal economy. The most important will be the 'revolutionary taxation' of income and wealth, sometimes through voluntary action by the donor, more often through pure extortion. While kidnapping yields one-time results, revolutionary taxation can produce an ongoing cash flow.

In the third stage the guerrilla movement succeeds in taking over a piece of territory from which the state is effectively excluded. At this point it may well need to upgrade its arsenal to include material essential to defend its gains. To its previous expenses are added those arising from the provision of social services to the general population of the controlled area, and from the need to build infrastructure necessary for the growth and development of a parallel economy. As a result, fund-raising ceases to be parasitic with respect to the formal economy controlled by the state. Instead it becomes symbiotic with the parallel economy being developed by the insurgent group.

In this advanced stage, the most important sources of revenue come from indirect taxation—sales taxes on domestic commerce and/or export and import taxes on foreign trade. These taxes produce revenues in the form of foreign exchange, which is crucial for tapping into the international arms black market. Taxing the growth and/or transit of 'recreational drugs' has played a role in financing insurgencies almost everywhere in the world. Such fees used to be commonplace among Burmese ethnic factions and some of the better-placed Lebanese paramilitary groups during that country's long civil war, and they remain the most important source of income for Colombia's FARC guerrillas. Income from taxing commodities that are inherently legal—everything from tea to teakwood—is likely much greater, or at least far more wide-spread. Particularly desirable are high-valued items like gemstones or ivory. Across Southeast Asia and sub-Saharan Africa, through-out Central Asia and the Indian subcontinent, this pattern of insur-gencies financed through controlling the export of valuable natural products is repeated.

During the Cold War era, this third stage was usually a prelude to a final assault on the state. However, one of the main things dif-ferentiating many of the current round of insurgent wars from their predecessors is that there is often no incentive to do so. The desir-ability of capturing control of the existing state decreases as ethnic concerns replace more strictly political ones, and as the old state structure gets closer and closer to financial and political bank-ruptcy. Instead, the strategic objective becomes the creation of eco-nomically differentiated and ethnically homogenous mini-states built around control of one or a few major resources. With the guer-rilla group in firm control of a piece of resource-rich territory, its relations with the 'legitimate' business world beyond its borders also change. Corporations will come, quietly, to the guerrilla group seeking deals—protection of current operations and/or future con-cessions—in return for contributions to the cause.

Under such circumstances, which vary widely from place to place and even from time to time in the same place, a gun-runner dealing with a non-state actor may have to accept payment in a number of forms, some unconventional.

If the insurgency has the support of an outside group, payments may take the form of a transfer from the accounts of a registered 'charitable, educational or religious foundation' to the accounts of the gun-runner. From the gun-runner's perspective, this situation is among the most desirable of situations, as payment is assured on delivery, and in hard currency instruments transferred through le-gitimate banks. Alternatively the payment may come from money the exiles have raised from various forms of rackets, and this is a decidedly riskier situation for the gun-runner. Although payment might be offered in a hard currency such as dollars, deutsche marks or Swiss francs, a police investigation into extortion or heroin traf-ficking might by accident also blow the gun-runner's cover.

When payment is accepted from actors on site, there are a num-ber of possible variations: Although over-romanticised, exchanges of guns for gold do sometimes occur. Or the gun trafficker might be offered cash on site, which always entails a risk of counterfeit. If cash payment is made in soft currency, the fair exchange value must be determined. Any currency, no matter how nominally inconvertible and seemingly undesirable, can fetch something on the foreign exchange markets of the big financial centres, especially in the Far East. But the danger here is that the gun-runner might flood a weak market and see the profits on a deal swallowed by a rapidly sinking exchange rate.

Checks drawn on bank accounts in the country where the deal occurs are safer in that respect, though they produce complications of their own. The country likely has exchange controls, and in order to get a permit to convert the local bank balance into hard currency for export, it will be necessary for the trafficker to pretend to be engaged in trading commodities for which the government has chosen to give priority access to limited supplies of foreign exchange.

The gun-runner might decide to engage in counter-trade. However, basic commodities, which are often quite safe when dealing with an embargoed state, are risky when dealing with an insurgent group. Their sheer bulk creates all manner of additional dangers of detection, and, since they can scarcely be sold forward to lock in current values, the world price could shift adversely before they are safely brought to market. Precious items like gemstones are superior in this respect, but it takes a special skill to assess their value. Although arms trade lore abounds with stories of guerrilla bands exchanging rough diamonds for arms, in fact (much as with counter-trade deals in oil) the standard is to work a mixed commercial-financial exchange. Bag-men for the guerrilla groups sell the illegally mined or stolen diamonds to buyers acting for legitimate diamond dealers, who deposit the appropriate sum in the guerrilla group's secret bank account from which arms purchases can be financed. And the diamonds are then resold on the Antwerp exchanges or directly to cutting and polishing centres.

Thus, although a gun-runner may prefer to negotiate a deal using normal bank facilities, there are many alternatives. And even where banks are involved, their role is highly variable depending on the stage a transaction has reached. This reality has important policy implications. At a minimum it must serve to moderate the enthusiasm of those who, inspired by recent changes in narcotics enforcement trends, urge a shift from tracking the traffickers to chasing the money. The rationale behind this shift is a belief that it is more efficient to attack crime by removing the motive (profit) and the means (working capital). The only problem is that such a 'follow the money' strategy has proven to be grossly overblown in drug enforcement, and it is likely to be even more disappointing when imported uncritically into the realm of arms control.

Implications for Arms Control

Arms control policy can be directed at three logically distinct levels. The first and most popular is to attack trafficking—the actual process of intermediation between the supply and demand sides of the market. This approach runs afoul of a number of obstacles. For a start, there is the problem of the growing sophistication of the means of evasion: the proliferation of bank and corporate secrecy havens, free trade zones and flag-of-convenience shipping centres, the democratisation of client lists and the rapid diffusion of information about how to use them. These same global features permit a steady flow of recreational drugs, despite ever harsher laws with ever more countries nominally committed to cooperation and enforcement, and with ever larger budgetary allocations for stopping the drug supply. How, then, to curtail weapons trafficking when laws are vague and inconsistent, and genuine international cooperation is the exception, rather than the rule?

Furthermore, there are glaring asymmetries in national regulations producing a multitude of cracks through which an arms deal can fall. In some cases, these cracks in the system were deliberately created by governments to let certain deals get through.[24] Governments also play games with their own rules, declaring material to have been destroyed in combat or in accidents, and then quietly selling it, or insisting that certain militarily essential components and supplies are really 'non-lethal.'

There are also administrative handicaps. Few countries rigorously check exports. Even in the United States, of about 20,000 employees in the Customs service, some 500 (2.5%) are put to work examining outbound cargoes.[25] The simple rule is that an arms shipment will be intercepted only if there is a tip-off or if the exporter does something particularly foolish to make it stand out.

Yet another, often overwhelming, obstacle is that arms merchants, however profit driven, have proven in too many cases in the past to be working not solely on their own account. Governments, usually through their intelligence services, have long made a practice of deliberately diverting deals to the black market to give themselves deniability. Unless there has been a dramatic wave of internal reform among powerful governments, they can hardly be relied upon to crack down on the movement of arms or on the people—often 'retired' spies—who move them. Veteran intelligence operatives from the former East Bloc countries numbered among the most prominent suppliers in the Balkan wars, and much of the material originated in state inventories.

In any case, law is irrelevant unless the will and the means exist to enforce it. Lacking those, the main impact of harsher laws will be more to permit officials to extract higher bribes rather than to reduce the international flow of arms. Nor should it be forgotten that the enormous stocks of weapons accumulated in present and former zones of conflict are quite beyond the control of any government, even one zealously committed to arms control.

Not least of the problems with attacking trafficking, if gunrunners get caught, they are easy to replace. Indeed, it could be argued that the result of any success of enforcement in the short run makes the problem worse in the long run. In almost any black market, the response to regulatory pressure is to increase the number of intermediaries, reduce the size of each load and find more circuitous means of moving the merchandise, while the overall market continues to serve its clients much as before. Contrary to the fantasies of police and regulators, illegal markets are not structured and hierarchical, under the control of great crime 'cartels.' Instead they are anarchic and diffused, and underground entrepreneurs come and go. Rather than deferring to orders from the local godfather, they engage in a series of ad hoc arms-length commercial transactions with each other.[26]

Critique of 'follow the money' approach

Precisely because it has proven so difficult to stanch the flow of arms by focusing on the actual trafficking, some have suggested shifting attention to the resulting flow of money, removing the profit and the means for further crimes by seizing and forfeiting the 'proceeds.' Applied to arms control, such proposals range from subjecting weapons traffickers to anti-money laundering laws, to forcing the opening of bank-secrecy havens and freezing the assets of known weapons traffickers.

This 'follow the money' approach, which has been applied to drug trafficking, has succeeded in recent years in subverting the

traditional presumption in favour of financial privacy and clutter-
ing national financial systems with reporting regulations of dubious efficacy without any measurable effect on the volume or price
of recreational drugs. Particularly in the United States, where the
follow-the-money strategy first developed and from where it has
spread across the globe, such an approach to crime control has led
to all manner of prosecutorial abuses and helped turn police forces
into self-financing bounty-hunting organisations. Yet the United
States continues to be the world's most lucrative market for criminal goods and services.[27]

Contrary to the hopes entertained by law enforcement officials
that tracing financial flows will provide a technological magic bul-
let, the great majority of crimes will continue to be solved by old-
fashioned police work—cops pounding the pavement, laboriously
sifting evidence, cultivating informants and, from time to time, just
getting plain lucky. If the proceeds-of-crime approach pays such
poor dividends with 'regular' crime, then with arms trafficking—
where states and their intelligence services are often complicit, and
where the commodity itself is often legal—there is even less chance
of such a strategy having a significant impact.

For one thing, banks can only report to the authorities what they
know. In an arms deal, the bank itself probably has no useful
knowledge of what is going on unless it is actively involved in offering dedicated letters of credit. Even then, phoney documents to
disguise the nature of the transaction have long been standard procedure. Furthermore banks enter the process in different ways at
different times. One bank may issue credit, with or without knowledge of what is really being negotiated; another may merely
transmit payments from one party to another; others may wire
funds from place to place at the behest of one party; and yet another may simply act as financial manager for profits derived from
it knows not where.

Law enforcement often points its finger at the supposed barrier
to investigation posed by bank secrecy laws. This claim is exagger-
ated. There are many degrees of bank secrecy, and most present little obstacle to bona fide law enforcement. Mutual legal assistance
treaties and Memoranda of Understanding permit states to waive
bank secrecy and to exchange information. Even where secrecy is
extremely tight on paper, the key to penetrating it is usually no
more complicated than a $100 bill. Precisely for that reason, it has
long been an adage among users of foreign banks for illicit pur-

poses that real bank secrecy comes not from legislation but from
keeping one's mouth shut—and working where possible using
multiple or false passports as identification. Under those circumstances, a bank in New York open to the full force of the law can be
just as effective, and just as discrete, as one in Nauru protected by
all manner of legal barriers to information flows.

Secrecy is aided by the fact that, in the gun-running trade, discretion is a proverb, not only with respect to one's own business,
but everyone else's. By an unwritten but well-respected code, gun-
runners, however anxious to cut each other's commercial throats,
will not rat out each other the way drug dealers routinely do. Even
if the gun trafficker is a regular informant to the intelligence services, those services in turn typically have a circumspect relationship
to law enforcement. Intelligence agencies are often deeply implicated in committing many of the crimes law enforcement agencies
are trying to combat.

Finally, even if a country through which a gun-runner's money
has passed stands prepared to cooperate in chasing the proceeds of
gun trafficking, the techniques of effective laundering are now so
well known that only the most incompetent or unlucky person will
be caught. The occasional gun-runner might lose his bank balance,
provided it is in a jurisdiction that is actually accessible to law enforcement, but as long as there are stocks of weapons for sale and
enthusiastic users ready and able to buy, intermediaries will always
be quickly replaceable.[28]

None of this is meant to imply that the 'free market' should
simply be left to work its magic in distributing the world's weapons stockpiles to ready and willing users. Rather, it is a warning
that conventional crime control tactics biased towards attacking
intermediation fail in dealing with crime derived purely from individual greed, and it would be unwise to expect greater results
when these same tactics are applied to acts in which at least one
level of participants have profoundly political motivations. Moreover, the more energy and resources that are put into actions that
inevitably yield low results, the greater the ability of politicians to
avoid more serious actions that might involve real political risks.

Critique of supply-side approaches

Supply-side control initiatives are also liable to critique. The
supply side can be subdivided into primary (production of new

equipment), secondary (distribution of old stocks) and tertiary (dispersion of arms into the hands of the 'end-user' population) levels. On all three levels the obstacles to control are formidable.

For decades governments in the West used military expenditure as the central instrument for spurring their economies in times of recession. They would increase the productive capacity of the arms industry and, with it, the flow of new weaponry. In spite of the loss of the legitimisation formerly provided by the Cold War, economic pressure on politicians to maintain elevated levels of military spending has persisted. Since today's primary flows of weapons are tomorrow's stocks, the longer high levels of military spending continue at home, the larger will be the eventual secondary stock of weapons abroad.

This reality has been exacerbated by the fact that, unlike the situation just after the two world wars, conversion today is difficult. The reasons are partly technical and partly commercial— namely the absence among arms producers of a corporate culture and infrastructure for success in the civil sector. Nor has there been any evidence of governments' willingness to provide sufficient funds to cover the enormous overhead costs of conversion. Failing any broad commitment to industrial restructuring, the only result of reducing domestic expenditures for arms procurement will be arms manufacturers pushing export sales all the harder. They will then run up against competition from a host of other eager producers. For many developing countries, stimulating weapons production is a deliberate tool of industrial development.[29] And for former Communist countries arms export is often the most immediately viable source of desperately needed foreign exchange.

This problem is made worse by the fact that in many countries the military has its own budget, quite distinct from that of the state. It might get tax exemptions and guaranteed subsidies, or even an assured cut of export revenues. Militaries run their own businesses, military-related and civilian, legal and illegal. Therefore, even if arms production is running at a loss, the military can use the profits from other businesses, or from various kinds of rackets, to subsidise the weapons industry.

Even if industrial and industrialising economies could be weaned from their addiction to war industries for jobs, technical change and money, and even if the political and financial autonomy of their armed forces could be curbed, that is not enough. Effective supply-side control also requires addressing the problem of accumulated stocks. Each time an army upgrades, whether through strategic necessity or simply greed of purchasing officials, it sells off its old stock. Since the rate of psychological obsolescence in formal armies is higher than the rate of technical obsolescence on the second-hand market, the result is that the stockpile keeps growing. The current glut, compounded by the growing ease with which upgrading services can be obtained, means that even if primary flows fall temporarily below the rate of physical depreciation, there will be plenty of secondary stock to fuel conflicts well into the future. Even if sheer logistics were not enough to defeat any effort to remove from the market the accumulated stocks of weapons, the cost would be prohibitive.

Furthermore, no supply-side control can be truly effective without addressing the dispersion of arms into the hands of the population at large, particularly in areas subject to insurgencies and civil breakdown. Efforts can be made to do so through increased policing. But rarely, if ever, in the face of a pressing need for the weapons, have repressive tactics had much success. The alternative is buy-backs and amnesties to encourage the voluntary handing in to the authorities of illegal weapons already acquired. These approaches work sometimes in countries where the state has both power and legitimacy. But outside those narrow borders, the record of success is spotty and geographically very limited. All too often only junk is handed in. If payment is made, it might well be recycled back into buying even better arms. Furthermore, the most dangerous elements in society, those most prone to using their weapons, are the least likely to surrender their weapons.

This tertiary form of supply-side control ultimately bumps up against the three most basic lessons of the arms black market. One is the fact that the arms supply business is subject to the law of entropy: the further the material moves away from the primary source and the greater the degree of dispersal, the greater the problems of putting the process in reverse. The second is that arms are durable goods: the economics of control for a flow of new products are radically different and far simpler than the economics of control for a second-hand stock of durable goods. The third is that the product is not a consumer good, but a capital good: it is demanded not for what it is, but for what it will do. Therefore, illicit weapons will remain in demand until the underlying conditions that created the demand disappear. Since the market for illegal weapons is driven from the demand side, it is to that side that the primary efforts at arms control should be directed.

Need for demand-side approaches

Demand-side controls can take three forms. One, which compliments the repressive form of tertiary-supply-side control, is to mete out increasingly severe punishment for unauthorised possession. This strategy has historically done little besides raise the profits garnered from satisfying repressed demand. It also raises the question, rarely addressed by arms control advocates, of whether in all cases it is justifiable to try to disarm populations without guaranteeing the legitimacy of the governments under which they live.

The second is to attack the capacity to buy. Today economic sanctions are imposed not just on 'rogue states,' but even on insurgent groups in control of a piece of territory, creating the interesting situation where the international community attempts to deny political legitimacy to a group through an act that implicitly confers political recognition. Time after time the main result of economic sanctions has been to starve the population at large and ruin the civil economy, while the elite siphon off yet more national resources and divert them to paying inflated arms bills.[30]

The third way in which demand-side controls can work is to recognise that arms are a capital good, demanded not for their own sake (except by a handful of oddball collectors), but for what they will accomplish. In all too many cases the demand for weapons is ultimately a surrogate for the demand for social justice. Therefore to reduce demand directly requires addressing squarely the real causes of violent conflict, of which the most important is the prevailing maldistribution of income, wealth and ecological capital. In the final analysis, the most effective way to attack the economy of weapons production and the infrastructure for arms distribution is to render the weapons that do exist irrelevant.

Notes

[1] The author would like to thank the John D. and Catherine T. MacArthur Foundation of Chicago and the Social Sciences and Humanities Research Council of Canada for financial support of the research that permitted the writing of this chapter. For an earlier analysis of the arms black market, see

R. T. Naylor, 'Loose Cannons: Covert Commerce and Underground Finance in the Modern Arms Black Market' in *Crime, Law & Social Change*, Vol. 22, 1995.

2 William Hartung, *And Weapons For All* (New York: Harper-Collins, 1994) p. 255.

3 A superlative examination of this process in Saudi Arabia is provided by Said Aburish, *The Rise, Corruption and Coming Fall of the House of Saud* (New York: St. Martin's Press, 1994).

4 George Thayer, *The War Business* (New York: Simon & Schuster, 1969), p. 129.

5 Running electoral slush funds through offshore accounts of brokers did not prevent corruption scandals from rocking the military and political establishments of Thailand, Taiwan and South Korea in the early 1990s. In addition, corruption scandals related to arms deals plagued India's late Rajiv Gandhi, Belgium's Willy Claes and—most recently—Germany's Helmut Kohl. For summaries of some of the more notorious recent scandals, see R. T. Naylor, *Patriots & Profiteers* (Toronto: McClelland & Stewart, 1999), chapters 16, 17 and 20.

6 Hartung, *And Weapons for All*, p. 268.

7 One especially interesting example of the use of such cut-outs is when an Israeli gun-runner using phoney Bolivian end-user certificates acquired Bulgarian arms for Croatia during the Balkan wars of the early 1990s. See Peter Fuhrman, 'Trading in Death,' *Forbes*, 10 May 1993.

8 Legitimate cargo provides physical cover for the weapons and serves as a device for laundering the ensuing payments. An excellent exposition of gun-running in practice that details this practice is Ragnar Benson, *Gun-running For Fun and Profit* (Boulder, Colorado: Loompanics, 1986).

9 Russia, for example, accepted from Malaysia palm oil in payment for past debts and new arms, transferred at a cut rate to allow Russia to break into a traditionally Anglo-American market. China sold aircraft and parts to the Sudan, taking payment partially in cotton, gum arabica, sesame seeds, corn, camels and meat, and partially in long-term credits. Taiwan immediately followed suit, setting up the 'Islamic Oriental Establishment' to give millions to the Sudan which could be used for arms. See *Far Eastern Economic Review*, 14 December 1995.

10 Ronald Matthews, 'Butter for guns: the growth of under-the-counter trade,' *The World Today*, May 1992; Grant Hammond, *Countertrade, Offsets and Barter in International Trade* (London: Pinter, 1990).

11 See chapter 3 for more on state-sponsored gun-running to insurgents.

12 The payment mechanics are analysed in *Euromoney*, October 1990.

13 On diamond concessions granted by UNITA in Angola for weapons procurement, see *Report of the Panel of Experts on Violations of Security Council Sanctions Against UNITA*, UN Doc. S/2000/203, 10 March 2000.

[14] *Jane's Intelligence Review*, 21 August 1997 and 1 September 1997; *Evening Standard*, 8 August 1997; private communication.

[15] *The Independent*, 16 October 1994; Paul Halloran and Mark Hollingsworth, *Thatcher's Gold: The Life and Times of Mark Thatcher* (London: Simon & Schuster, 1995) p. 218.

[16] Benson, *Gunrunning For Fun and Profit*, p. 11.

[17] Robert Turp, *Gunrunner: the Confessions of an Arms Dealer* (London: W. H. Allen, 1972) recounts a sale to India when he was offered—and refused—a letter of credit drawn on the State Bank of India. To clinch the deal, they had to find another, guaranteed neutral bank to guarantee the LC.

[18] *Globe and Mail* (Toronto), 1 May 1984.

[19] As one London-based banker commented, 'I have no sherrif's badge when acting as a banker.' *Middle East*, December 1983.

[20] See, for example, Godfrey Hodgson, *Lloyd's Of London: A Reputation at Risk* (London: Viking, 1986) p. 175; and Hermann Moll and Michael Leapman, *Broker Of Death* (London: MacMillan, 1988), pp. 30-31.

[21] See Mike Levi, 'Regulating Money Laundering: The Death of Bank Secrecy in the UK,' *The British Journal of Criminology*, Vol. 31, No. 2 (1991).

[22] These issues are examined in depth in R. T. Naylor, 'The Insurgent Economy: Black Market Operations of Guerrilla Groups,' *Crime, Law & Social Change*, Vol. 20 (1993).

[23] For the hysterical, Moscow-directed plot hypothesis, see Claire Sterling, *The Terror Network* (New York: Holt, Rhinehart and Winston, 1981).

[24] The opinion of the managing director of Sam Cummings' Interarms Co expressed in *Business Week*, 29 December 1986.

[25] The result is that in the United States in 1992, for example, Customs managed 500 convictions for smuggling narcotics into the country and 21 for illegally moving weapons out. (Deborah Lutterbeck, 'License to Deal,' *Common Cause Magazine*, Summer 1994.)

[26] On this confusion and its consequences, see R. T. Naylor, 'Mafias, Myths and Markets: the Theory and Practice of Enterprise Crime,' *Transnational Organized Crime*, Vol. 3, No. 3 (1997).

[27] For an examination of the 'proceeds' strategy, see R. T. Naylor, 'Wash-Out: A Critique of Follow-the-Money Methods in Crime Control Policy,'*Crime, Law & Social Change*, forthcoming Summer 2000.

[28] For an examination of the mechanisms of modern money laundering, see Jack A. Blum, Michael Levi, R. T. Naylor, and Phil Williams, *Financial Havens, Banking Secrecy And Money-Laundering* (Vienna: United Nations Office of Drug Control and Crime Prevention, 1998).

[29] See chapter 4 for more on local licensed production of weapons.

[30] This is the main theme of R. T. Naylor, *Patriots & Profiteers*.

part 4
FORWARD
STEPS_____

8/Combating Arms Trafficking: Progress and Prospects

by Sarah Meek

Previous chapters have well illustrated the ease and complexity with which the black market in arms operates today. Each step of an illegal arms deal, however, represents an opportunity for law enforcement or other officials to uncover the broader picture and de-rail the transaction. Therefore, to maximise possibilities of success, effective action against arms trafficking needs to address all of the aspects previously raised—the sources of weapons, methods of transport, false documentation and other forms of official corruption, issues fuelling demand and payment mechanisms. Underlying any such efforts, of course, is a need for sincere political will by governments to tackle this issue.

Pushed by investigative journalists and nongovernmental activists, policymakers around the world have recently begun to target each of these links in the chain—albeit with varying degrees of seriousness. Thus, at the beginning of 2000 dozens of unilateral, bilateral, regional and global initiatives are underway to help countries reduce the likelihood that their territory will be used for criminal gun-running activities. Many of these efforts are related to, or drawing from, approaches being taken to prevent other types of trafficking, including those of drugs, women, children and endangered species.

Remedial actions are needed at all levels. The national arena is key since domestic and international law are, for the most part, actually enforced by states. And it is important to note that governments in the North as well as in the South, and in the West as well as the East, all need to strengthen their national laws and practices with regard to weapons production, export and brokering. In addition, regional efforts are important to bring all states up to a similar level of understanding and capacity, so that criminals will not simply exploit some countries' weak laws and practices against stronger ones in neighbouring states. And, as cross-border trade increases and criminal organisations operate transnationally, effective international cooperation and agreed norms are imperative.

A critical first step in control efforts has been the development and harmonisation of legal frameworks to combat illicit traffic. Gaining greater agreement among countries as to what types of sales can be considered legal makes it easier to identify what is illegal (for example, if all countries agree not to supply weapons to an embargoed country, weapons that appear in that country can be deduced to be illegally trafficked). Not surprisingly, it is easier to develop consensus around those sales that are clearly black-market transactions, for example the supply of arms to a country under a UN-mandated arms embargo or to a well-known violent criminal organisation. Reaching broad agreement on how to restrict grey-market deals, like covert arms supply by one state to insurgents in another, becomes more elusive.

This chapter examines the practical effect of ongoing efforts to stem the illegal arms trade, first at the national, then regional, and finally at the global level. As many of these initiatives are quite nascent, and in many cases still being negotiated, much of this analysis is necessarily prescriptive.

Approaches to Curtailing Trafficking

In addition to guns and drugs, many other illicit commodities are frequently trafficked, including currency, cars, women, children and endangered species. Various efforts to stem these trades over the years have focused on the suppliers of the commodities, the users and the ways in which the commodities and their proceeds are moved and stored. The following common objectives have been derived as necessary for combating all types of trafficking:

- establishment of adequate national laws and regulations to criminalise offences related to trafficking;
- effective national law enforcement of these provisions;
- international intelligence and law enforcement cooperation to assist in enforcement of these provisions;

- curbs on money laundering;
- restrictions on corporate shells and front companies; and
- measures to address the more difficult factors that perpetuate demand.

Efforts to curb illegal drug trafficking receive the lion's share of attention and resources. In 1995 US citizens spent an estimated \$48 billion on cocaine and heroin.[1] The US government, which has identified drug trafficking as 'one of the greatest threats to Americans and their communities,'[2] spent \$15 billion on drug control activities in 1997. These activities included research and development, law enforcement, demand reduction, interdiction and international programmes.[3] Several other countries have also declared 'war on drugs,' although not generally as militantly as has the United States.

While industrialised countries are affected by the problem of drugs, they are seldom the main suppliers. Efforts to reduce supply, therefore, have often been directed outwards, towards the countries in Asia and Latin America that produce the drugs, and at stopping their importation into the United States.

Arms trafficking, by comparison, commands little of the industrialised states' resources. Rarely do those countries with the strongest laws and greatest enforcement capacity face significant illegal arms importation. Rather, these countries are often the suppliers of weapons, while the recipients reside in countries too poor to put in place the comprehensive controls necessary to prevent their exploitation by arms traffickers.[4] This disparity in the availability and application of resources demonstrates the tremendous need for strong international support to countries suffering under the direct impact of arms trafficking.

Fortunately, many efforts aimed at combating other types of trafficking will also serve to inhibit gun-running. For example, efforts to combat money laundering promote control of the illegal gun traffic, as well as of illegal narcotics and other illicit commodities. In addition, improved information sharing among law enforcement and customs officials, increased bank transparency and better detection and interdiction techniques benefit efforts to control the illegal trade in cars, people, currency, arms and drugs alike.

Yet gun-running also poses some distinct challenges, and governments need to focus sustained attention and adequate resources on efforts to curb this traffic. The threat posed by illicit arms trade first emerged recognisably within the Americas in the context of drug networks, and the nexus between the illegal trade in drugs and arms became the focus of early control efforts. It was also recognised that the illegal trade in arms had some unique features, and so the two processes, while advancing in parallel, were kept distinct.[5] In other regions, control efforts centred around the negative impact of the free circulation of arms on war and peace. From Europe to Southeast Asia, Africa and South America, the overabundance of weapons appears to prolong conflicts, drive up armed crime and threaten democratic governance.[6]

Beyond simply recognising this new problem, governments began to respond in the later part of the 1990s. Initial efforts were largely focused on national concerns. Later, however, as the regional dynamics of illegal weapons trade were better realised, regional and international cooperation increased. Today, in Europe, the Americas and parts of Africa, regional frameworks and conventions are in place in an effort to reduce illicit arms trafficking. And, at the international level, almost every agency within the United Nations has been drawn into identifying ways of preventing arms trafficking.

To address effectively the scope of illicit arms trafficking, efforts need to occur in parallel within countries and regions, while being complemented by international momentum. Ideally, each level of effort would reinforce and support what is happening elsewhere. To some degree such complementarity has occurred, although less perfectly than desired.

National Efforts

Without the creation and implementation of effective national controls, little meaningful action to curtail arms trafficking can occur. The focus of national efforts vary, depending on a country's assessment of the principal threats posed by these weapons and by the approaches available to it to combat these threats.

Contrary to other current security threats, which tend to be more narrowly confined, weapons trafficking affects almost all countries in the world—to a greater or lesser degree. A useful typology is to think of countries as either the suppliers of weapons, transit countries or demand countries.[7] In many instances, a country can fit into two or even all three categories. For example, South Africa is not only a producer of arms, but it is also affected by weapons passing through its lax ports of entry to other destinations, and it faces a seemingly unlimited demand for new weapons. Since 1996 South African citizens have made an average of 200,000 applications for new firearms each year.[8]

States that allow the civilian possession of firearms, have domestic arms production and are also exporters of arms face the greatest challenges in controlling gun-running. As discussed in previous chapters, each of these factors can feed into the illicit market in weapons, and each requires its own method of control.

Many national governments have recently embarked on specific efforts to reduce arms trafficking. These efforts include reviewing existing or implementing new legislation to control the ownership and use of firearms by individuals; improving legislation on export controls; prioritising tracing weapons seized from criminals; cracking down on suspect gun dealers; drafting legislation to control arms brokering; and destroying stocks of weapons surplus to national needs. Some of the states recently taking these steps include Australia, Brazil, Mexico, Hungary, Poland, South Africa, the United Kingdom and the United States.[9]

Others, however, still have yet to respond demonstrably to the weapons trafficking from and within their national jurisdiction. There are two main reasons for this lack of response: either a government is reluctant to address the issue due to ignorance or a lack of political will to take action; or the government is simply unable to respond and control the movement of goods across its borders.[10] The latter problem is the more conducive to amendment, and regional and global initiatives to assist these countries are underway and will be discussed in following sections.[11]

A closer look at one national case brings into focus the many difficulties a government faces when trying to combat arms trafficking on its own. Mexico has long had a strict gun control policy in place: Mexican law bars civilian ownership of any gun larger than .22-caliber, requires a permit before purchase, mandates the registration of firearms with the Ministry of Defence and bans carrying weapons in public. Although Mexico has produced military-style assault rifles under license from European gun manufacturers, it does not make or sell weapons approved for the general population.

Efforts to regulate guns, however, have suffered from the laxity of US domestic gun sales policies just across the long border. Individual and/or organised traffickers have often found it easy to purchase guns in the United States, often legally, and then bring them across the border illegally.[12] During 1995-1996, Mexican police seized 24,000 illegal firearms and asked the United States for assistance in tracing over 4000 weapons used in drug-related crime.[13] Many of these weapons are believed to be connected to larger criminal cartels involved in smuggling drugs and people.

While the Mexican government had long requested US assistance in preventing the easy trafficking of arms across the common border, it was through the OAS convention (discussed below) that bilateral cooperation opened up most dramatically. After signing the convention in 1997, the two governments in February 1998 established a High Level Contact Group for Drug Control, which includes cooperation on firearms tracing.

According to a November 1999 report of the Contact Group, the two governments continue to improve their ability to trace seized weapons through new procedures and better training. The US Bureau of Alcohol, Tobacco and Firearms completed 1344 of 1948 tracing requests between February and November 1999, of which 700 proved to originate in the United States.[14] This reality shows that Mexico can not go it alone in combating arms trafficking. However, Mexico also replaced 1972 legislation with a new federal law in 1999 that clamps down on possession of illegal firearms and criminalises possession of illegal firearms or ammunition.[15]

States have increasingly found that regional approaches are necessary to address factors present in illicit arms trafficking that cannot be controlled nationally, such as lax regulation of firearms, the presence of multinational criminal organisations or armed conflict in neighbouring countries.

Increasing Regional Cooperation

The complex and 'borderless' nature of illicit arms trafficking has prompted coordinated regional action. Such efforts have proven to be the most successful approaches to date, in areas as diverse as Southern Africa, West Africa, Europe and the Americas. While almost all regional organisations, including the North Atlantic

Treaty Organisation (NATO), the Organisation for Security and Co-operation in Europe (OSCE) and the 54-member Common- wealth have issued statements endorsing the need for work on small arms, the focus in this section is on regional organisations that have specifically prioritised illicit trafficking of weapons within their regions and have taken or are developing concrete measures to prevent arms smuggling.

The Organisation of American States (OAS), the European Un- ion (EU), the Economic Community of West African States (ECOWAS) and the Southern African Development Community (SADC) have, over the past five years, all prioritised common ap- proaches—suited to regional concerns and needs—to dealing with light weapons. The measures concluded thus far have focused variously on violent crime, conflict or drug trafficking, and they have all tended to put the building of common capacity within law enforcement, customs and other government departments at the top of the list of priorities.

Not surprisingly, regional groupings have been able to move forward more quickly on identifying common approaches to illicit arms than have global bodies. It is easier for regions with common problems to devise applicable solutions than it is for all the mem- bers of the United Nations to agree to common solutions to dif- fering problems and realities. However effective solutions are within regions, it is equally important that measures at the global level continue to evolve, since arms migrate from region to region as easily as from state to state.

The Americas

The illicit traffic in firearms first appeared on the radar of the OAS in 1990, in the context of its relationship to drug trafficking.[16] Momentum around the issue resulted in the negotiation in 1997 of the Inter-American Convention against the Illicit Manufacturing of and Trafficking in Firearms, Ammunition, Explosives and Other Related Material.[17] The convention entered into force in 1998, and as of February 2000 ten of the thirty-one signatories had ratified the treaty. These states are: Bahamas, Belize, Bolivia, Brazil, Ecua- dor, El Salvador, Mexico, Nicaragua, Panama and Peru. Two of the main backers of the treaty, the United States and Canada, have not yet ratified the agreement.

The convention is the first of its kind, and it is remarkable that it was negotiated in only seven months. The purposes of the agreement are 'to prevent, combat and eradicate the illicit manufacturing of and trafficking in firearms, ammunition, explosives and related materials' and 'to promote and facilitate cooperation and exchange of information and experience.' The six main provisions are:

- development of a harmonised system of licensing for the export, import and transit of weapons;
- a requirement that firearms be marked at the time of manufacture;
- a requirement that states put in place legislation to make the illicit manufacture and traffic in firearms a criminal offence;
- an exchange of information on legislation and national practice, known smugglers, smuggling routes and methods used for concealing and detecting firearms, ammunition and explosives;
- cooperation between law enforcement agencies in the hemisphere; and
- provision of technical assistance and training for states in the region.[18]

The most important feature of the convention is that it is legally binding. The provisions requiring regulation and control over legal firearms and arms transfers should effectively diminish the ability of traffickers to exploit a weak rule of law in Western Hemisphere countries. In addition, the treaty is particularly strong in four areas.

First, it includes a broad definition of both the goods to be controlled (in this case arms) and of 'trafficking.' The fullest possible widely agreed definition of terminology is an important consideration in the fight against arms trafficking.

Second, the agreement makes important gains in the area of documentation. By requiring standard export, import and transit licenses, the convention begins to close one loophole frequently exploited by traffickers. The Model Regulations, which complement the convention, provide the technical information to be included in these licenses and the standard format they should follow.

Third, the convention promotes capacity building and assistance. Noting that traffickers will work to exploit countries with weak legislation and enforcement, it sets out measures to provide training, assistance, and information sharing on smuggling routes and methods, and requires the criminalisation of arms trafficking offences—all important to limit the space within which traffickers can operate.

Fourth, by requiring that firearms be marked at manufacture and by putting in place standard licensing procedures, the convention helps regulate the legal trade in arms. An important factor in the Model Regulations is that they suggest in-transit licences, so that any shipment crossing a third country will need authorisation from that country. The Model Regulations also suggest that no amendments be allowed on a licence. If a licence is changed, it is invalidated.

The Model Regulations, negotiated separately from the convention but also within the OAS, are an important part of the approach to combating firearms trafficking in the Americas.[19] The regulations are not binding on states. Rather, they give detailed information on preparation and issuance of export, import and in-transit documentation, information on authentication of certificates and responsibilities of members for record keeping, information sharing and steps to be taken if an irregularity is noted on a commercial firearms shipment. The Model Regulations simplify the process of certification and make it possible for countries to issue common certificates. This system should reduce fraudulent certification of arms shipments and make fraudulent documentation more easily identifiable.

One criticism of the agreement is its relatively narrow scope. The convention does not address the broader issues that arise from the proceeds of criminal activity in arms trafficking nor the individuals involved in the process of arms trafficking. These facets need attention to combat arms trafficking effectively. Nor does it address the more difficult area of non-commercial arms transfers; arms exports negotiated directly by governments—often considered military assistance—do not fall under the jurisdiction of this agreement.

Moreover, as with all agreements, the biggest challenge for the convention lies in its implementation. Most countries in the region seem committed to the principles of the convention, but their ability—financially and politically—to enact necessary measures to comply with the agreement remains less clear.

The first hurdle is ratification by more states. Legislative processes have taken longer than anticipated in many countries, including Canada and the United States. Nevertheless, the United States has publicly adopted the Model Regulations into its regulatory system and, as a result of the as yet unratified convention, ended unlicensed firearms exports to Canada in 1999. Other states that did not already have in place specific legislation on arms export controls have had to enact legislation to criminalise offences, as required by the convention, prior to being able to ratify it. Even for some countries that have ratified the agreement, it is unclear whether on-the-ground realities have changed significantly as a result of required legislative and regulatory changes.

In March 2000, the ten states that had ratified the convention met for the first session of the Consultative Committee, the body that will serve as the forum for information exchange and improving cooperation for tracing the illegal movement of firearms.[20] However, without the participation of the United States and Canada, the two states most able to provide direct financial and technical assistance, the level of practical assistance that will derive from the Consultative Committee process is in question. To date, while they await ratification, the US and Canadian governments are relying on direct bilateral cooperation and assistance in firearms tracing rather than utilising the mechanisms within the convention. Meanwhile, having signed the convention, both are apparently abiding by its provisions.

Despite its limitations and lack of proven efficacy (due to its recent enactment and limited ratification), the convention is regarded as a success by the OAS and countries in the region. The Mexican government stated that the number of weapons it confiscated has doubled since the convention was signed. The United States, meanwhile, has increased its cooperation and training assistance in weapons tracing and identification to customs and police officials in the region, including most notably Mexico and Jamaica.[21]

Southern Africa

Southern Africa is experiencing a different set of serious problems with the illicit arms trade. Unlike in the Americas, where the link is principally to drug trafficking, in this part of the world the impetus for regional action is the effect illegal weapons have on

crime, conflict and stability. Significantly, in recent years Southern
African states have begun to marshal the political will necessary to
take effective action against arms trafficking. In addition, by prioritising the issue within the context of regional crime, and especially
the growing threat of transnational organised crime, countries
have been able to develop a constructive framework for specific
actions to tackle it.

In cooperation with the European Union, in 1998 the Southern
African Development Community (SADC) endorsed the Southern
African Regional Action Programme on Light Arms and Illicit
Arms Trafficking.[22] This programme sets out steps to be taken to
combat arms proliferation in four keys areas:

- combating illicit trafficking, including strengthening laws and
  regulations, strengthening operational capacity and improving
  information exchange and systems to trace illicit arms flows;
- strengthening regulation and controls on accumulations and
  transfers of arms, including controls over civilian possession of
  firearms, controls over arms transfers and improved capacity to
  monitor and trace arms possession and transfers;
- promoting the removal of arms from society and the destruction of surplus arms, including voluntary weapons collection
  programmes and the destruction of surplus military weapons;
  and
- enhancing transparency, information and consultations on arms
  in the region.[23]

The Action Programme has led to increased regional cooperation
within the SADC and the Southern African Regional Police Chiefs
Co-ordinating Organisation (SARPCCO). In July 1999 SARPCCO
adopted a declaration that stated:

> among the issues which will be considered [by SARPCCO] are
> prohibitions on civilian possession of automatic and military
> weapons; co-ordination of procedures for the import, export and
> transit of small arms shipments, ensuring the registration of
> small arms in a country, and, where appropriate, ensuring that
> proper controls be exercised over the manufacture of small arms
> to prevent their entrance into the illicit market; to promote the
> destruction of surplus arms.[24]

This declaration was followed by the initiation of negotiations on a regional protocol on illicit firearms trafficking, to complement the global protocol being negotiated in the United Nations. A draft of the regional agreement was circulated among SARPCCO members in February 2000, and it is expected to be completed in late 2000 or early 2001. The protocol will set out legislative requirements and common practice within the subregion for reducing trafficking.

This protocol is an important first step in making operational the programme of action, which to date has not resulted in many projects under its aegis. In part, this inaction has been due to a preoccupation among countries in the region with other security concerns (including the penetration of organised criminal groups into the subregion and the war in the Congo), combined with a lack of clarity between recipient countries and EU donor states on fundable projects.

As with the OAS convention, too little time has passed to allow an assessment of the real impact of the regional programme of action and related activities. Especially in the case of Southern Africa, where the degree to which countries are affected by arms trafficking varies greatly, it may be difficult to sustain current motivation for action. In addition to completion of the regional protocol, another important way to sustain focus and enthusiasm is to build on successful joint operations that have been conducted within SADC—both on illicit arms (such as the joint weapons destruction operations between Mozambique and South Africa, known as 'Operations Rachel') and on other types of trafficking, including commodity and vehicle smuggling.[25]

West Africa

West African governments have also identified weapons flows as contributing to insecurity and armed conflict in their region. In October 1998 the 16 heads of states belonging to the Economic Community of West African States (ECOWAS) signed a Moratorium on the Exportation, Importation and Manufacture of Light Weapons. The entire declaration is contained in only one paragraph, with the operational part as follows: '[the heads of state of ECOWAS] declare a moratorium on the importation, exportation and manufacture of light weapons in ECOWAS member states which shall take effect … for a renewable period of three years.'[26]

This statement is politically, although not legally, binding upon the 16 states, and it represents the first and thus far only regional initiative of this kind. The agreement is an acknowledgement of both the threat to stability posed by light weapons trafficking within West Africa and an appreciation that collective action is necessary to tackle this problem.[27] Armed only with this vague outline, however, those tasked with its implementation were left scrambling to clarify the scope and coverage of the agreement, including which weapons were included. According to a knowledgeable UN disarmament official, the moratorium extends to all small arms and light weapons imports, exports and domestic manufacture in the region.[28]

The elaboration in March 1999 of the Programme for Co-ordination and Assistance on Security and Development (PCASED) was an important step toward implementing the political agreement. This programme, supported financially by external donor states, is intended to operationalise and reinforce the moratorium by building internal capacity among states to sustain efforts against arms trafficking. Among other things, it promotes arms collection efforts and the development of legal and regulatory measures relating to weapons possession and transfer. During 1999 programme officials worked to establish an implementation office in Bamako, Mali. This office organised several conferences on various aspects of regional security sector reform, including a September 1999 workshop on the establishment of a regional arms register.[29]

Despite this progress, it appears that many of the functionaries within ECOWAS states responsible for implementing and monitoring the moratorium are unaware of the mechanism and its requirements. Moreover, the PCASED fails to address some of the fundamental questions of those working to support the moratorium, both inside the region and among the donor community. Continuing lack of certainty about the meaning of the moratorium was denoted by the fact that, during 1999, the secretariat implementing the agreement received:

- three requests for arms imports to be exempted from the moratorium;
- three reports by countries outside ECOWAS for clarification on acquisition attempts by signatories to the moratorium;
- four reports for deferring acquisition of arms; and
- two information requests for export details.[30]

The exemption requests were granted to states in the region that wanted arms for training purposes or to replace weapons for use by national security forces.[31]

While limited, these queries and reports indicate that the moratorium agreement is recognised as a control regime, although one needing more specific operational guidelines and greater technical and financial support. In response, in December 1999, one year after it was enacted, the annual summit of ECOWAS heads of state adopted a code of conduct for the arms moratorium that sets out objectives and priorities, including establishing national commissions, regional focal points and more support within ECOWAS to manage the moratorium.[32] Most significantly, perhaps, this code of conduct establishes a waiver procedure for ECOWAS states wishing to import, export or manufacture light weapons while the moratorium is in operation. The provision requires prior authorisation from ECOWAS before importing arms for peacekeeping operations, hunting, training or sports shooting. Such weapons must be registered when they arrive in an ECOWAS country, and their removal is required after the event for which they are intended.[33]

In addition to political will among states in the region, the role of exporters, especially private companies, is key to the success of this initiative. In this regard, the Wassenaar Arrangement—a grouping of 33 arms-exporting states, based in Vienna—stated in December 1998 that its members would 'undertake an appropriate collaborative role with ECOWAS member states to respect the provisions of the Moratorium and will be open to providing advisory and/or technical assistance in the implementation of the Moratorium.'[34] Such assistance will be of great value to states in the region that face enormous challenges in halting arms trafficking. Equally important, however, is the need for each member state of the Wassenaar Arrangement to implement domestic procedures notifying its arms manufacturers and brokers that arms exports to West Africa are largely off limits.

The moratorium example underlines the many challenges for a regional control mechanism developed among politicians with little regard as to how the controls would be implemented or the political promises delivered. No criticism, however, should diminish the significance of the moratorium and what it could achieve once it has both political and operational clarity and commitment. And most important is the heightened and coordinated focus by states within the region on arms trafficking and the increased pledge of technical and legal assistance from external states to combat the trade.

Europe and North America

Outside of those regions most affected by conflict and arms trafficking, governments have also been active in promoting regional approaches to the problems of arms trafficking. Representing some of the largest weapons suppliers, states of Europe and North America have given significant political support to efforts to stem illicit exports and have begun to fund programmes in affected regions.

The members of the European Union have prioritised issues related to illicit arms trafficking. In 1998, the 15 EU member states agreed the Code of Conduct on Arms Exports, which requires members to take into consideration issues such as human rights and regional stability when authorising arms transfers. Previously, the EU had adopted a Programme of Action for Preventing and Combating Illicit Trafficking in Conventional Arms in June 1997.

This programme commits EU members to strengthen national efforts to prevent and combat arms trafficking, provide assistance to other countries affected by arms trafficking and ensure cooperation among national authorities.[35] The EU programme is a political declaration and places no legal obligation on EU members to implement any of the suggested approaches. However, the EU programme is significant as it addresses the problem of arms trafficking within a broader context that incorporates the need for capacity building, long term development and disarmament measures in regions where weapons are abundant.[36]

In December 1998 the European Union adopted a Joint Action on Small Arms, which commits EU members to providing financial and technical assistance to countries combating illicit arms trafficking. A joint action is legally binding, though it is up to the member states to implement the directive through national laws and policies. To date, through the joint action, the EU has been working with countries in Southern Africa, Albania and Cambodia and has identified West Africa as another region for assistance. In addition, the agreement also commits member governments to bar exports to non-state actors in other states without the permission of the recipient government officials.[37] Many states outside the

European Union—and those waiting for accession to the EU—have also agreed to the principles of the joint action, including endorsements from Canada, the thirteen associated countries (including Poland, Hungary, the Czech Republic, Slovakia, Estonia and Cyprus) and the United States. These and other states have also endorsed the programme of action and the EU Code of Conduct.

In 1995 the 'Group of Eight' leading industrialised states[38] added firearms trafficking to the list of issues on transnational crime that they identified as needing greater attention. A subgroup on arms trafficking was formed within the 'Lyon Group,' which brings together law enforcement officials from the G-8 countries to study the problems associated with financial crime and organised crime. This subgroup has considered how arms trafficking can be addressed at an intergovernmental level. At the G-8 summit in 1997, a set of priorities on arms trafficking were adopted. These included support for the development of an international instrument to combat arms trafficking, stronger import/export regimes for weapons transfers and a standard system for firearms identification.

Table 8.1 Comparison of Anti-Arms Trafficking Initiatives

	National efforts	OAS Convention	EU initiatives	SADC Cooperation	UN Firearms Protocol
Assistance and training		✓	✓	✓*	✓
Legislation and regulation	✓	✓		✓*	✓
Close loopholes (e.g., money laundering, trade agreements)	✓				✓
Regulate Brokers	✓				✓

*Assistance and training within the SADC region is both devised to be intra-regional and open for outside assistance from donor countries and organisations. SADC cooperation also recommends the review and regional harmonisation of relevant legislation but sets no common standards or frameworks.

In large part due to the political backing of the G-8 states, the United Nations Economic and Social Council (ECOSOC) initiated a process in 1997 to draft a protocol on illicit firearms (see below). The G-8 has continued to support these global efforts, most recently in its 1999 communiqué, while maintaining the Lyon Group. The political endorsement of the UN process by the richest countries in the world, and those which represent some of the largest arms exporters, has been significant in promoting the negotiation of the UN firearms protocol. Meanwhile, the subgroup on firearms continues to meet and works to develop common understanding among the G-8 on language and technical concepts related to the protocol.

Progress at the International Level

Several regions—such as Southeast Asia, Northeast Asia and the Middle East—have not yet undertaken specific initiatives to combat arms trafficking, and beginning in 1998 momentum shifted to the global arena. Approaches within the United Nations system have focused on the need to identify the magnitude of the problem and on finding means of reducing the availability of weapons. Efforts have largely centred on two aspects of the problem—the availability and misuse of military-style weapons and the criminal use of firearms. There is a great deal of similarity between the two foci, especially where the illicit traffic in arms is concerned. The latter approach is leading to the creation of a legal instrument to prevent arms trafficking in the form of negotiations on a Protocol against the Illicit Manufacturing of and Trafficking in Firearms, Ammunition and Other Related Material.[39]

The protocol represents the first global regime for all commercial transfers of firearms and ammunition, devised to prevent illegal diversion of these weapons. Negotiations began in early 1999, within broader UN negotiations of a convention on transnational organised crime by the Economic and Social Council's Commission on Crime Prevention and Criminal Justice. The goal for completion of both the umbrella treaty and the firearms protocol is October 2000, although this target date might slip.

Many of the protocol's main provisions mirror those found in the OAS convention, including its strict focus on commercial transfers of arms and its exclusion of state-to-state transfers. Many provisions have been modified in order to gain global consensus.[40] While it is still a work in progress, the protocol is expected to:

- establish an international, legally binding definition of 'illicit arms trafficking';[41]
- create common international standards for the export, import and in-transit movement of firearms, ammunition and their parts and components, including licensing and end-use certification;
- improve international cooperation on commercial transfers of firearms;
- regulate the activities of those engaged in commercial arms brokering;
- require record keeping of arms transfers, potentially for a minimum of ten years;
- establish a comprehensive system for marking firearms at manufacture and possibly at each subsequent point of entry into a new state; and
- encourage widespread and systematic international information sharing and cooperation to improve the identification and tracing of firearms.

Like the OAS convention, the UN Firearms Protocol will improve transparency and controls over the legal shipments of firearms and, by doing so, make the illegal trade easier to distinguish. In adopting this approach, those negotiating the protocol have been willing in some cases to include issues that were left out of the OAS convention. Most importantly, provisions to register and license arms brokers are included in the current draft. In addition, through being supplementary to the Convention on Transnational Organised Crime, the protocol will also benefit from provisions within the draft convention on combating money-laundering and corruption.[42] These elements will make the protocol the most far-reaching instrument available to combat illicit arms trafficking at the international level (see table 8.1).

However, even this agreement does not cover the full spectrum of illicit arms trafficking occurring around the world, and the protocol has been criticised for not using its potential for a wider scope and broader objectives. Specifically, it has been suggested that the scope should encompass government-to-government transfers of firearms (including those for national security) in addi-

tion to commercial transactions. The rationale for the inclusion of
these state-controlled weapons is that such arms are often diverted
from state control into illicit markets through either criminal motivation or negligence. Some states, however, remain unconvinced
that the protocol should go beyond a narrow focus on illicit trafficking into areas which touch on legal arms transfers, and several
feel strongly that the protocol should only take on what is clearly
within the realm of law enforcement.

A second area that should—and might be—included in the protocol is a commitment by signatories to destroy illicit weapons that
have been seized by security forces. South Africa has been a vocal
proponent of including such a destruction clause in the protocol,[43]
but other countries have suggested more temperate language calling only on states to take adequate steps to prevent seized weapons from falling into private hands.[44]

A third area of contention, which represents a significant opportunity for improving states' ability to trace the movement of illicit firearms, centres on provisions relating to marking weapons.
There is general agreement that firearms being sold commercially
should be given a unique and indelible mark at the time of manufacture (although some governments resist even this fairly common practice). There is no consensus, however, that weapons
should be marked at each place of import, or that weapons produced for military purposes should be marked at the time of
manufacture. Retroactively marking unmarked firearms already
stockpiled or in circulation would pose an even greater challenge.

Objections to this comprehensive approach to marking are
technical, financial and political. On the former, the question exists
of how, logistically, states would mark weapons at import and under whose authority (police, military, foreign ministry). Financially, the most onerous costs would be associated with marking
already manufactured weapons and with marking arms at the
point of import. Most challenging, however, are the political objections. Some national governments either are not convinced that
marking will have a significant impact on reducing illicit arms trafficking, or they do not want routes and destinations of their arms
exports known.[45]

Clearly, significant challenges remain before the protocol is
completed and enough states ratify it to ensure its implementation.
However good the protocol looks on paper will be moot without
its implementation by as many states as possible. As illustrated

throughout this book, arms traffickers are masterful at exploiting weak links, and without high common levels of detection and enforcement capability, arms trafficking will continue to flourish.

A second relevant international effort is the forthcoming UN conference on the illicit trade in small arms and light weapons in all its aspects. The first preparatory meeting for this event was held in February 2000, and the UN conference is scheduled to take place in mid-2001. It will focus on developing a programme of action that should reinforce, coordinate and extend measures already being taken at national and regional levels, while also pushing the boundaries to extend control over illicit arms into areas such as improving transparency in, and restraint of, government-to-government sales, improving the security of government stocks of arms and developing standards for the regulation of arms brokers and shipping agents.[46] Expectations have been high among those within and outside governments for the achievements of this conference; however, following the first preparatory meeting, during which Russian and Chinese officials, among others, voiced strong objection to discussion of limits on state-authorised transfers, these expectations have been diminished. Reservations by a few governments—even ones that are major sources of small arms supply, like China and Russia—should not prevent states that are committed to preventing illicit arms trafficking from finding a way to bring international momentum beyond the rhetorical realm and into the practical.

Progress against Prospects

In a few short years governments around the world have begun to take concrete steps to limit the threats to security and stability posed by the unchecked proliferation of small arms. While the illegal arms trade represents only one element in the larger problem of reducing the supply of and demand for weapons, the billions spent on illegal weapons acquisitions that are used to prolong wars and destabilise societies must be effectively addressed. This chapter has illustrated some of the actions to do so that are taking place within countries, regions and at the global level. The progress that has been made within several regions thus far is significant, and with the conclusion of the UN protocol the legal and political framework to address the criminal aspects of the problem will be in place. The challenge will then become for countries to prioritise the implementation of these mechanisms and to assist each other in narrowing the space available for arms traffickers to operate.

Notes

1 US State Department, *International Crime Control Strategy,* June 1998.

2 *Ibid.*

3 US General Accounting Office, *Terrorism and Drug Trafficking: Responsibilities for Developing Explosives and Detection Technologies,* GAO/NSIAD-97-95 (1997), p. 4.

4 Consider, for example, that the $15 billion spent by the US government in 1997 on drug control represents nearly half of the combined total Gross National Products of Ghana, Kenya, Mozambique, Tanzania and Zimbabwe. (GNP estimates from *World Development Report 1998/1999,* as found in *South Africa at a Glance* [South Africa: Editors Inc, 1999], p. 157.)

5 James McShane, 'Light Weapons and International Law Enforcement,' in Jeffrey Boutwell and Michael T. Klare, eds., *Light Weapons and Civil Conflict* (Lanham, Maryland: Rowman & Littlefield, 1999), p. 174.

6 Sarah Meek, 'New Democracies under the Gun: Small Arms in Southern Africa,' in Abdel F. Musah and Niobe Thompson, eds., *Over a Barrel: Light Weapons and Human Rights in the Commonwealth* (London/New Delhi: Commonwealth Human Rights Initiative, 1999), p. 166.

7 Concept developed by the Arms Management Programme at the Institute for Security Studies in South Africa.

8 Katharine McKenzie, *Domestic Gun Control Policy in Ten SADC Countries* (Johannesburg: Gun-free South Africa, September 1999), p. 22.

9 Various UN General Assembly documents provide updates on states' actions in this regard. See, in particular, Report of the Group of Governmental Experts on Small Arms, UN Doc. A/54/258, 19 August 1999. This and other relevant UN documents are available on the UN Department of Disarmament Affairs' website (www.un.org/Depts/dda/CAB/).

10 Laurie Nathan, draft paper presented to the BICC Expert Seminar on Smart Sanctions, Bonn, Germany, 21-23 November 1999.

11 In addition to more formal regional and international programmes, there are also extensive bilateral assistance programmes, especially on implementing export controls for countries of the former Soviet Union and East Europe. For detailed information on legislation being put in place, see the website of the Stockholm International Peace Research Institute (projects.sipri.se/expcon/expcon.htm).

12 For more information, see Susannah Dyer and Geraldine O'Callaghan, *One Size Fits All? Prospects for a Global Convention on Illicit Trafficking by*

2000 (Washington, DC/London: BASIC, 1999), p. 6; Lora Lumpe, 'The US Arms Both Sides of Mexico's Drug War,' *Covert Action Quarterly*, Summer 1997, No. 61, pp. 39-46.

[13] *Arms Sales Monitor*, Federation of American Scientists, Washington, DC, No. 38, November 1998, p. 1 (available at www.fas.org/asmp).

[14] 'US/Mexico Drug Control Group Issues Communique,' *USIS Washington File*, 10 November 1999 (available at www.fas.org/irp/news/1999/11/991110-drugs-usia1.htm).

[15] 'Mexico's New Gun Law Goes into Effect,' 30 March 1999 (available at www.jointogether.org/gv/wire/). See also info4.juridicas.unam.mx/unijus/fed/120/default.htm

[16] James McShane, 'Light Weapons and International Law Enforcement,' p. 173.

[17] Full text available at www.oas.org/en/prog/juridico/english/treaties/a-63.html

[18] See also, Geraldine O'Callaghan and Kate Joseph, 'The International Response to the Light Weapons Crisis: Lessons for the Commonwealth,' in Musah and Thompson, eds., *Over a Barrel*, pp. 307-309; Sarah Meek, 'The Organisation of American States,' in Virginia Gamba, ed., *Society under Siege: Licit Responses to Illicit Arms* (Halfway House, South Africa: Institute for Security Studies, 1998), pp. 49-54; and James McShane, 'Light Weapons and International Law Enforcement,' pp. 176-177.

[19] Available at www.cicad.oas.org/en/legal_development/legal-regulations-arms.htm

[20] Organisation of American States, 'Consultative Committee Meets on Hemispheric Firearms Convention,' Press Release, 9 March 2000 (available at www.oas.org).

[21] O'Callaghan and Joseph, 'The International Response to the Light Weapons Crisis: Lessons for the Commonwealth,' p. 309.

[22] The text of the regional action programme can be found at www.iss.co.za/pubs/ASR/7.4/regional.html.

[23] Andrew McLean and Elizabeth Clegg, eds., *Towards Implementation of the Southern African Regional Action Programme on Light Arms and Illicit Trafficking* (Pretoria/London: Institute for Security Studies and Saferworld, 1999), pp. 71-85.

[24] *Ibid.*, p. 114.

[25] For more information on these initiatives, see Virginia Gamba, *Small Arms in Southern Africa: Reflections on the Extent of the Problem and its Potential Management* (Pretoria: Institute for Security Studies, November 1999); and Martinho Chachiua, *Arms Management Programme: Operations Rachel 1996-1999* (Pretoria: Institute for Security Studies, June 1999).

[26] The text of the moratorium agreement, a related chronology, news and analysis are available on the NISAT website (www.nisat.org/west%20africa/african.htm).

27 For analysis of the evolution of the ECOWAS moratorium, see Joseph Smaldone, 'Mali and the West African Light Weapons Moratorium,' in Boutwell and Klare, eds., *Light Weapons and Civil Conflict*, pp. 129-145.

28 Conversation between the author and the director of the United Nations Regional Centre for Peace and Security in Africa in Lomé, Togo, August 1999.

29 UN News Centre, 'Workshop on Arms Register in Africa Opens in Accra,' Press Release AFR/175 DC/2661, 23 September 1999.

30 Information based on a presentation made by the director of PCASED, Ivor Richard Fung, to the seminar on Small Arms and the European Union, Helsinki, Finland, 8-10 October 1999.

31 UN News Centre, 'West African States Adopt Code of Conduct on Light Weapons, Launch Regional Arms Register and Database,' Press Release AFR/199-DC/2675, 27 December 1999.

32 For the text of the ECOWAS Code of Conduct, see Jacqueline Seck, *West Africa Small Arms Moratorium: High-level consultations on the modalities for the implementation of PCASED*, United Nations Institute for Disarmament Research and the United Nations Regional Centre for Peace and Disarmament in Africa, Geneva and Lomé, 2000.

33 UN News Centre, 'West African States Adopt Code of Conduct on Light Weapons, Launch Regional Arms Register and Database.'

34 Wassenaar Arrangement on Export Controls for Conventional Arms and Dual-Use Goods and Technology, 'Public Statement,' Vienna, 3 December 1998 (available at www.wassenaar.org/docs/press_4.html).

35 Sarah Meek, 'International Initiatives on the Control of Weapons,' in Gamba, ed., *Society under Siege*, p. 10.

36 O'Callaghan and Joseph, 'The International Response to the Light Weapons Crisis: Lessons for the Commonwealth,' p. 316.

37 European Union Joint Action on Small Arms (1999/34/CFSP), 17 December 1998 (available at www.sipri.se/projects/expcon/euframe/eusmja.htm). The operative language in the agreement is that the states of the EU 'shall aim at building consensus in the relevant international forums, and in a regional context as appropriate, for a commitment by exporting countries to supply small arms only to governments (either directly or through duly licensed entities authorised to procure weapons in their behalf) in accordance with appropriate international and regional restrictive arms export criteria.'

38 United States, United Kingdom, Germany, France, Italy, Canada, Japan and Russia.

39 The phrasing was originally 'other related material' as in the OAS convention. However, during negotiations in October 1999 it was recommended that the phrasing change to mirror that of the relevant ECOSOC resolution, which reads 'parts and components.'

40 Notably, the protocol is unlikely to include explosives within its mandate, unlike the OAS convention.

41 The precise wording of the definition is unlikely to be resolved until the protocol is close to completion. Currently, the definition of illicit trafficking reads: 'the import, export, acquisition, sale, delivery, movement or transfer of firearms, ammunition and parts and components from or across the territory of one State Party to that of another State Party if any one of the States Parties concerned does not authorise it.' UN Doc. A/C.25/4/ Add.2/Rev.2, p. 8.

42 See United Nations, *Revised draft United Nations Convention against Transnational Organised Crime*, UN Doc. A/AC.254/4/Rev.4.

43 United Nations, *Contribution from the delegation of South Africa*, UN Doc. A/AC.254/CRP.6, January 1999.

44 British American Security Information Council, *Strengthening the UN Firearms Protocol: Recommendations* (London: BASIC, February 2000).

45 *Ibid.* and International Alert, 'Developing the Firearms Protocol,' paper circulated at the meeting of the ad hoc Committee of the Protocol against the Illicit Manufacturing of and Trafficking in Firearms, Ammunition and Other Related Materials, Vienna, October 1999 (available at www. international-alert.org).

46 For more information, see Owen Greene, Elizabeth Clegg, Sarah Meek and Geraldine O'Callaghan, *Framework Briefing: The UN 2001 Conference—Setting the Agenda* (London: BASIC, International Alert and Saferworld, February 2000).

9/ Law Enforcement and International Gun Trafficking

by Ted Leggett

This book has principally looked at the ways gun traffickers evade the law. This chapter explores the ways frontline law enforcement can make life difficult for them, and how the international community can assist in this effort.

While the process of globalisation is making the nation-state increasingly superfluous in many respects, laws binding the conduct of individuals continue to be made and enforced at the national and local level. Criminals still must be arrested, convicted and imprisoned in one or another national system of justice. Meanwhile, approaches to the problem of crime vary today as widely as they ever have, reflecting various nations' deeply held beliefs about ethics and human nature. These values can be difficult to reconcile internationally.

In contrast to this fragmentation, international commerce is increasingly unfettered, as business appears less contentious an issue than crime and punishment. In this respect, post-Cold War gunrunners are no different than other global entrepreneurs. They are suppliers responding to demand and making profits from regional disequilibria. Like other dealers in forbidden merchandise, evading law enforcement is just part of the cost of doing business. Since they are creatures of the free market, the focus of control efforts must lie in making the business itself unprofitable. This is unfamiliar territory for most law enforcement officers, however, and will require substantial international cooperation.

Of course, sovereign nations are free to set whatever standards they feel are appropriate regarding civilian access to firearms, and these standards rightly vary in response to local conditions. The most effective form of regulation is also likely to vary from context to context. Those used to the harsh punishments of Islamic *shariah* are unlikely to respond to more Western forms of persuasion. The task, then, is for nations to cooperate in assuring that the laws of each nation are enforced by limiting the opportunities for international evasion.

This task is clearly more of a challenge for some states than others. The willingness of well developed nations to cooperate may vary, but developing or transitional states may be seriously challenged in their capacity to comply, whatever their intentions. And it is in these countries that the problem of uncontrolled access to arms is most acute.

This chapter explores the various contexts in which gun trafficking is an issue. It then focuses on a single case study—the newly democratic South Africa. Next, cooperative international enforcement efforts currently in place are reviewed. Finally, the chapter discusses ways in which cooperation can be enhanced and local performance improved.

Gun Cultures

Having a lot of guns about does not necessarily equate to having a 'gun problem.' Some countries, such as Switzerland and Israel, are able to maintain remarkably high levels of armament without much violent crime. Indeed, these nations see a generally armed populace as essential to maintaining national security. However, in countries such as South Africa and Brazil, easy access to guns and high levels of crime seem to be two sides of the same coin.

Looking at just these examples, the most obvious distinction between these two sets of countries is in level of development. But the United States, despite its industrialisation, also suffers from high levels of gun-related crime. A better predictor of gun violence would be levels of income inequality, or the relative deprivation of the poor. Another would be the level of social fragmentation, the extent to which the stresses of rapid change and dislocation play themselves out in violent conflict. It is in highly polarised, transitional societies where demand for guns may be high, but where the state has a strong interest in controlling access to these weapons. These conditions create a market for illegal gun-running.

In more industrialised states, illegal guns are in demand for three principal reasons:

- they circumvent the regulatory controls that link a particular gun to its owner, allowing the gun to be used for further criminal purposes;
- they allow convicted felons, youth or illegal aliens, who may not be able to acquire guns legally under local laws, to have access to them;
- they allow collectors, survivalists and militia movements to have access to firearms normally prohibited to civilians.

Each of these sources of demand has undertones of further criminality. In the developing world, however, demand is far more general and not necessarily linked to other types of crime. Particularly in countries that have only recently democratised after years of guerrilla warfare, having a gun may be seen as an essential part of daily life. Registration drives are unlikely to succeed where relations between the people and the state are strained, or where the threat of confiscation or licensing fees hang in the air. The populace may rationally resist relinquishing illegal guns where the protections of a functioning criminal justice system are not yet in place.

Of course, guns are also the tools of the trade for young males unable and unlikely to find employment in any field other than crime. As such, they are a kind of productive capital, sometimes the only sort a poor household may have. Fear of falling victim to crime promotes further unlawfulness as, ironically, people purchase stolen guns to protect themselves from robbery.

Besides public resistance, an additional impediment to gun law enforcement in the developing world is the sheer diffusion of the problem. In industrialised countries, rural areas are generally the most socially stable and conservative areas of the country. Crime tends to be conveniently concentrated in the inner cities or public housing projects, often among minority groups or recent immigrants. These are often areas of anonymity, where the rapid flow of people erodes any sense of community, where few of the residents have any ownership stake in the neighbourhood and where equally disadvantaged groups vie for scarce resources.

In the developing world, the problem is not so conveniently packaged. Large areas of rural instability may form, populated by displaced or impoverished agriculturists or those seeking to take

advantage of multiple means of creating a livelihood. Squatter set-
tlements spring up in urban areas as people come seeking opportunities. Retrenchments attendant to the shocks of global economic
integration further feed the pool of the marginalised, and the
sprawl of the disadvantaged widens further still. Adding guns to
this mix creates a potentially explosive situation.

Police Cultures

Rural instability poses major challenges for law enforcement. Even
in developed urban areas, the threat of law enforcement is largely a
bluff, made workable only by the willingness of the majority to police themselves. Police forces focus on visibility to maintain the illusion of ever present authority. In some developed urban areas, even
small offences may be vigorously prosecuted in a 'zero tolerance'
approach, the idea being to restore a sense of order to previously
neglected areas. But these techniques are woefully ineffective when
high crime patrol areas encompass hundreds of square kilometres,
crossing jurisdictional and international boundaries.

When the subject matter is gun trafficking, the problem becomes
more complicated still. Where unstable rural areas adjoin borders,
smuggling becomes trivially easy. Since the illegal sale of guns is a
'willing seller/willing buyer' situation, it has much in common
with other 'victimless crimes,' such as the sale of drugs and sexual
services. There is generally no complainant, and these transactions
tend to take place in secrecy. The situation is aggravated by the fact
that guns are not illegal in themselves in most countries. It is only
by checking government records that the legality of a weapon is
determined. This reality greatly reduces the ability of third parties
to act as informants to the police.

Thus, nearly all successful gun law enforcement is reliant on
police initiative and, by extension, the interest of the state. The
presence of state interest cannot be conclusively established on the
basis of acquiescence to international conventions. States may have
many reasons, both political and economic, for wishing to appear to
be in line with global trends on arms control, while actually fostering illicit commerce. This is true of both supplier and recipient
countries.

State support for illicit commerce can take a variety of forms,
from direct participation to lax enforcement. Customs and other

regulatory agencies may be assigned other priorities, such as narcotics. These agencies may be underfunded, understaffed, burdened with excessive administrative duties or otherwise hindered in enforcing international conventions.

This low priority status need not imply a conspiracy to promote gun-running. The power of the market ensures that a nation will behave in ways consistent with the interests of its domestic political economy. Principled decisions at national level to adhere to global standards may have little effect on the day-to-day business of local enforcement. Additionally, of course, graft and corruption can undermine even the most sincere national efforts.

Because the level of enforcement is entirely reliant on police initiative, guns and other illicit commodities tend to generate corruption. Since the law enforcement officer is not directly accountable to a complainant, and much of his work is necessarily conducted in secrecy, his discretion in enforcing the law is subject to influence by bribery. This can often lead to a situation where the perpetrators and the police form a working relationship of sorts, in which the police selectively enforce the law to the benefit of the insider syndicate—allowing the illusion of enforcement while enriching both the insider and the police. One ironic side effect of this arrangement may be a reduction in the violence generated by illicit commerce, as competition between rival syndicates is minimised. But the core concern—the flow of arms—continues unabated.

In developing countries, the tendency towards corruption can be augmented by a real inability to effectively enforce the law even where the will exists. Often undertrained, underpaid and lacking basic equipment (including basic transport and communications equipment), law enforcement officers in developing countries may be left to their own devices in remote areas with little supervision and backup. As would be expected, chief priorities quickly become self-protection and extortion. When oversight is limited, incentives for performance few, the personal threat from local criminal groupings high and the financial incentives for cooperation outrageously disproportionate to the salary offered by the state, it is little wonder that corruption ensues.

Many of these dynamics are well illustrated by the concrete example of the newly democratic South Africa.

The Case of South Africa

South Africa defies easy classification as a developed or a developing country. In many respects, South Africa's technological capabilities are world class—including its capacity for the production of light weaponry. But the majority of its people live in poverty or near-poverty, many without the basic amenities of development, such as running water, electricity, telephones and sewerage.

The police likewise face significant capacity challenges, especially in rural areas. The low salaries that the state is able to offer do not secure the most qualified workforce. The National Commissioner himself estimates that 30% of the South African Police Service (SAPS) is functionally illiterate,[1] and 40% of police officers in the largest metropolitan area in the country are not licensed to drive a car.[2] In many areas, there are not even cars to drive, as rural police departments may lack such basic amenities as vehicles and telephones.

The resources that do exist are not evenly spread. While the targeted number of citizens per police officer in South Africa is a respectable 240 per 100,000,[3] in rural areas the ratio may be many thousands to one. In the Tugela Ferry police district, for example, one report showed the ratio to be nearly 50,000 to one.[4] The chances of significant arms interdiction through routine policing in such areas are limited.

South Africa is also facing a crime wave that seems to follow almost inevitably after years of absolutist rule. During the struggle for democracy, both the repressive state and resistance movements employed violent and illegal methods to achieve their ends, including widespread smuggling of arms and other contraband. This legacy has had spill-over effects into the democratic era.

Perhaps most importantly, the history of repressive rule has damaged the relationship between the public and the state, especially with regard to the institutions of social control. During the struggle, rural areas were the basis of revolutionary power, although many of the more dramatic events occurred in those areas where black bordered white. It is thus in rural areas where the need for reconciliation between the police and the public is greatest, and also where it is most difficult.

There have also been problems with the transition within the police service:

- During the apartheid era, human rights were widely abused and police work largely reduced to a matter of extracting confessions by force. The police service is thus lacking in basic investigative skills compatible with human rights, including the gathering and use of sophisticated intelligence.
- Much of the command structure has of necessity been retained from the apartheid era, and members of this grouping may be more susceptible to corruption. Recent investigations into the Organised Crime Unit in Durban, including the seizure of the property of the Unit's head, illustrate this risk.[5]
- Within the service, relations between white commanders and black 'lateral transfers' from the revolutionary forces have been understandably strained, and some black commanders face serious capacity challenges due to their systematic miseducation under apartheid.[6]
- Language barriers can make interaction between minority police members and the black public difficult.
- High risks, low morale and dismal pay make police officers of all colours very susceptible to brutality, negligence and corruption.

The dire situation in South Africa with regard to guns is well known. But while firearms are used in 85% of the car hijackings and bank robberies in South Africa,[7] they are less important than might be expected in several other crime areas. Knives are the weapons of choice in 40% of South Africa's murders, nearly 80% of its rapes and the majority of its armed robberies.[8] Of all murders by firearm, the vast majority involve handguns and shotguns, with military weapons playing only a minor role.[9] Even three quarters of all bank robberies involved handguns, with assault weapons generally being a feature only in attacks on armoured bank vehicles.[10]

The number of murders per year in South Africa has declined slightly since the first democratic elections in 1994, dropping from over 26,000 to under 24,000.[11] The percentage committed with a firearm, however, has increased, from just over 40% to just under half.[12] Of these 12,000 murders, about 200 of the victims each year are police officers, of which over a fifth are shot with their own service pistols.[13]

Since the elections, the number of armed robberies with firearms has decreased. Most of these are performed with handguns. Although the number of military-style cash-in-transit robberies dropped by nearly 50% between 1996 and 1998, the number of security personnel killed in these crimes increased slightly during the same period.[14]

Despite the stability or decline in the number of firearm-related offences, seizures of guns have been on the rise since the transition to democracy began. There has been a steady increase in the number of arrests for possession of illegal firearms and ammunition, with a sharp upturn in 1998.[15] The SAPS seized over 20,000 illegal firearms in 1998, up from just over 14,000 in 1994.[16]

Seizures are up, and firearm-related offences are down. Does this mean that South Africa has its gun problem under control? Only if 12,000 firearm murders are something the country is prepared to live with! But it should be kept in mind that guns are only part of the problem of violent crime in South Africa.

While the estimates of illegal guns vary widely, according to the Central Firearms Registry there are over four million licensed firearms in South Africa, in the hands of over 3.5 million owners, and this figure is growing by about 10% a year. A recent study revealed that 20,000 South Africans with criminal records had firearms licenses and that 15% had been convicted of serious violent crimes, such as assault and murder.[17] With legal guns in the hands of such people, the illicit trade is clearly only part of the country's problem. Moreover, another study of 2458 license holders showed that the Central Firearms Registry is less than 30% accurate in gun owner details.[18]

Border controls are lax. Fences dividing South Africa from its neighbours are, in most cases, barbed wire less than a metre high, riddled with gaps.[19] Migrants from the north wander in at will. Between January and September of 1999, South Africa deported nearly 32,000 Zimbabweans and 75,000 Mozambicans.[20] Many of those deported to Mozambique, for example, brag that they will be back in Johannesburg in 24 hours. According to interviews with Mozambicans conducted in connection with the investigative news programme *Special Assignment*, they may pay R100 to corrupt officials for the right to jump off the deportation train, or simply walk back through the hole in the fence that they used the last time. When they return, they may bring with them arms, cannabis from Malawi and any other contraband that will sell in South Africa.

In addition, scores of airstrips dot the countryside, hold-overs from the sanctions-busting days. Only a few of South Africa's many international airports and border posts have an immigration, customs and police presence.

Aside from smuggling, massive numbers of legitimate weapons are diverted into the illicit economy each year. In 1998 29,694 firearms were reported lost or stolen, of which only 1764 were recovered by the police. The incidence of reported theft of firearms increased 56% between 1994 and 1998, and loss increased 32% between 1996 and 1998.[21] The South African Police Service and the South African National Defence Force are significant sources of lost and stolen firearms. A study of theft of police firearms in KwaZulu-Natal showed that 77% were lost while the officer in question was off duty, with most of the alleged thefts occurring without resistance and without witnesses, calling into question the role of corruption in the situation. In the same study, it was shown that in 74% of cases in which suspects were found in illegal possession of firearms, no conviction was secured.[22]

A more recent study showed that, of 788 dockets concerning firearms-related crime, of which 63% were robbery or murder: 63% were closed as 'undetected'; 24% were withdrawn by the complainant, prosecutors, or the police; and 4% resulted in acquittals. In only 9% of the cases was the accused tried and convicted.[23]

Thus, even if the cross-border flow of arms into South Africa were stemmed, sizeable numbers would continue to make their way into the hands of criminals. These criminals are unlikely to be punished even if they are caught in possession of illegal arms or commit another crime with the weapon.

To counter this situation, South Africa has employed the full range of internationally recognised measures at one time or another, including amnesties, buy-back schemes and clean sweep operations. While many of these have shown some success, they mostly seem to be a case of too little too late. Gun Free South Africa, a gun control campaign, launched a 24-hour buy-back in 1994 which, despite nearly $200,000 in funding and the endorsement of Nelson Mandela, netted a disappointing 900 guns and explosive devices. Subsequent assessment indicated that the programme had cast its net too widely in attempting to embrace the entire country at once, and that educational efforts should have played a greater role.[24] Part of the problem may be that, while communities believe that guns cause more violence than they prevent, between a quarter and a half of the members of three communities surveyed indicated that they were willing to own a firearm.[25]

In February of 1999, a South African Gun Control Charter was signed by 62 organisations and 30 individuals. It was followed in March by draft legislation to strongly limit rights granted under the previous Arms Act, including the right bear a firearm licensed to another person if in possession of a letter of permission. Police find that a large percentage of those found with firearms justify their possession with such a letter.

This draft bill was fiercely debated, scrapped and resurrected with some modifications. On 17 November 1999 a general policy document was approved by the cabinet. A draft bill was subsequently published for public comment, and over 2000 submissions were received. The Ministry for Safety and Security is presently redrafting in response to this input. At time of writing, the content of the bill that will finally be presented to Parliament is anyone's guess, but the most recent published draft contains the following provisions:

- The bill provides for stricter control over the issuing and renewal of firearm licences, including allowing only one gun for personal protection purposes and revocation of the right to lend weapons.
- It provides for stricter control of state-owned firearms.
- New presumptions have been developed on the illegal possession of firearms, together with heavy penalties; being in illegal possession of an unlicensed firearm carries a sentence of up to 15 years.
- It provides for extended policing powers. Significant, for instance, is the ability of the police to fingerprint all occupants of a motor vehicle in a case where an illegal firearm is found and seized, to establish ownership or possession.
- Provision is made for the relevant civil authorities to levy administrative penalties for non-compliance. This is intended to avoid clogging the courts with minor offences.

Incorporated into the bill are measures that ensure that state departments and other institutions of the state are not hampered in their work, but at the same time they must carry responsibility for ensuring proper control of their official firearms.

South Africa, however, is developing a reputation for passing sterling legislation without the capacity to enforce it. It is not clear how the bill will affect the vast pool of illegal weapons already in the country, or the cross border flows that feed it. Some indication of the size of individual caches was revealed in the run-up to the last elections, when several minor arsenals were discovered in rural KwaZulu-Natal, some of which included rocket launchers and other military weaponry. While few of these arms are likely to be used in street crime, the potential is truly frightening.

Thus South Africa, like many developing countries, is facing a long, hard road ahead as it cleans up its troubled past. In this task, it is limited by systemic weaknesses in its domestic law enforcement and in its economy—weaknesses that are aggravated by the continued threat of violent crime. The international community has a long history of providing humanitarian aid to developing countries, but the provision of law enforcement assistance is often considered problematic. The establishment of order is a prerequisite for economic growth, and the flow of illegal guns is a threat to all nations, whatever their state of development. It therefore becomes incumbent on the 'international community' to find ways for international agencies and local law enforcement to cooperate and more effectively limit the flow of illegal arms.

International Law Enforcement

Police agencies are notorious for not working well together. Whether it is national and local police, enforcement officials of different national agencies or police of different countries, most police personnel are used to a hierarchical chain of command that does not allow for multiple authorities. Police intelligence is a little too close to military intelligence for many countries to feel comfortable about sharing it, especially in the field of arms or anywhere large volumes of money are involved. Furthermore, police investigations are often, by nature, covert, and information is spread on a 'need to know' basis. This secrecy is essential for the protection of undercover operatives and the success of sting operations. Trust is all-important, and this trust does not often extend beyond borders.

Protections surrounding human rights also vary widely from country to country, which interferes with joint operations. Local police cannot permit violation of national standards of evidence collection, and foreign courts may not admit evidence gathered contrary to their own rules.

In a world of diverse approaches to the crime problem, the question of jurisdiction becomes very important. Does the jurisdiction over a criminal act lie in the site where the act was committed, in the country in which the perpetrator holds citizenship, in the country s/he is apprehended or in the country where the damage is ultimately felt? Unfortunately, various national governments answer these questions in different ways, and, even within a single government, the laws surrounding these matters can be quite complex and vary from offence to offence.

In addition to establishing jurisdiction over the act and the actor, there is often a need to gather evidence abroad. This need can lead to conflicts, particularly in matters of financial secrecy. The tension between a country's economic self-interest and its desire to assert its sovereignty on the one hand, and international pressure to distance itself from the criminal classes on the other, often renders these negotiations more political than principled.

While a nation-state can claim extraterritorial effect for its laws, no nation has an independent right to enforce its laws or demand evidence outside its borders. Police officers who show up on foreign soil and begin to conduct their business are as unwelcome as unauthorised military personnel, and may be subject to arrest for simply making inquiries. Extraterritorial law enforcement rights can only be established by agreement between the countries concerned. A request from one nation to another to acknowledge personal jurisdiction generally involves extradition agreements, while exchanges of evidence and information are facilitated by mutual legal assistance treaties (MLATs). In either case, law enforcement activity on foreign soil usually involves local agencies acting as an intermediary. Sometimes these agreements take the form of multilateral or regional conventions to extradite fugitives or share information, but oftentimes these agreements are simply bilateral.

The multilateral agreements are often spearheaded by international organisations, such as the United Nations, as part of broader documents declaring a unified position with regard to certain offences. The state of international arms trafficking agreements is discussed elsewhere in this book (see chapters 2 and 8, in particular). As with many such documents, the long process of negotiation and ratification often reduces these to the least common denominator of agreement. This reality leads some countries, such as the United States, to negotiate agreements bilaterally, as doing so allows leverage to be applied for optimal extraterritorial penetration.

As a result of all these negotiations, extradition and information exchange agreements vary in their strength. Among closely cooperating states, a request to seize a fugitive or his property may be accorded the same priority as local matters, while requests from more distant partners become mired in bureaucracy. Many extradition agreements require that the offence concerned be illegal in both jurisdictions. Some nations are highly resistant to extraditing their citizens, no matter what the offence. Where extradition is impossible, some national governments are even willing to try the offender locally for offences committed elsewhere.[26]

US agencies

The country that has most pushed the envelope with regard to extraterritorial jurisdiction is the United States, particularly with regard to its war on drugs. The United States Drug Enforcement Administration (DEA) has aggressively conducted operations outside American borders and, more than any other single law enforcement body, has challenged traditional notions about territorial sovereignty. With approximately 500 personnel stationed abroad in 65 countries, the DEA emphasis is on 'joint operations,' where US nationals actively work in the field with local officers. While some other US agencies have also moved in this direction in recent years, none comes close to the impact of the DEA, and most emphasise training and information sharing.

In the field of arms control, the US Bureau of Alcohol, Tobacco, and Firearms is constrained by founding legislation that limits its mandate to domestic enforcement. Nonetheless, it has established a presence in Mexico, owing to the importance of that country to the US illicit arms trade. It has focused on training foreign agents and maintaining an international database on firearms and explosives.

US Customs has been active in preventing international smuggling of high-tech weapons, as well as money laundering. Firearms have not been a focus in the past.

Interpol

The premiere international policing organisation in the world today is Interpol. While it can claim most of the states of the world as members, Interpol is a very small organisation. At the beginning of 1999 it had a global staff of 360 people, including seconded and contract employees. Its 1999 budget of 161 million French francs came mainly from the donations of member states. It exists primarily to facilitate cooperation and communication between the police departments of member countries, and it is extremely deferential to principles of national sovereignty. Contrary to its popular image, Interpol does not have teams of detectives with supranational powers who travel around investigating cases.

Interpol is prohibited by its constitution from undertaking, 'any intervention or activities of a political, military, religious or racial character.' A 1984 resolution stipulates that offences are not considered to be political when they are committed outside a 'conflict area,' and when the victims are not connected with the aims or objectives pursued by the offenders. Once again, though, drawing the line between political and criminal activity can be difficult, especially in the developing world.

Major policy decisions are made at the annual meeting of Interpol's General Assembly, which is comprised of delegates from member countries. These decisions are enacted by an Executive Committee, comprised of thirteen Assembly delegates, who reflect the geographic diversity of its members.

Interpol's Criminal Intelligence Directorate contains four sub-directorates, concerned with General Crime, Financial Crime, Drugs and Criminal Intelligence. The Criminal Intelligence sub-directorate manages the Interpol Criminal Information System and maintains databases of fingerprints, fugitives, missing children, stolen vehicles and stolen works of art, among other things.

A database (Interpol Weapons and Explosives Tracking System, or IWETS) contains information on traffic in firearms, the use of explosives for criminal purposes and data on improvised explosive devices. Access to this database is restricted to ensure maximum confidentiality. An electronic messaging format has also been developed so that member states can supply information to the system and share information multilaterally. Reports have been produced at various times on the sale, possession, carrying, use, import and export of firearms.

In addition, the FOPAC Branch (an acronym deriving from the French title of the branch, *Fonds Provenant d'Activités Criminelles*) gathers information about the movements of funds derived from such criminal activities, which can involve gun-running.

All this adds up to is simple coordination of international intelligence, but this is a vital function. Unfortunately, Interpol is limited by its small size in the amount of active intelligence gathering and analysis it can do. Levels of member participation vary greatly, and thus coverage is uneven.

Other international organisations

Europol was created partly out of frustration with the limitations of Interpol. While it initiated activities in 1994, it only became fully operational in 1999. It has primarily focused on narcotics, but has targeted other areas of organised crime as well. Firearms have not been a special area of focus thus far, which reflects the relatively low levels of gun violence on the continent. Although slightly smaller than Interpol, its narrower geographic focus and the relative affluence of its members has allowed it to engage more fully in direct operational matters. Europol is establishing a secured computer network (TECS), which is not yet fully operational.

The World Customs Organisation has a broad mandate that extends far beyond smuggling and criminal matters to include many aspects of international commerce. It is especially concerned with the harmonisation and uniformity of standards relating to legitimate cross-border travel and trade. While it shares information with Interpol and other law enforcement organisations, its potential for operational gun interdiction is limited.

Once fully operational, the International Criminal Court will take on cases involving genocide, terrorism and other crimes against humanity. Its jurisdiction is based on ratification of its enabling legislation by all UN member states, and it will preside over cases involving either the territory or the citizens of members. While a case could be made for prosecuting those who illegally arm combatants or criminals, it is unlikely this venue will accept any but the most egregious cases.

What Should Be Done?

Given the limitations discussed above, how can interested parties contribute to the capacity of police agencies worldwide to reduce firearm violence?

Firstly, a variety of regulatory activities discussed elsewhere in this book need to be enforced. The job of the police is greatly facilitated if it is clear which arms are legitimate and which are not, if ownership rights are easily ascertained and if the sources of arms seized can be easily determined.

Secondly, international agencies, such as Interpol, should be supported in their campaign to track illicit weapons supplies and dealers. A single agency should be designated as the data collection point for information from police agencies all over the world, whether this is the IWETS database or a new and independent body. The presentation and access of data should be easy and immediate, perhaps via a secured Internet link, a technology spreading even into the most remote corners of Africa.

In practical terms, when a police officer seizes a weapon anywhere in the world, it should be possible to log the make, model and serial number in the database immediately, and to get back information on the source of this weapon and the last legitimate owner. National police departments should be notified if, for example, a weapon logged as destroyed surfaces at another location. Regular notices should be sent analysing the most significant global weapons flows and describing the activities of the most notorious brokers. Certainly information on convicted traffickers should be shared among national police intelligence agencies and international policing bodies.

On the patrol side, border control and customs agents could greatly benefit from training in international best practices. Targeted border points should be lent portable x-ray technology, including the equipment necessary to scan entire containers. The possibility of international bounties on seized contraband should be explored. In developing countries, a little hard currency can go a long way. If nothing else, such funds could be used to pay border guards more, thereby increasing the cost of doing business for those who attempt to bribe their way through border controls.

In certain dire cases, the international community may wish to take on responsibility for border controls in countries that simply lack the capacity to provide even the most rudimentary enforcement. Again, given resource constraints, these efforts should be mobile and targeted. International peacekeeping should not be confined to areas of political conflict, since for many people the greatest threat to safety lies in the hands of criminals.

The whole concept of 'borders' should be reviewed critically in contexts where very little control exists. Regional law enforcement initiatives, such as those described in chapter 8, should be fostered, especially among developing countries. Collective efforts should be made to clean sweep entire regions for guns and to halt flows entering areas where borders are permeable. An excellent example of a successful regional police sweep is the joint South Africa-Mozambique venture dubbed 'Operation Rachel,' which, with foreign financial assistance, recovered nearly 12,000 firearms and more than three million rounds of ammunition.

Whatever the context, each intervention to curb gun-running or illegal gun supplies should be tailored to the distinct interests of the players in the region, which should be determined by solid intelligence work. As the example of South Africa shows, doing so can mean exploring an incredibly complex network of fears and desires, but it is essential if interventions are to be effective in a long-term way.

Notes

[1] T. Lamberti, 'The Great Trek to Crime Deterrents,' *Business Day*, 4 November 1999.

[2] T. Salgado, 'Too Few Police Officers have Drivers Licences,' *Business Day*, 17 October 1996.

[3] Institute for Security Studies, untitled report, in press in 2000.

[4] Institute for Security Studies, untitled report, in press in 2000.

[5] P. Kirk, 'The Downfall of "Durban's Biggest Gangster",' *Mail and Guardian*, 23 July 1999.

[6] M. Marks, 'Making Waves: The Black Officers' Forum,' *Crime and Conflict Quarterly*, No. 14.

[7] E. Hennop, 'Firearms and Violent Crime in South Africa,' *Nedcor ISS Crime Index*, No. 1, 1999.

[8] V. Barolsky, 'Victims and the Police: The National Victims of Crime Survey,' *Crime and Conflict Quarterly*, No. 16.

[9] A. Minnaar, 'A Plague of Guns: The Proliferation of Firearms,' *Crime and Conflict Quarterly*, No. 14.

[10] Hennop, 'Firearms and Violent Crime in South Africa.'

[11] Crime Information Analysis Centre (CIAC), South African Police Service, 'The Incidence of Serious Crime,' January 1998.

[12] E. Hennop, 'Firearm Related Crime: Lead-Up to New Legislation,' *Nedcor ISS Crime Index*, No. 3, 1999.

[13] Minnaar, 'A Plague of Guns: The Proliferation of Firearms.'

[14] A. Maree, 'Cash in Transit Robberies,' *Crime and Conflict Quarterly*, No. 15.

[15] Crime Information Analysis Centre (CIAC), South African Police Service, Pretoria, 'The Incidence of Serious Crime,' January 1998.

[16] Crime Information Analysis Centre (CIAC), South African Police Service, Pretoria, 'The Incidence of Serious Crime,' January 1998.

[17] H. Ludski,, '20,000 South Africans with criminal records have firearm licences,' *Sunday Times*, 14 February 1999.

[18] C. Hansmann and E. Hennop, 'The Central Firearms Registry: Assessing Data Accuracy,' *Nedcor ISS Crime Index*, No. 4, 1999.

[19] P. Kirk, 'A Border Violated Day and Night,' *Mail and Guardian*, 1 October 1999.

[20] D. Masunda, 'An Express Train to the Border,' *Mail and Guardian*, 19 November 1999.

[21] Crime Information Analysis Centre, South African Police Service, Pretoria, 'The Incidence of Serious Crime,' January 1999.

[22] Crime Information Analysis Centre, South African Police Service, Pretoria, 'Firearms and their impact on crime: KwaZulu-Natal,' unpublished report, 1996.

[23] E. Hennop, 'Firearm related crime: Lead-up to new legislation,' *Nedcor ISS Crime Index*, No. 3, 1999.

[24] S. Meek, *Buy or Barter: The History and Prospects of Voluntary Weapons Collection Programmes*, ISS Monograph Series, No. 22.

[25] C. Hansmann, 'Public Perception about Firearms: A Survey of Three Communities,' *Nedcor ISS Crime Index*, No. 6, 1999.

[26] E. Nadelmann, 'The Role of the United States in the International Enforcement of Criminal Law,' *Harvard International Law Journal*, Vol. 31, No. 1.

Summary of Recommendations
for states and citizens

Political will is the thread that runs through all of these chapters—
the need for it and, in many cases, the lack of it.

The authors in this volume have noted the enormous obstacles
to effective state control of the thriving black market in arms. Brian
Wood and Johan Peleman, for instance, show how easily brokers
and transporters change identities, bases of operation and plane
registration numbers to outwit customs and law enforcement officials. And Brian Johnson-Thomas demonstrates the ease with
which dealers obtain false or forged documentation to provide a
sufficient veneer of legitimacy. Most confounding, Tom Naylor and
Lucy Mathiak/Lora Lumpe note that states themselves are often
the problem—running guns and fostering networks of brokers for
some perceived short-term political or financial pay off. And Ted
Leggett identifies the many financial, practical and political obstacles to enforcement of anti-trafficking measures, even when states
have the sincerest of intentions. The net result is few criminal investigations and even fewer prosecutions of illicit traffickers.

Despite this grim assessment, progress has been made in that
states are paying greater attention to arms trafficking then ever before. The authors, with the help of other participants in this project,
have mapped out many areas where states committed to doing so
can overcome these obstacles and reduce the deadly and illegal
trade in arms. Priority recommendations, culled from chapters in
this book, follow.

Comprehension of the Problem

Government officials gathered in New York in February 2000 to
begin preparations for the United Nation's global conference on
'the illicit trade in small arms and light weapons in all its aspects.'
This conference, authorised in 1999 by the UN General Assembly, is

to be held in June or July 2001. During a week of preparatory discussions, however, the assembled representatives could not agree
on the date or venue for the conference, let alone the scope and
goals of the meeting. States have widely varying interests in and
definitions of the 'illicit trade.' Many were strongly opposed to the
inclusion in the 2001 conference of any topics relating to what they
consider to be legitimate arms sales.

Emanuela Gillard's chapter fleshes out the many dimensions of
what is already illicit—that is, proscribed by international law—in
relation to small arms exports. She reminds states of their direct responsibilities relating to the UN Charter—including a duty to implement fully within their jurisdiction UN Security Council-
mandated arms embargoes. In addition, she notes the derivative
obligation of states to consider the situation in recipient states and
their possible violation of international law, when authorising arms
transfers. Relevant offences include violations of international humanitarian law or human rights law.

A principal goal of this book, and its central recommendation to
concerned states and citizens, is to work to enlarge the commonly
held definition of 'illicit' arms supply to embrace the above notion
of state responsibility regarding arms supply and respect for international law.

External enforcement mechanisms generally do not exist for international law, and all too often in the past acts of commission or
omission by states relative to arms trafficking have occurred with
impunity. With its report to the UN Security Council in March
2000, however, a panel chaired by the Canadian Ambassador, Robert Fowler, has challenged this culture of impunity by naming specific governments and private individuals implicated in violating
the UN arms embargo on UNITA rebels in Angola.

Among its recommendations, the Fowler report suggests several
mechanisms for enforcement of embargo obligations. First, it recommends that Security Council sanctions be applied against governments found to have deliberately broken the sanctions. The
panel suggests an embargo for three years on arms transfers to
states identified as complicit in violating the embargo. Second, it
suggests that compliance with UN sanctions regimes should be
among the criteria considered by NATO and the European Union
when evaluating new candidates for membership.

Support for this ground-breaking report, which ends the pattern
of impunity that has prevailed within the United Nations system

for so long, and for the panel that prepared it, should be among the highest priorities of states and citizens opposed to arms trafficking.

New Norms on Covert Arms Supply

In addition to reminding states of their current international law obligations, there is a need to develop or strengthen laws or norms against certain state practices. One area particularly in need of clarification is the supply of arms, generally covertly, by states to non-state actors in other countries. As shown in the chapter by Mathiak and Lumpe, while many states currently interpret this practice as illegal under the UN Charter, others do not.

This practice has been, and left unaddressed will likely continue to be, a major source of small/light arms proliferation, as evidenced by the legacy of weapons and brokering networks established during the 1970s and 1980s to arm combatants in South Asia, Southern Africa and Central America. These arms outlived the original purpose for which they were shipped and have since been recycled to other conflicts, bandits or terrorist networks.

In 1998 the Canadian government introduced a discussion draft of a potential treaty that would prohibit the transfer of military small arms to non-state actors. This draft represents the first attempt by the international governmental community to prohibit the provision of official military aid to insurgent forces. It touches upon fundamental and sometimes competing concepts of people's right to self-defence (and perhaps self-determination) versus states' right against external aggression (through the arming of insurgent forces). Lumpe and Mathiak argue that this effort deserves serious consideration and support by the coalition of governments and nongovernmental organisations seeking to curb the most dangerous aspects of illicit arms supply. At a minimum, the international community should debate the legal, practical and humanitarian record of covert arms supply to insurgent groups.

Standard Documentation

One of the many issues raised in Brian Johnson-Thomas' narrative, but true, account of ammunition-running from East Europe by

West Europeans to Africa is of official corruption around sales of end-user certificates.

A priority area for international cooperation should be the establishment of an international system of authenticated end-use certificates, which would minimise forgery of documentation. The form should be used for all arms grants and sales, including those conducted by brokers. Most effective would be the requirement of positive import certification by states granting export permits. As part of this effort, states should improve the official documentation required by transport forwarding agents and sub-contractors so that Customs inspectors can better monitor and check for trafficking. For instance, carrier and air waybills could be cross-referenced with arms export licences and end-user certificates.

In addition, states should investigate and prosecute theft and sale of end-use certificates and other official trade documentation.

Controlling Production

The world is awash in surplus guns, many of them flowing from state arsenals. Yet, as Pete Abel notes, private manufacturing companies and national governments continue to export the production of their latest-model firearms through licensed production agreements. Abel's chapter shows in concrete terms how this practice has undermined the stated human rights policies of several licensing governments, as licensee countries exported arms to states that the licensing country was prohibited from exporting to, due to the imposition of European Union arms embargoes.

Abel suggests that 'at a minimum, to protect against diversion and undermining of their own national laws and policies, as well as the undermining of supranational arms embargoes,' national governments should:

- license the export of arms manufacturing capacity *at least* as stringently as they license weapons exports;
- ensure that licensed production agreements include provisions that spell out the production quantities being authorised and the terms under which export of licensed produce is acceptable; and
- enforce adherence to these provisions.

Domestic Gun Markets

Wendy Cukier and Steve Shropshire show the multitude of ways in which lax regulation of domestic firearms markets contributes to the illicit trafficking and use of guns. They note that, 'the illicit firearms market does not recognise distinctions between criminals, warring factions, insurgents or freedom fighters. Nor does it observe national borders. Inadequate domestic gun control procedures, gaps in import/export control regimes and insufficient enforcement all fuel illegal firearms markets. ' In particular they make the following recommendations:

- careful domestic gun regulation through licensing and registration, national standards to help control secondary markets, measures such as safe storage requirements to reduce gun theft and restrictions on the types of guns that may be owned;
- careful securing of state police and military arsenals against theft or corruption; and
- responsible border control policies, which emphasise unlawful gun exports as well as unlawful imports.

Regulating Brokers and Shippers

While not all arms brokering activity is suspect or illegal, almost all embargo-busting trafficking is carried out by brokers. States, therefore, need to regulate brokering activities of their nationals and within their jurisdictions carefully, in order to comply with their obligations to support UN embargoes and other international law.

Currently, many states do not regulate the full range of brokering activities. Exploiting the absence of harmonised laws and practices, brokers often base their activities in states with more lax rules, therefore technically often not violating national law.

Wood and Peleman call for states to enact the strongest possible national laws, along the lines of that which the United States has in place to register arms brokers and license their individual transactions. To be most effective, such laws need to apply not only to persons or corporations domiciled in a given country, but also to that country's nationals abroad, as does the US law.

Wood and Peleman write: 'This [US] approach would … cover the arms brokering and trafficking activities of all citizens at home and abroad, regardless of their shifting residences or company registrations. Such a law, if accompanied by criminal sanctions, would act as a stronger deterrent to arms brokers and traffickers who migrate from country to country to escape proper regulation.'

Many states have expressed opposition to such extra-territorial application of national laws. And yet without it even the few national laws that do exist to regulate brokering are rendered ineffective by the easy movement of brokers to states that do not have or do not enforce relevant laws. Some states opposed in general to extra-territorial application of laws have nevertheless implemented such legislation in regard to child sex crimes, war crimes, torture and the enforcement of UN arms embargoes. This precedent provides some cause for optimism that, given the humanitarian impact of gun-running, anti-trafficking laws might be implemented equally aggressively.

Focus on Demand

R. T. Naylor is sceptical about the efficacy of proposals that would seek to diminish gun-running primarily by subjecting weapons traffickers to anti-money laundering laws and forcing open bank-secrecy havens so that the assets of known traffickers could be seized and frozen. He points out that such methods have been applied to drug trafficking for a decade without any measurable effect on the volume or price of recreational drugs being trafficked. 'If the proceeds-of-crime approach pays such poor dividends with "regular" crime, then with arms trafficking—where states and their intelligence services are often complicit, and where the commodity itself is often legal—there is even less chance of such a strategy having a significant impact.'

Instead, Naylor agrees with Leggett that the great majority of arms trafficking crimes will continue to be solved by 'old-fashioned police work—cops pounding the pavement, laboriously sifting evidence, cultivating informants and just getting plain lucky.'

He advises states to focus on helping reduce demand for arms by directly addressing the causes of violent conflict, of which he says 'the most important is the prevailing maldistribution of income, wealth and ecological capital.'

In addition to focusing on the root socio-economic causes, Cukier and Shropshire urge states to limit gun marketing efforts as a way of diminishing demand. They make this proposal in the context of domestic gun markets, but it holds valid for the international trade, as well.

Negotiation

Although rhetorical and policy attention to the nature and impact of gun-running has increased dramatically in recent years, as Sarah Meek notes, this attention is often not backed up by adequate resources. Moreover, the interest in combating the trade has not yet spread to all corners of the globe, nor has consensus emerged about priorities for action among the Western democracies or the states where conflict and repression are fuelled by illicit arms. These realities threaten to lower outcomes of the two major international anti-trafficking initiatives currently under way—the firearms protocol and the UN conference in 2001. Through an assessment of recently negotiated regional agreements, Meek calls for clarity in goals, attention to operational effectiveness and full implementation of any future agreements.

She explores the interaction between national, regional and global initiatives focused on the black-market arms trade. Of course, universal and aggressive application of any measure is ideal, but states committed to reducing illicit arms flows need not be held back by others. While waiting for China, Russia and other sceptics to come around, committed states can revise their own policies and practices to narrow the area of operation for traffickers. For example, they could initiate greater transparency around their legal arms exports (thereby casting light on possible fraud or diversion), improve their legislation with regard to implementing UN or regionally-mandated embargoes within their national jurisdiction and by their nationals abroad and provide more resources for investigation and enforcement of such legislation.

Enforcement

Ted Leggett lays out the variety of obstacles to on-the-ground enforcement of even the best of governmental intentions, as well as obstacles to international cooperation for enforcement. On the former, he cites lack of resources, which results in low pay, low moti-

vation, insufficient forces and high corruptibility as a most serious
obstacle. On the latter, differing national, legal and police cultures,
the sensitivity of intelligence gathering and sovereignty issues all
inhibit effectiveness. With these realities in mind, he makes the
following recommendations:

- States should enact clear regulatory measures.
- An international agency, perhaps Interpol, should be designated as the data collection point for information from police
  agencies all over the world regarding weapons trafficking.
- An international system should be established to permit rapid
  tracing of weapons to the source and last legitimate owner.
- Border control and customs agents in much of the developing
  world could greatly benefit from training in international best
  practices and from the provision of modern equipment.
- International donor funds could be used to pay border guards
  more, thereby increasing the cost of doing business for those
  who attempt to bribe their way through border controls.

In a democracy, national political will is often forged by motivated
groups of citizens—religious leaders and their followers, business
interests, human rights workers, etc. As more businesses lose investment or profit, as more aid workers are kidnapped and as more
people are killed in conflict, terrorist attacks and banditry, citizens
increasingly are calling on their governments to take effective action to curb the spread of small arms. A positive sign in this regard
is the coming-together in May 1999 of groups from the North and
South into the International Action Network on Small Arms, a coalition working against policies that proliferate guns and armed
violence. In addition, in November 1999 the council of delegates of
the International Committee of the Red Cross/Crescent voted to
endorse ICRC advocacy against the scourge of small arms similar
to the very important role that the ICRC played during the 1990s in
combating the scourge of anti-personnel landmines.

It is hoped that the analysis in this book will give impetus to the
work of concerned citizens, nongovernmental organisations, intergovernmental organisations and governments on behalf of people
around the world who suffer under these weapons.

Glossary *of* Terms

air waybill: the document prepared by the carrier that describes
Customs purposes the contents of the cargo, its consigner, consignee, route and value.

bill of lading: states that the goods loaded onto a specified commercial carrier (ship or cargo plane) are in good order and are
bound for a specified destination. It is signed by the skipper and is
normally presumed to be conclusive proof that an order has been
filled. Bills of lading are negotiable instruments—that is, possession
of an endorsed bill will eventually give the holder possession of the
actual goods.

cargo manifest: details the weight, dimensions, packaging and any
peculiarities (*e.g.,* explosive content) of the cargo on board.

countertrade: an act of international trade in which the purchase of
goods is paid for not in cash or financial credit instruments, but at
least partially in other goods or services. At its simplest, counter-
trade represents a pure barter arrangement of one set of goods for
another. But it is usually more complicated, involving networks of
exchanges paid for partially in goods, in which money may enter in
the final analysis to cover any residual payment obligations.

end-user certificate: a statement signed by a responsible official of
an arms-importing country that the items to be imported are for
that nation's exclusive use and that the receiving country would
seek permission of the selling government before re-transferring
the items to a third country.

letter of credit: a document used to finance international trade. It is
opened by a bank at the request of the would-be buyer of the goods
in favour of the seller. The issuing bank instructs the seller's bank
to make the specified sum available to the seller when the seller

presents documents (of which a bill of lading is the most important) confirming that the goods have been shipped.

offsets: the practice, very common in large-scale arms transactions, of the seller's attempting to reduce the cost to the buyer and win a competitive advantage over other would-be sellers by offering to build certain manufacturing facilities or conduct other related operations like maintenance and construction of infrastructure in the buyer's country. The use of offsets makes pricing of arms deals very difficult to determine, since the prices used to determine the value of investments and subcontracts in the buyer country can often be very arbitrary.

performance bond: a pledge frequently required in contractual dealings by which the seller of the goods or services agrees to make restitution to the buyer of a certain sum or a certain percentage of the value of the deal in the event of failure to comply satisfactorily with the terms of the contract. Usually the supplier's bank will (for a fee) issue the required pledge and convey it to the buyer's bank.

private banking: originally referred to as private partnerships that, while called banks, really restricted their role to managing family fortunes rather than taking deposits and making loans to the general public. Today most major banks have a 'private banking department' to cater to the super-rich.

supercargo: an agent on board a ship who is responsible for the care *en route* and the eventual sale of the cargo. The supercargo exists to ensure the fulfilment of the terms of the contract.

About *the* Authors

Pete Abel is Information Manager at the Omega Foundation (UK), which investigates military, security and police equipment production and transfers and provides research services for human rights organisations, other nongovernmental groups and journalists.

Wendy Cukier is a Professor of Information Technology Management and Justice Studies at Ryerson Polytechnic University, Toronto. She is also the Coordinator of the Small Arms/Firearms Education and Research Network (SAFER-Net) and has consulted to governments around the world on various aspects of firearm research and regulation. She has published over 200 articles on firearm injury, crime and trafficking and has been active in the UN Commission on Crime Prevention and Criminal Justice. Cukier is President of the Coalition for Gun Control (Canada), a network of 350 NGOs. She is completing a PhD in Management Science at York University and has a *Docteur d'Université* from Laval University and an LLD degree from Concordia University.

Emanuela-Chiara Gillard works in the Legal Services branch at the International Committee of the Red Cross in Geneva. She is a qualified English solicitor, with a number of years' experience working in the field of international law. She previously served as assistant to Prof Sir Elihu Lauterpacht, as a Legal Officer at the United Nations Compensation Commission and as a Legal Officer at the International Organisation for Migration (Geneva). Her contribution reflects her views alone and not those of the International Committee of the Red Cross.

Brian Johnson-Thomas began his career in the lowest possible grade of the British Diplomatic Service and later worked in the Ministry of Defence and other British government departments and agencies. He became a journalist some 20 years ago and has specialised as a war correspondent over the past decade, reporting from Baghdad in 1991, Bosnia, the genocide in Rwanda, civil war in the Congo and Kosovo. These war experiences motivated Johnson-Thomas to focus on gun-runners, which he has increasingly done, most frequently for the *Sunday Times* and the *Observer* (London). In addition, he continues to broadcast for the BBC and has worked on several television investigative series in Britain and elsewhere. In recent years he has undertaken assignments for the United Nations, other international organisations and national governments.

Ted Leggett is a former police officer and prosecutor presently engaged in research in crime and development at the University of Natal in Durban, South Africa. His special focus is on the international illegal economy and its ties to street crime in the developing world, including the illicit sale of drugs, sex, guns and stolen automobiles. He edits *Crime and Conflict Quarterly*, a journal aimed at creating a dialogue between researchers and the law enforcement community. He has a Juris Doctor from New York University (focusing on criminal law) and a Masters degree in Social Science (Development Studies) from the University of Natal.

Lora Lumpe is a senior associate at the Peace Research Institute, Oslo, where she was based during 1998-1999. She also currently serves as a consultant to Amnesty International USA on military/human rights matters. In 1991 she founded the Arms Sales Monitoring Project at the Washington, DC-based Federation of American Scientists and directed the research and advocacy programme until 1998. Lumpe has written many book chapters, magazine articles, speeches and op-eds on a variety of disarmament topics, including the booklet *Arms Trade Revealed: A Guide for Investigators and Activists* (Federation of American Scientists, 1998). Most recently, she edited *Small Arms Control: Old Weapons, New Issues* (UNIDIR and Ashgate, 1999).

Lucy Mathiak is based at the University of Wisconsin-Madison, where she is completing work on a book entitled *American Jihad: The Reagan Doctrine as Policy and Practice*. Mathiak is the author of 'The Light Weapons Trade at Century's End,' in Virginia Gamba, ed., *Society Under Siege: Crime, Violence, and Illegal Weapons* (Institute for Security Studies, 1997), and 'Light Weapons and Internal Conflict in Angola,' in Boutwell et al., eds., *Lethal Commerce: The Global Trade in Small Arms and Light Weapons* (American Academy of Arts and Sciences, 1995). She has written on sexual violence as a tool of

236

war, the linkages between the traffic in weapons and drugs and the role of violent nongovernmental groups in the spread of weapons and violence. She is a co-founder and advisor to the British-American Security Council's Project on Light Weapons.

Sarah Meek heads the Light Weapons and Peacebuilding Programme at International Alert (UK). Previously, she was a senior researcher on the Arms Management Programme at the Institute for Security Studies in South Africa, and before that she worked at the Centre for Non-proliferation Studies in Monterey, California and the United Nations Department for Disarmament Affairs in New York. She has published numerous articles and reports. Her current research focuses on assessing the impact of weapons availability on countries emerging from conflict and identifying ways to improve controls over weapons movements, including to prevent the illicit trafficking of weapons.

R. T. Naylor is Professor of Economics at McGill University in Montreal. His fields of specialisation are black markets, smuggling and international financial crime. He is author of several books including *Hot Money and The Politics Of Debt* (on money laundering, tax evasion and capital flight) and *Patriots And Profiteers: On Economic Warfare, Embargo Busting and State-Sponsored Crime* (McClelland & Stewart, 1999). Naylor helped author the recent study by the United Nations Crime Control and Drug Prevention Office, *Financial Havens, Banking Secrecy and Money Laundering*. His work on topics such as gun-running, gold smuggling, 'organised crime' and black market operations of guerrilla groups appears regularly in journals such as *Crime, Law & Social Change* and *Transnational Organized Crime*.

Johan Peleman directs the International Peace Information Service in Antwerp, Belgium. He conducts research on war financing and the political economy of conflict. He is the co-author of *The Arms Fixers* (PRIO/NISAT/BASIC, 1999). Peleman works as a consultant for various research projects, including in 1999-2000 the Fowler Commission of the UN Security Council, investigating violations of the UN arms, oil and diamond sanctions against UNITA guerrillas in Angola.

Steve Shropshire is an independent researcher based in the United Kingdom. He has recently studied firearms injury, death and civilian firearms ownership for the Small Arms/Firearms Education and Research network (SAFER-Net). From 1995-1999 Shropshire was on the research staff of Saferworld, a British think-tank that works closely with the UK Ministry of Foreign Affairs. While there, he served on the management committee of the International Action Network on Small Arms and helped organise a number of international conferences on small arms and export controls, which involved both governments and private organisations.

Thorvald Stoltenberg is the President of the Norwegian Red Cross. Previously, he has served in a number of Norwegian government posts, including Minister of Defence during 1979-1981 and Minister of Foreign Affairs during 1987-1989 and again from 1990-1993. In the Foreign Service of Norway, Stoltenberg was posted to Nigeria, Yugoslavia and the United States, and he has served as Ambassador to Norway's Permanent UN Mission and to Denmark. He also served three terms as International Secretary of the Federation of Norwegian Trade Unions during 1969-1983. In 1990-1991 he was the United Nations High Commissioner of Refugees, and in 1993 he began three years' work negotiating for peace in the former Yugoslavia.

Brian Wood has been responsible since 1994 for the international coordination and development of Amnesty International's work on military, security and police relations. In this capacity he has authored, co-authored and edited many publications and reports, including several on arms trafficking. He is currently on sabbatical leave from Amnesty's London headquarters, working as a senior associate with the International Peace Research Institute, Oslo. While there, he has co-authored *The Arms Fixers* (PRIO/NISAT/ BASIC, 1999) and is establishing a pilot project with poor communities and police in Malawi to diminish firearms proliferation. Between 1978 and 1990, Wood carried out economic, social and military research and journalism on Southern Africa and coordinated operational projects for refugees on behalf of human rights organisations, churches and the United Nations.

Index